Urban Enclaves

Identity and Place in the World

Second Edition

Contemporary Social Issues

George Ritzer, *Series Editor*

Urban Enclaves: Identity and Place in the World
(second edition)
Mark Abrahamson

Hollywood Goes to High School: Cinema, Schools, and
American Culture
Robert Bulman

Society of Risk Takers
William C. Cockerham

The Wilding of America: Money, Mayhem, and
the New American Dream
(third edition)
Charles Derber

Global E-litism: Digital Technology, Social Inequality,
and Transnationality
Gili Drori

Sex Trafficking: The Global Market in Women and Children
Kathryn Farr

Between Politics and Reason: The Drug Legalization Debate
Erich Goode

The Myth of Self-Esteem: Finding Happiness and
Solving Problems in America
John P. Hewitt

Speculative Capitalism: Financial Casinos and
Their Consequences
Dan Krier

Post-Industrial Peasants: The Illusion of Middle Class
Prosperity
Kevin Leicht and Scott Fitzgerald

Just Revenge: Costs and Consequences of the Death Penalty
(second edition)
Mark Costanzo

Contemporary Social Issues
Series Editor: George Ritzer, *University of Maryland*

Urban Enclaves

Identity and Place in the World

Second Edition

Mark Abrahamson
University of Connecticut, Storrs

Worth Publishers

Acquisition Editor: Erik Gilg
Executive Marketing Manager: John Britch
Associate Managing Editor: Tracey Kuehn
Project Manager: Richard Rothschild / Print Matters, Inc.
Art Director/Cover Designer: Barbara Reingold
Text Designer: Lissi Sigillo
Production Manager: Barbara Anne Seixas
Composition: Matrix Publishing Services
Printing and Binding: R. R. Donnelly and Sons Company

ISBN: 0-7167-0636-9 (EAN: 9780716706366)

Printed in the United States of America

First printing 2005

Library of Congress Cataloging-in-Publication Number 2005923893

Worth Publishers
41 Madison Avenue
New York, NY 10010
www.worthpublishers.com

About the Author

M ark Abrahamson has been a professor of sociology at the University of Connecticut since 1976 and has also served that university in a variety of administrative positions. He is a former Program Director (for Sociology) at the National Science Foundation and was a professor of sociology at Syracuse University before moving to Connecticut.

His main scholarly interests are in classical theory and urban sociology. He has authored more than 30 papers and one dozen books, most recently including *Global Cities* (Oxford University Press, 2004).

Contents

Foreword

A s we move further into the twenty-first century, we confront a seemingly endless array of pressing social issues: urban decay, inequality, ecological threats, rampant consumerism, war, AIDS, inadequate health care, national and personal debt, and many more. Although such problems are regularly dealt with in newspapers, magazines, and trade books and on radio and television, such popular treatment has severe limitations. By examining these issues systematically through the lens of sociology, we can gain greater insight into them and be better able to deal with them.

Each book in the series casts a new and distinctive light on a familiar social issue, while challenging the conventional view, which may obscure as much as it clarifies. Phenomena that seem disparate and unrelated are shown to have many commonalities and to reflect a major, but often unrecognized, trend within the larger society. Or a systematic comparative investigation demonstrates the existence of social causes or consequences that are overlooked by other types of analysis. In uncovering such realities the books in this series are much more than intellectual exercises; they have powerful practical implications for our lives and for the structure of society.

At another level, this series fills a void in book publishing. There is certainly no shortage of academic titles, but those books tend to be introductory texts for undergraduates or advanced monographs for professional scholars. Missing are broadly accessible, issue-oriented books appropriate for all students (and for general readers). The books in this series occupy that niche somewhere between popular trade books and monographs. Like trade books, they deal with important and interesting social issues, are well written, and are as jargon free as possible. However, they are more rigorous than trade books in meeting academic standards for writing and research. Although they are not textbooks, they often explore topics covered in basic textbooks and therefore are easily integrated into the curriculum of sociology and other disciplines.

Each of the books in the "Contemporary Social Issues" series is a new and distinctive piece of work. I believe that students, serious general readers, and academicians will all find the books to be informative, interesting, thought provoking, and exciting. Among the topics to be covered in forthcoming additions to the series are the global digital divide, the declining wealth and increasing indebtedness of the middle class, and the risk-taking nature of contemporary Americans.

—*George Ritzer*

Preface

In the ten years since the first edition appeared, the contemporary enclaves described in this book were significantly altered by the arrival of newcomers, the expansion of businesses and changes in local institutions. One major objective of this revision was to systematically update those chapters so that they accurately described the enclaves in the first years of the twenty-first century.

A second objective was to bring a more global focus to the contemporary enclaves. This entailed noting the growth of import-export businesses linked to firms in their homelands and/or the way enclaves have attracted international tourists. Most important are two entirely new chapters focusing upon enclaves outside of the U.S. One examines American writers, artists and musicians in the Montparnasse district of Paris during the 1920s when they formed a large and lively lifestyle enclave. The second new chapter traces the growth and development of communities formed by German immigrants to Brazil's southernmost states over a period of over 150 years.

Readers familiar with the first edition will notice that the maps included in each chapter are much improved aesthetically. I am indebted to Erik Gilg for taking the initiative on the maps as well as for other editorial contributions which improved the final product. Finally, in addition to those people I acknowledged in the previous edition, I would like to add my thanks to the many readers who were kind enough to share comments with me.

An Overview

Robert Park, a pioneering urban theorist, once described cities as comprising "a mosaic of little worlds that touch but do not interpenetrate."[1] With a bit of elaboration, Park's description fit most large American cities not only when he first offered it in 1925 but even today. He was primarily calling attention to the fact that various types of people tend to seek out others like themselves and live close together. Located within these distinctive clusters are specialized commercial enterprises and institutions that support the inhabitants' special ways of life. Examples include grocery stores and restaurants that offer food from people's countries of origin; bars, nightclubs, theaters, and newspapers that cater to particular lifestyles and interests; and churches of various denominations, synagogues, and mosques.

Each distinctive group, along with its stores and institutions, occupies a geographic area that becomes intimately associated with the group. Through this linkage, areas acquire symbolic qualities that include their place-names and social histories. Each place, both as a geographic entity and as a space with social meaning, also tends to be an object of residents' attachments and an important component of their identities. For example, Chinese people living in Chinatown are likely to think of themselves not only as Chinese but as Chinese who live in Chinatown, as opposed to those who live in areas where their ethnic group does not predominate. Thus place of residence is also a prominent part of self-concepts. Park also concluded that people who live in these "little worlds" have their most meaningful relationships with those who cohabit in their worlds. Many of the residents' neighbors are also their kin, for example, and there are ongoing and diffuse relationships between customers and local store owners.

The little worlds Park wrote about, when given the above clarifications, come very close to constituting what we shall refer to as *enclaves*. To use the term *enclave* in this manner requires some broadening of its customary referents, though. In prior writings it has most frequently been used to refer to racial or ethnic minorities living in economically self-contained communities such as Miami's Little Havana.[2] We shall retain this usage and in addition we shall use *enclave* to refer to concentrations of residents who do not have the same ethnic or minority status in the conventional sense but who share a significant commonality based on wealth, occupation, lifestyle, or a combination of these attributes. The Castro district of San Francisco, for example, includes a residential area populated largely by men who are openly gay. This distinctive group supports a complete array of gay-oriented commercial and institutional activities: gay nightclubs and bars, bookstores, churches, therapists and clinics specializing in the treatment of gay patients, and so on. In San Francisco, the *Gay Yellow Pages* directory is comparable to the *Chinese Yellow Pages* or *Hispanic Yellow Pages*. The Castro as a place is also an important part of residents' identities. Therefore this community based on lifestyle should also be regarded as an enclave.[3]

Our use of the term *enclave* will expand on prior usages in still another way. Enclaves have traditionally been viewed as existing only in inner cities, but as the metropolitan areas around cities have grown in size and complexity, communities with all the features of enclaves have recently formed in otherwise conventional suburbs. Enclaves located outside city limits tend to be newer, physically more attractive, with wealthier residents, and more economic opportunities.[4] Despite their dissimilarities to central-city concentrations, these suburban communities still possess the major characteristics that define enclaves.

Finally, past studies have emphasized the commercial self-sufficiency of enclaves to differentiate them from ghettos, which involve only distinctive population concentrations. Although we shall regard the commercial dimension as an important component in defining enclaves, in addition we shall place a similarly strong emphasis on institutional developments consisting of distinctive churches, periodicals and other media, community centers, and so on. We expect that an enclave will typically possess a reasonably high degree of commercial as well as institutional development. In special circumstances, however, the presence of either may be sufficient to warrant enclave designation.

Both the suburban and institutional features described in the preceding paragraphs are illustrated by Kiryas Joel, the "Village of Joel." In 1977, several thousand Hasidic Jews moved from Brooklyn to Orange County, New York, about forty miles northwest of the city. Within a decade the village had grown to about twelve thousand people. They were seeking a place where they could follow, without compromise, the teachings of their religious leader, Rebbe Joel Teitelbaum. It was for him that they named the new community Kiryas Joel. In homes and in the religious schools that all the Hasidic youngsters attend, Yiddish and Hebrew are the main languages. English is a "second" language, and most youngsters in the village know little about the world outside. Most of the adults who work are employed outside the village, either in New York City or in an industrial park about twenty miles away. Only a few of the residents operate local businesses (such as kosher food stores) that meet the Hasidic residents' special needs. What most makes this suburban community an enclave lies in the institutional realm. Its residents share an identity, a commitment to a place, and a way of life in which local religious organizations provide the central themes.[5]

As all of the preceding examples imply, an enclave involves a special relationship between a distinctive group of people and a particular place. Thus an enclave has some characteristics of a subculture, in which a group of people shares common traditions and values that are ordinarily maintained by a high rate of interaction within the group. Not all subcultures have the requisite place ties to be classified as enclaves, however, and not all groups with place ties necessarily share the features of a subculture.

Contemporary Romany provide an example of a subculture without a place tie. There are some sizeable concentrations of Romany in major cities of the United States; as many as fifteen thousand have been estimated to live at least part of the year in Los Angeles neighborhoods. However, as the derogatory name affixed to them ("Gypsies") implies, they are highly mobile. They migrate across the country, working in traveling carnivals, sometimes sealing driveways, telling fortunes, working temporarily in automobile repair shops. They undertake much of this travel in order to visit friends and family, especially to celebrate Romany holidays. Their high rate of within-group interaction has enabled them to perpetuate shared values and a distinctive way of life, but this has not been accompanied by the establishment of ties to a place. For this reason, the Romany provide an example of a subculture but not of an enclave.[6]

On the other hand, many of the homeless in Austin, Texas, provide an example of a group that is tied to a place but does not have the shared values and meaningful interactions ordinarily associated with a subculture. According to sociologists David A. Snow and Leon Anderson, who spent two years studying the homeless in Austin, a large number of these homeless people remain in Austin spending years together on the streets in some well-defined areas and regularly sleeping and eating in shelters such as the Salvation Army's.[7] Given their shared human needs and lack of resources with which to meet them, most of these homeless people tend to respond similarly to similar circumstances. However, the overt commonalities in their behavior are not the result of meaningful relationships with each other. Furthermore, most hate the life they are living and would not care to celebrate, in terms of rituals, for example, anything about that life. The existence of a subculture generally presupposes an emotional attachment to a group, which in turn usually implies positive feelings about it. Such attachments transcend a cognitive assessment of membership in the group ("I belong") and entail a subjective sense of happiness about belonging.[8] Thus these homeless people appear not to share a subculture, which is why, despite their apparent ties to a place, they are best viewed as not constituting an enclave.

The Formation of Enclaves

Enclaves typically grow by serving as magnets that attract other people who share the same significant quality as the pioneers. For a place to seem as though it is dominated by a particular group and then to act like a magnet to others, the group need not make up 100 percent, or even a majority, of the local population. If no other group is present in sizeable numbers and the distinctive group's institutions and stores are concentrated in conspicuous locations, then an area could appear to be dominated by a group that comprised 25 percent or less of its total population.[9]

An interesting and logically prior question concerns why enclaves form where they do. Closeness to places of work associated with members of the distinctive group is often one reason the "settlers" chose a particular residential area. During the early part of the nineteenth century, for example, the first of many Norwegian immigrants settled in Brooklyn, New York, near the East River. They selected this part of Brooklyn because of its proximity to the docks and harbors, where they were initially employed.[10] Many years later, a young and politically active gay enclave formed in West Hollywood, California, apparently because of its closeness to the film, recording, television, and design industries in Hollywood, where many of West Hollywood's residents were employed.[11] In addition, an enclave's pioneers may have selected a particular site because of its physical features. For example, the Norwegians were attracted to the area near the Brooklyn shipyards because the saltwater and ships made them feel at home.[12]

Sometimes a specific place seems to have been selected simply because it is available when a distinctive group needs a place, and no one else wants it. For example, right after the notorious stock market crash of 1929, a large reservoir in New York's Central Park was drained and taken out of service. A few homeless people immediately set up residence in the reservoir but were evicted by the police. Over the next two years, however, as the Great Depression worsened, more homeless people moved to the park and built small shacks. Evictions and arrests for vagrancy slowly declined, and the shantytown's population grew into the hundreds. Most of the shacks had chairs and beds, some had carpets, and the shack of some unemployed bricklayers even had an inlaid tile roof. In a sarcastic reference to the then-president, the shantytown became known as "Hoover Valley," and its unpaved road, "Depression Street." With the growth of the homeless village, City officials became concerned about sanitation in the settlements and the possibility that the homeless men were really just disorderly vagrants. In 1933 the City resumed work on the reservoir landfill, and Hoover Valley was dismantled.[13]

The prior settlement of a place by people with similar characteristics has always been a major magnet to later migrants. The movers who follow later know of the enclave's existence before they relocate, and it becomes their intended destination. The pioneers who become established in the enclave often intentionally recruit potential migrants and they typically provide many types of help to newcomers, such as monetary assistance, employment, or help in finding an apartment.

Attraction to an enclave can also be based on the goods and services that are exclusively offered in its specialized stores and institutions. It is usually only in enclaves that there are the concentrated numbers of potential customers or clients necessary to support purveyors of various types of specialized goods and services. Access to them may serve as a magnet to members of the distinctive group. In Houston, for example, there is a substantial community of Iranian exiles. For those who wish to follow traditional Muslim practices in arranging and negotiating marriages, observing communal religious rites, and the like, life outside the enclave would be impossible. To illustrate, consider how a death in the family is to be handled. The proper traditional response includes assembling mourners in a mosque for a prayer service to ensure the deceased's passage to the next world, ritual washing of the corpse, burial in an exclusively Muslim graveyard, digging the grave exactly to the prescribed depth, and making certain the deceased faces Mecca. Within the enclave it is difficult enough to find the technical skills and communal cooperation that are needed for such tasks; outside the enclave, it would probably be next to impossible.[14]

6

Enclave Boundaries

Some enclaves have intentionally designed entries that unambiguously mark some or all of their boundaries. In San Francisco, for example, portals over main streets leading into Chinatown have elaborate decorations to mark them as entrances and thereby serve as boundary markers. Some neighborhoods in Chicago have erected signs on major thoroughfares leading into particular areas (such as "Welcome to Rogers Park") or put neighborhood name signs on light poles at major intersections. More often, however, there is no concrete designation of an entrance or a boundary, and people have only mental images of where socially significant places begin and end.

Around 1920, Ernest Burgess, who spent many years collaborating with Robert Park, prepared a "Fact Book" for Chicago. This book identified seventy-five communities, almost all of which were informal rather than formal entities; their names did not appear on city maps and they did not correspond with legal jurisdictions. Most consisted of residential areas surrounding a local shopping area, park, or school that residents regarded as the center of the community and that often provided its name. About fifty years later, Albert Hunter, while a graduate student in sociology at the University of Chicago, found that some of the communities Burgess noted had simply disappeared, others had changed names, and still others had merged into larger areas. However, nearly one half persisted intact, suggesting to Hunter that community names are part of a shared local culture and therefore endure. He also asked his respondents to identify, if they could, the boundaries of the community in which they lived. About 70 percent could name four boundaries, typically involving boulevards, expressways, parks, and so on.[15]

Regardless of their obtrusiveness, boundary markers are rarely associated with abrupt and total changes in community composition. Places usually change from each other in subtle ways that become dramatic only after they have accumulated. Residents' dress, their skin color, the music they are playing, and the food in store windows all provide clues to the changes that are occurring in the composition of an area. The distinctive features of an enclave in most instances gradually crystallize as one moves from its periphery to its core. For example, the Greenpoint section of Brooklyn contains a white, European (largely Polish), residential and commercial area. Packed into several blocks are Polish restaurants and meat markets, busts of Polish heroes, and billboards written in Polish. Adjacent to this enclave is a section with a Hispanic concentration, many of whose residents work in local factories. A resident described how one could see the racial differences between the geographical center of Greenpoint and its boundaries: "You go to Greenpoint Avenue and down . . . you'll see . . . white and Hispanic. But if you go all the way up . . . they're all white."[16]

It should also be recognized that distinctions made by local residents are likely to be more precise than those made by people farther away. Outsiders may simply be unaware of boundaries that separate enclaves (or subenclaves) from each other within an area. For instance, during the late 1950s Herbert Gans studied an inner-city Boston area called "West End." The single largest group in the area consisted of first- and second-generation Italian households. Other large immigrant groups were Polish, Jewish, and Irish. There was also a "skid row" area populated mostly by single men who drifted and drank. To the average person who resided elsewhere in Boston, Gans wrote, the West End was one undifferentiated slum. However, "the concept of the West End as a single neighborhood was foreign to the West Enders themselves."[17]

Corresponding to the tendency for different West Enders to see themselves as residing in separate enclaves were the specialized stores and institutions of each group. The Jewish area, although holding only about 10 percent of the total West End population, maintained two synagogues with a full range of social and religious activities, a Hebrew school, Jewish restaurants, and kosher food stores. Despite some intermingling of Jewish and Italian commercial and residential sites, especially near the enclaves' shared borders, the Jewish residents thus appeared to have formed a separate enclave within the larger community.

The difference between the self-views of people who lived in the West End and the views of non–West Enders existed because the latter tended to avoid the area. Outsiders knew too little about it to make many distinctions. In addition, to non–West Enders, many of the differences emphasized by the people of the West End would likely have been of trivial importance. Almost all of the residents were recent immigrants, they were generally poor, and they lived in a run-down neighborhood. For purposes of social placement, that was probably all the other Bostonians cared to know.

The general absence of unambiguous boundaries makes it impractical to study enclaves using any of the large-scale databases that have been compiled. Census Bureau publications, zip code directories, and other publications contain voluminous information about communities and neighborhoods, but they do not indicate where enclaves exist between and among neighborhoods. To locate enclaves with any precision ultimately requires detailed, firsthand information about a place that can be obtained only by walking its streets and talking to residents.

8

Imposed Separation

In the preceding pages we have noted many of the ways in which enclaves form and persist by attracting residents. However, enclaves are only partially maintained by the inducements they offer or by the desires of residents to remain in homogeneous concentrations. Segregation also results from the desires of people outside the enclave to preserve their own neighborhoods by keeping out the various categories of people they consider undesirable.

The boundaries of residential areas are, of course, sometimes maintained by violence. When outsiders' encroachments are defined as trespasses and physically punished, it sends a clear message to all outsiders to remain "in their place." The boundaries of enclaves are most often maintained in more subtle ways, though. In the Greenpoint section of Brooklyn, for example, white ethnic and Hispanic enclaves sit side by side. People of European descent with apartments for rent take care to find tenants who are racially like themselves, even though such discrimination is against the law. The women in Greenpoint have taken the place of local real estate agents, informing family and friends when housing becomes available within their enclave. Information spreads through the women's network, in butcher shops and churches. People attached to the network then sponsor their friends or family members, and outsiders are excluded. The experience of one unsponsored couple—she is Irish and he is Puerto Rican—is illustrative. When they somehow learned of a vacant apartment in the white ethnic enclave, they were still unable to rent it. They were asked by a prospective landlord, "What are you?" She said Irish, he said Hispanic. "What kind?" the landlord asked him. When he said Puerto Rican, the landlord asked if they had "any crawling things" in their current apartment, and then refused to rent to them.[18]

People in enclaves are also kept in their places by the actions of others that set them apart. Filipinos in Salinas, California, for example, tended to remain in the Filipino enclave for fear of being rejected by Anglos. They were self-conscious about their ability to speak English, and in the work settings where they had regular contacts with Anglos, they felt ridiculed by the way Anglos spoke to them: slowly and often using incorrect grammar, asking questions such as, "Work . . . difficult . . . here?"[19] In suburban Atlanta, to illustrate further, the Cobb County Board of Commissioners once passed a blanket resolution condemning homosexuality and eliminated *all* funding for the arts for an entire year out of fear that some funds might support "life styles advocated by the gay community."[20] To understand the context, one must know that in the preceding year the City of

Atlanta had granted domestic partnership status to the partners of gay City employees. This was too close to home for Cobb County officials, who felt it was important to make a statement telling homosexuals that their lifestyle might be accepted in Atlanta but would not be tolerated in Cobb County.

The most effective large-scale means of keeping people in their place is probably through the official actions of national governments, cities, counties, and other municipalities. Such actions take the forms of zoning ordinances, fire and safety regulations, dress codes, and so on. In parts of some French cities, for example, nearly everyone is Arab Muslim. That is the case in the Rue du Bon Pasteur neighborhood on the north side of Marseille, where women wear head coverings, newspapers and magazines are flown in from across the Arab world, and Arabic is spoken. However, the French government has "publicly" banned the full head covering traditionally preferred by Muslim women. They cannot wear it on public transportation, in public schools, and so on. To most of the Arab population of Rue du Bon Pasteur, the government's ban symbolizes the alienation of the Arab Muslim population from French society. One woman who worked in a food market near the largest mosque in the community viewed the ban as racist and claimed, "I don't feel French." In the enclave, she added, "I feel safe, because everyone is Arab. But the France outside is a France of racism."[21]

Local governments can also play an active role in maintaining the segregation of enclaves by imposing constraints on people's movement. The former are often indirect ways of putting out an "unwelcome mat" to some groups. For example, the selective enforcement of vagrancy laws is a time-honored way of discouraging minorities or the homeless from settling in a new area, even temporarily. In many cities the location of expressways similarly reinforces enclave boundaries in a very direct manner. In Los Angeles during the 1950s, for example, a number of freeways were constructed that bounded (on all four sides) a Chicano community in East Los Angeles. The freeways effectively isolated the enclave, but its generally poor and unorganized residents were virtually powerless to stop the freeway construction.[22]

Identity and Place

We have referred to enclaves as areas containing residents who share something significant. This formulation is intended to convey not only that residents are alike in some regard, but that the residents themselves are aware of the commonality and that the shared quality is important to their identities. From a social-psychological perspective, the term *identities* refers to meanings and definitions attached to people's selves both by the people themselves and by others. Because one's sense of self tends to be linked to roles and relationships, a person typically has multiple identities. Thus people think about themselves in their occupational and student roles, familial roles, gender and racial roles, and so on.[23]

Some identities are highly situational for most people, and the subjective significance of the roles associated with them also tends to vary situationally.[24] For example, suppose a person were markedly older than everyone else in one particular group. While in that group, in contrast with an older or mixed-age group, the one older person would likely see age as a more salient aspect of his or her identity. Similarly, people might take their city of residence for granted most of the time and attribute little significance to it for purposes of self-definition; but when they are traveling abroad and making new international acquaintances, it would probably become subjectively more prominent.

Other identities and their corresponding roles are less prone to situational change. They remain central features of the self. One useful way to characterize the latter is by the identity salience of roles.[25] High salience can be indicated when a person employs the same role in many different situations. For example, a hypothetical physician, Dr. Smith, might make restaurant and hotel reservations as *Dr.* Smith, insist on being described as *Dr.* Smith in voter registration files, be introduced as *Dr.* Smith in social settings, and so on. This cross-situational reliance upon the occupational title would likely signify that, for this physician, the doctor role had high identity salience.[26]

Like roles, a built environment can attain very high salience in people's identities because physical settings become associated with the bonding of people. That, according to sociologist Melinda Milligan, is the basis of people's attachments to a place, such as an enclave.[27] The names of communities of this type, simultaneously conveying both physical and social space, can similarly attain very high salience in people's identities.[28] Saying that one is from the Castro district or from Kiryas Joel is a personal statement that acts as a calling card, providing others inside and outside the enclave with information about the person's identity.

Another way to differentiate among roles or places in terms of their salience for people's identities is to note the emotional difficulty that people ordinarily experience when they go through the process of disengaging from them. The role exits that usually create the greatest turmoil for people—sex changes, giving up custody of children, or leaving a profession—are the ones associated with people's most salient identities.[29] Disruptions in the roles associated with people's place attachments, due to natural disasters, for example, have similarly been found to have profoundly adverse effects. The more enclave qualities that communities have before a flood, landslide, or the like, the greater the long-term depression, sadness, and stress former residents report feeling after they are forced to move. Some go through a grieving process for the destroyed place similar to a mourning for the dead.[30]

Residents can also experience emotional aftereffects when urban renewal projects or racial and economic changes dramatically alter a neighborhood's composition. The transformation of Rosedale, a community in the southeast corner of Fort Worth, Texas, is illustrative. As late as the 1950s, Rosedale was a homogeneous and cohesive suburban-type neighborhood. Its residents were reasonably prosperous and almost entirely white. (Every community in the Dallas–Fort Worth area was highly segregated at the time.) Over the next few decades, the neighborhood changed as a result of several processes that were also occurring in metropolitan areas across the country. Specifically, migration into the area increased competition for housing. A few middle-class black families, trying to move out of increasingly crowded ghettos, finally managed to buy homes in Rosedale, despite opposition from many residents and real estate brokers. That triggered panic-selling by whites and flight to suburban areas then being developed. As property values fell, more black (and later Hispanic) families moved in; but those who arrived later were generally poorer and had fewer intact families than the blacks who initially entered Rosedale. White flight increased, and many businesses and churches closed or relocated. By the 1990s, about the only whites remaining in the now-multiracial neighborhood were poor and old.[31]

The elderly whites who remained in Rosedale resented both the changes and their inability to have prevented them. They felt a profound sense of sorrow and loss for the neighborhood that used to be and the emotional security they associated with it. Many saw themselves as too old or too poor to move, so they felt trapped. Others' long-standing commitments to Rosedale—despite its profound changes—were too great to leave, so they immersed themselves in memories and the self-definitions of the past. The elderly residents of Rosedale were not unusual in this respect. Dramatic changes to neighborhoods typically result in identity discontinuity and nostalgia, and residents' longing for the past creates a new identity based on their shared experience of loss.[32] The only way they can still visit "their" Rosedale is by collectively reliving the significant events of their shared past.

Dominant Statuses

There appear to be many instances in which "outsiders" attempt more or less to equate people with a single master status. For example, to whites, blacks may be only blacks—it does not matter whether they are fat or thin, smart or dumb. Of course, blacks may also disregard similar differences among whites. In the same way, straight people may equate gay people with a sexual orientation, and vice versa. The one status that is dominant or overwhelming in the eyes of others (who do not share that status) can be highly diverse, based on a person's occupation (e.g., movie star), past history (e.g., ex-con), physical condition (e.g., blind), or so on.

Because others tend to recognize only the one status, it is important for people with a potentially dominant status who are committed to multiple statuses to interact with others like themselves. Such others are often the only ones who can "validate" the full range of a person's salient identities. If a woman is to continue to view herself as humorous, for example, it is necessary for people to laugh when she tells stories; if a man is to continue to think of himself as physically attractive, it is necessary for others to respond to him in an interested way. When people with a potentially dominant status interact with others who do not share that status, the others may be overwhelmed by that one master status. As a result, the others may not respond to the person's humor, intelligence, physical attributes, or other qualities. That leaves the person with only the single identity when interacting with others who are different. Thus people with such dominant statuses often prefer each other's company.[33] The homogeneity of enclaves with respect to a dominant status translates into opportunities for people to establish their other identities and provides one explanation for why many people are reluctant to leave.

With respect to enclave formation, people with two or more potentially dominant statuses present an especially interesting case. One strategy such persons have followed is to play the roles associated with the different statuses sequentially and to play the roles with different others (i.e., keep audiences segregated). This tactic may minimize the role conflicts a person experiences, but it does not eliminate all the stress that person may feel. To illustrate, an African-American lesbian explained that there is always a debate in her mind over whether to emphasize being black or gay, but added, "You can't stop being one. We've done that too long. Saying, 'I'm going to be black when I go to the N.A.A.C.P. meeting, so I'll stop being gay right now.' Or, 'I'm going to sit in on the Gay Pride community meeting, so I'm going to stop being black.'"[34]

In large cities people are less likely to be forced to choose among dominant identities because of the possibility of forming organizations that combine multiple statuses. In New York, for example, there are all-white gay clubs, all-black gay clubs, all-Latino gay clubs. These combinations of dominant statuses can also be a factor in encouraging people to establish subenclaves. Thus a gay subenclave may form within a larger enclave in which the residents are predominantly African American or young professionals, for instance. Or within a predominantly gay enclave there may be subenclaves that differ from each other in terms of such aspects as social class or race. The places where these multiple-status subenclaves form are often "social borderlands"—fringe areas in which, by straddling different groups, people create new social forms in terms of language, dress, style, or the like.[35]

As the above examples illustrate, race has frequently been a dominant status in America. That makes it interesting to conjecture about the impact of future increases in the interracial population, because that is likely to be associated with an increase in multicultural identities. Will race then become a less prevalent master identity in the future? Or will multicultural identities simply take their place alongside conventional single-race identities?[36]

Summary and Preview

This chapter has presented an overview of enclaves as containing concentrations of residents who share a distinctive status that is important to their identity and specialized stores and institutions that provide local support for the residents' distinctive lifestyle. A strong tie is ordinarily formed between that lifestyle and the geographic space the residents occupy, leading to place attachment and the ability of the place to serve as a calling card, symbolizing the social identities of the residents of the enclave.

Given the above view of enclaves, the tradition that confines use of the term to racial or ethnic concentrations is too limiting. Lifestyle, religion, income, or occupation—or combinations among them—can also be the primary bases of enclaves. In the following chapters we shall examine in detail a number of enclaves that represent a diverse array of historical and contemporary types. To distinguish them from each other entails creating ideal types, that is, deliberately exaggerating some distinctive characteristics of each.[37] Presented in each chapter are detailed case studies of one or two representative enclaves that in at least some respects are exemplars of that (ideal) type of enclave.

The three chapters following this one are historically grounded, focusing upon enclave forms that were common one hundred years ago but, due to changes in social organization, are rarely found in contemporary metropolitan areas.

Chapter Two describes elite enclaves based on residents' wealth and lifestyle. These typically small enclaves usually involved a number of extended families connected by kinship ties. Boston's Beacon Hill is the primary focus of the chapter, with secondary attention directed to Philadelphia's Chestnut Hill and San Francisco's Nob Hill. These were the exemplars of elite enclaves that developed in Eastern cities early in the nineteenth century and later that century in the Midwest and West.

Chapter Three is an examination of the "Back of the Yards" area in Chicago's southwest side. This sprawling, working-class community was primarily comprised of European immigrants employed in the stockyards' meatpacking plants. The Yards complex illustrated the close association between neighborhood and work that occurred in many large American cities during the period of rapid industrial development in the late nineteenth and early twentieth centuries.

Chapter Four examines two concentrations of African Americans in Detroit near the turn of the twentieth century: a large and predominantly poor enclave on the near east side and a smaller and wealthier near-enclave that formed on what was then the edge of the city. Detroit was a rapidly growing and industrializing city with opportunities for factory employment that attracted African-American and white migrants from the South as well as international immigrants.

The next three chapters examine diverse groups in diverse places; but the chapters are all alike in that each traces a racial or ethnic enclave from the time of its residents' initial immigration through contemporary changes. In addition, each chapter notes the ways in which the enclave contributed to the economy of the nation in which it was located by helping to link it to global commerce.

Chapter Five, new to this edition, follows German immigrants to a couple of cities in Brazil's southernmost states. They were the original pioneers in this region and for many years they dominated the towns they settled. The towns became cities and more multicultural, and the Germans became more Brazilian, though evidence of German enclaves remain, and their influence upon Brazil is pronounced both culturally and economically.

Chapter Six analyzes two groups of Chinese immigrants who settled in California. In the nineteenth century, the first group came penniless to prospect for gold and silver; they established the Chinese Quarter in San Francisco, the predecessor to the city's contemporary Chinatown. In contrast, many more recent Chinese immigrants left professional and managerial professions to flee the communists and many of them have settled in upper-income suburban areas east of Los Angeles.

Chapter Seven provides a description of several diverse waves of Cuban immigrants and exiles, many of whom have settled in the Miami area. That city's Little Havana, the primary focus of the chapter, contains the largest concentration of Cubans anywhere in the world outside Havana. Cohesion is maintained within the community by opposition to Castro's regime and by the persistence of distinctively Cuban ways of life, but there are marked generational differences in acculturation.

The last three chapters prior to the conclusion focus upon enclaves that were or are primarily based upon lifestyle. None of them were based solely upon lifestyle, though; occupation, sexual preference, or religion were also involved and contributed in an important way to the lifestyle that distinguished the enclave.

Chapter Eight, also new to this edition, is another historical enclave. It describes Americans who were artists, writers, composers, or the like who, at least temporarily, immigrated to Paris during the first decades of the twentieth century. Particularly during the 1920s they formed a Bohemian enclave on the Left Bank that produced many of the century's most notable works but was also characterized by anomie and suicide.

Chapter Nine examines the largest and commercially and institutionally the most complete gay enclave in the United States: the Castro district in San Francisco. As an openly gay place, it is now about thirty-five years old. Like similar communities elsewhere in the United States, the Castro was a declining manufacturing area until it was revived by a gay influx. This chapter also describes the adjacent Mission district, where lesbian residents make up a near-enclave attached to the Castro district.

Chapter Ten describes Hasidic Jews who settled in Brooklyn, New York, after World War II. The Lubavitch sect in Crown Heights is examined in particular. This Hasidic enclave is illustrative of many closed religious communities that have formed in the United States since its founding, but it is unlike most in that the Hasidim reside in close proximity to African-American and Hispanic populations. This proximity has resulted in frequent intergroup conflicts.

Chapter Eleven presents some general conclusions by examining a number of changes that have tended to occur across all types of enclaves. Specifically, the effects of greater transnational contacts, more inclusiveness, more wealth, and less emphasis upon assimilation are examined in relation to the likely persistence of enclaves.

Notes

1. Robert E. Park, "The City," in Robert E. Park, Ernest W. Burgess, and Roderick D. McKenzie (Eds.), *The City,* Chicago: University of Chicago Press, 1967, p. 40, originally published 1925. Park's first career was as a newspaper reporter, but when he found himself more interested in the impact of newspapers on city life than in the stories he was covering, he became an academic sociologist. See Robert E. Faris, *Chicago Sociology,* San Francisco: Chandler, 1967.

2. See, for example, Kenneth L. Wilson and W. Allen Martin, "Ethnic Enclaves," *American Journal of Sociology* 88, 1982; John R. Logan, Richard D. Alba, and Wenquan Zhang, "Immigrant Enclaves and Ethnic Communities in New York and Los Angeles," *American Sociological Review* 67, 2002.

3. Stephen O. Murray, "Components of Gay Community in San Francisco," in Gilbert Herdt (Ed.), *Gay Culture in America,* Boston: Beacon Press, 1992.

4. Richard D. Alba, John R. Logan, Brian Stults, Gilbert Marzan, and Wenquan Zheng, "Immigrant Groups in the Suburbs," *American Sociological Review* 64, 1999.

5. Jerome R. Mintz, *Hasidic People,* Cambridge, MA: Harvard University Press, 1992.

6. The Romany's prohibition on economic dealings with each other also inhibits the development of local community businesses. See Ian F. Hancock, "Gypsies," in Stephen Thernstrom (Ed.), *Harvard Encyclopedia of American Ethnic Groups,* Cambridge, MA: Harvard University Press, 1980; and chap. 3 in William M. Kephart and William W. Zellner, *Extraordinary Groups,* New York: St. Martin's, 1994.

7. David A. Snow and Leon Anderson, *Down on Their Luck,* Berkeley: University of California Press, 1993.

8. For further discussion of these emotional attachments, see Pamela Paxton and James Moody, "Structure and Sentiment," *Social Psychology Quarterly* 66, 2003.

9. For further discussion of this issue, see Howard P. Chudacoff, *Evolution of American Urban Society,* Englewood Cliffs, NJ: Prentice-Hall, 2000.

10. Christen T. Jonassen, "Cultural Variables in the Ecology of an Ethnic Group," *American Sociological Review* 14, 1949.

11. E. Michael Gorman, "The Pursuit of the Wish," in Gilbert Herdt (Ed.), *Gay Culture in America,* Boston: Beacon Press, 1992.

12. Similarly, many Korean and Russian immigrants have recently established small suburban enclaves in the Catskills of New York because its woods and hills remind them of their homelands. *New York Times,* July 12, 1993, p. B5.

13. Roy Rosenzweig and Elizabeth Blackmar, *The Park and the People: A History of Central Park,* Ithaca, NY: Cornell University Press, 1992.

14. For further discussion of the (often humorous) difficulties faced by Iranians in Houston and elsewhere, see Michael M. J. Fischer and Mehdi Abedi, *Debating Muslims,* Madison: University of Wisconsin Press, 1990.

15. Albert Hunter, *Symbolic Communities,* Chicago: University of Chicago Press, 1974.

16. Judith N. DeSena, *Protecting One's Turf,* Lanham, MD: University Press of America, 1990.

17. Herbert Gans, *The Urban Villagers,* New York: Free Press, 1982, p. 11.

18. DeSena, op. cit., p. 61.

19. Edwin B. Almirol, *Ethnic Identity and Social Negotiation,* New York: AMS Press, 1985, p. 121.

20. *New York Times,* August 29, 1993, p. 18.

21. Elaine Sciolino, "A Maze of Identities for the Muslims of France," *New York Times,* April 9, 2003, p. A3.

22. See Rudolfo F. Acuna, "A Community under Siege," *Chicano Studies Research Center Publication #11,* Los Angeles: The Center, University of California at Los Angeles, 1984.

23. For further discussion of the concept of identity, see Sheldon Stryker and Peter Burke, "The Past, Present, and Future of an Identity Theory," *Social Psychology Quarterly* 63, 2000. See also Michael A. Hogg and Cecilia L. Ridgeway, "Social Identity," *Social Psychology Quarterly* 66, 2003.

24. The coherence among selves is examined in Steve Hitlin, "Values as the Core of Personal Identity," *Social Psychology Quarterly* 66, 2003.

25. Sheldon Stryker, *Symbolic Interactionism,* Menlo Park, CA: Benjamin Cummings, 1980.

26. Another way to think about salience is by the degree to which an identity is the basis for organized generalizations about the self. Social psychologist Hazel Markus calls those that are important bases, "self-schemas," and she defines them as dimensions on which individuals hold the most clear and distinct perceptions about themselves, the domains people are most likely to defend if challenged. Hazel R. Markus, "Self-Schemata and Processing Information about the Self," *Journal of Personality and Social Psychology* 35, 1977. For a review of studies of self-schemas and an analysis of racial-ethnic self-schemas, see Daphna Oyserman, Markus Kemmelmeier, Stephanie Fryberg, Hazi Brosh, and

Tamera Hart-Johnson, "Racial-Ethnic Self Schemas," *Social Psychology Quarterly* 66, 2003.

27. Melinda Milligan, "Displacement and Identity Continuity," *Symbolic Interaction* 26, 2003.

28. Hunter, op. cit. See also David M. Hummon, "Community Attachment," in Irwin Altman and Setha M. Low (Eds.), *Place Attachment*, New York: Plenum, 1992.

29. Helen R. F. Ebaugh, *Becoming an Ex*, Chicago: University of Chicago Press, 1988.

30. Barbara B. Brown and Douglas D. Perkins, "Disruptions in Place Attachment," in Altman and Low, op. cit.

31. Scott Cummings, *Left Behind in Rosedale*, Boulder, CO: Westview Press, 1998.

32. Milligan, op. cit.

33. Similar processes are described in Erving Goffman, *Stigma*, Englewood Cliffs, NJ: Prentice-Hall, 1963; and Ebaugh, op. cit.

34. *New York Times*, June 28, 1993, p. A12.

35. David Wellman, "Honorary Homey's, Class Brothers, and White Negroes," paper presented at the American Sociological Association meeting, August 1993.

36. For further discussion, see Kimberly McClain DaCosta, "Multiracial Identity," in Loretta I. Winters and Herman L. DeBose (Eds.), *New Faces in a Changing America*, Thousand Oaks, CA: Sage, 2003.

37. See Max Weber, *The Methodology of the Social Sciences*, New York: Free Press, 1949.

Boston's Beacon Hill and Other Elite Enclaves

Many cities initially formed on sites that offered favorable access to rivers, lakes, or oceans because of the importance of water routes for transportation. One disadvantage of proximity to water, however, is that flooding can be a recurring problem. Modern engineering technology has alleviated some of the problems but not eliminated them entirely. In earlier times, 150 to 200 years ago, the risks to life and property were even more substantial. Thus the most desirable places within cities where there was a threat of flooding were up high, on hills. Another aspect of bodies of water is that they seem generally to hold an attraction for people. People like residences from which they can look out over rivers, lakes, and oceans, and in addition to the safety from flooding it provides, higher ground translates into better views.

It is the wealthier and more privileged classes who almost always win in the competition for the most desirable residential areas. As a result, in many cities there is a marked correlation between the social status of communities and the number of feet at which they rest above sea level. It is therefore not surprising that elite nineteenth-century communities formed in places such as Nob Hill in San Francisco, Beacon Hill in Boston, and Chestnut Hill in Philadelphia.

By the beginning of the nineteenth century, large Eastern cities had growing numbers of families that had acquired great wealth and passed it on for a sufficiently long time that their family names became synonymous with high social standing: Adams and Cabot in Boston, Biddle and Ingersoll in Philadelphia, Roosevelt and Jay in New York. The sources of these families' wealth were varied. Some had brought their money with them from England; others had acquired it in conjunction with British appointments in the colonies as governors, judges, or the like; and some had earned it in America in manufacturing, trade, or banking. What these families had in common was a distinctive social status associated with their old wealth.

Elite Status Groups

The most important feature of *status* as we employ the term here was captured by Max Weber's distinction between status and class. By *class*, Weber meant the market, or economic, situation of people. He talked about class as comprising a person's life chances, which were determined by that person's position in the marketplace. One's *ability* to buy an elegant summer home, hire maids and cooks, acquire the best medical care, and throw lavish parties, for example, would obviously depend on having substantial wealth and would therefore be a function of one's class position. By contrast, status for Weber was primarily defined by one's *style* of life, with its attendant degree of prestige. He recognized at least a partial economic, or class, basis for status positions; some lifestyles are very expensive to maintain and hence require substantial wealth. However, he insisted on maintaining a distinction between class and status such that one would not be reduced to the other. An aspect of status separate from class would be involved in selecting a community in which one wanted a summer home, whether one entertained at home or at "the club," and the kinds of entertaining one did. Weber observed that nothing could be more foreign to those of high status than the vulgar pretentiousness of people who had recently acquired great wealth and were busy spending it but had not yet learned how to consume with taste.[1]

In marked contrast to the tactless flaunting of people with recently acquired wealth, the Beacon Hill residents whose families have possessed wealth for many generations tend to invert status symbols. For example, this elite community is full of well-to-do doctors and stockbrokers who park battered Chevrolets and rusted-out Fords in front of their Beacon Hill homes. One longtime resident, a local realtor, explained the local custom by observing, "The lousier looking the car, the more wealthy the person is."[2]

Nelson W. Aldrich, Jr., in reflecting on his experiences in the upper class, makes Weber's point clear when he states that the critical characteristic of the money of the "real" upper class is its longevity. In this respect money is like fine wine or cheese; it is better when aged. What is most important, of course, is not solely the age of the money, but the way its age tends to be related to the outlooks of its possessors. "Old Money," he writes, is seen by its holders as being like an estate with a history that is held in trust. The income it produces is used to support a family and its cultural undertakings. Old wealth is something one simply takes for granted and passes on, and its uses are determined by traditional standards. The earners of "New Money," in contrast, see wealth as a tool with infinite possibilities and take none of its characteristics for granted. Their stance is entrepreneurial, pushing aside traditional standards and seeking more and bigger marketplaces where everything is, presumably, for sale.[3]

Weber also argued that shared status, apart from class position, was an important basis for interaction among people. In other words, he viewed people as being attracted to others on the basis not solely or even primarily of similar purchasing power but of shared tastes in consumption. Associations were likely to form on the basis of common status or lifestyle characteristics such as taste in music, clothing, or vacation sites. It is common, Weber continued, for those of any status or lifestyle to restrict access to their group, thereby keeping people who are deemed to be "different" outside their social circle.

Aldrich again provides an interesting example in describing a typical old-money social club, in which the unattractive and vulgar ways of the business class ("New Money") are eschewed. Shoptalk is prohibited at the lunch tables. Conviviality and serenity are expected to reign supreme so people can "simply be." It is actually offensive for a man to identify his job, and even "bad form" to introduce oneself; others are expected just to know. The old-money club, Aldrich states, "is a refuge from the ugly world outside, with its pleading, cajoling, sleeve-plucking, breast thumping strivers and strugglers swirling through the streets."[4]

Weber concluded that restrictions on access to a social circle lead to endogamous marriages, especially in high-status groups. It is by keeping marriages within the status group that the group is in fact perpetuated. Researchers DiMaggio and Mohr illustrated Weber's marital endogamy contention with a longitudinal study of nearly three thousand eleventh-graders. They gave the students a questionnaire focusing upon their interest in such "high-culture" activities as attending symphony concerts or art events, reading literature, and so on. Each person in the sample was given a cultural capital score reflecting his or her exposure/expertise in the high-culture fields. Eleven years later, when most of the former students were nearly thirty years old, the investigators obtained information about the spouses of those who had married. DiMaggio and Mohr hypothesized that respondents who as high school students had scored high on the cultural scale would later marry people with higher levels of education. This hypothesis rested upon the assumption that higher education was positively associated with high-cultural involvement, so if people with high-cultural interests wanted to select spouses like themselves, they would marry persons with advanced education. The hypothesis was confirmed even when the investigators held constant measures of family wealth to make sure that class/wealth did not underlie the pattern. Thus marital selections seemed consistent with status endogamy.[5]

Because prior attainments of families, as opposed to those of individuals, are the primary basis by which the elite in America maintained the closed boundaries of their circle, Baltzell described the American upper class as having a "clan culture." Some of the most penetrating analyses of elite circles have been provided by Baltzell, himself both an offspring of the upper class and a sociologist. To illustrate "clan culture," Baltzell presents a letter of introduction that might have been written on behalf of a proper young Philadelphian:

> Sir, allow me to introduce Mr. Rittenhouse Palmer Penn. His grandfather on his mother's side was a colonel in the Revolution, and on his father's side he is connected with two of the most exclusive families in our city . . . and his family has always lived on Walnut street. . . . I feel certain that his very desirable social connections will render him of great value.[6]

(Note the kind of qualities the writer thought it important to emphasize—i.e., social background—and which type of characteristics—e.g., training, motivation, skills—seemed irrelevant.)

Following from their pronounced interest in their own ancestors, the nineteenth-century elite formed local historical and genealogical societies. The better the documentation of ancestry, the better could family background be erected as a barrier against potential invasion by the nouveau riche. The aristocratic families also established exclusive schools and private clubs for their own use. They later played central roles in both the creation and subsequent support of the first museums and symphony orchestras in their cities. In every realm of life they emphasized a genteel lifestyle (proof of "breeding") as well as family lineage to regulate access to their clubs, schools, and neighborhoods.

Elite enclaves in this country have tended to be composed of white Anglo-Saxon Protestants (WASPs), especially from the late nineteenth century onward. Prior to that time there were some Jews in exclusive clubs in New York, San Francisco, and elsewhere, and a few had even married into elite enclaves in Philadelphia. With increasing numbers of Eastern European Jews immigrating to American cities, however, anti-Semitism grew in the late nineteenth century, especially in Boston. Harvard University, reflecting its Boston Brahmin heritage and control over its board, instituted a quota system for Jewish students. The Brahmins also opposed, though unsuccessfully, the appointment of Louis Brandeis (a Jew) to the Supreme Court; and Jews were excluded from the "best" clubs and neighborhoods. While Boston's elite may have been the most actively anti-Semitic, local elites in other cities more or less followed the same pattern. In Los Angeles, for example, Jews had helped to establish several of the most select social clubs during the 1880s and 1890s, but after 1900 they were excluded from them.[7]

Similarly, persons of color were rarely included in elite communities, even though large numbers of nonwhite persons sometimes lived on the edges of WASP enclaves. There was a large upper-status African-American community located at the base of Beacon Hill, for example, but there was virtually no social contact between the people who lived in the enclaves at the bottom and at the top of the hill.[8]

Elizabeth R. Ameisen contends that for elite WASP communities to persist, they must continuously reinforce beliefs in the superiority of their way of life, requiring that their lifestyle be protected against any outsiders seen as trying to "infiltrate." Thus exclusion and discrimination are necessary practices of elite enclaves "to ensure that the way of life they know will continue."[9]

There was, as we would expect, a high rate of intramarriage among the elite, who shared the same values and lifestyle and whose social circles were closed to outsiders. As a result, kinship ties were widespread among them, which gave them even more of a clanlike quality and encouraged the formation of residential enclaves. They were also drawn toward the same areas for access to such institutions as the elegant Episcopal churches they built and their private clubs and schools. Around the turn of the nineteenth century, a group of wealthy Bostonians met and planned on Beacon Hill in Boston the community that would become the prototype of all elite residential enclaves.

Building Beacon Hill

Beacon was the tallest of three hills on which Boston was initially built. On its summit, the first Puritans set beacon fires to signal the approach of enemies—hence the origin of the name Beacon Hill. During the late 1730s, Thomas Hancock bought several acres on the south slope of the hill, abutting Boston Common, and built a two-and-one-half-story mansion with dozens of rooms, including one just for household china. The house was surrounded by a number of elegant gardens and imported trees.[10] For many years the Hancock mansion was the sole edifice on the hill. The remaining acres belonged to the town and were undeveloped.

Just before the turn of the nineteenth century, an elite group of Boston Brahmins began to develop the hill into a residential area for their clan. Working in concert, they bought up land and built stately mansions with servants' quarters and decorative gardens along tree-lined streets. Long and narrow private parks with grass, flowers, and trees also ran down the center of some of the streets, where the houses, set back from the roads on both sides, all faced the park.

The housing followed a number of different designs. Early in the nineteenth century, most were federal-red brick houses or more massive, Greek-style houses built of gleaming white granite. Later in the nineteenth century there was a revival of Queen Anne design, featuring homes that were asymmetrical (for example, no two windows were alike) and made extensive use of textured materials on their facades. Many were highly decorated, with conspicuous exterior red and yellow tiles, lavender window shutters, and the like.[11]

In the past 150 years or so, newer houses have been placed between the old ones, connecting them to each other and giving the area a more crowded look than it originally possessed. Most of the huge stables and servants' quarters have also disappeared. Nonetheless, a contemporary visitor to Beacon Hill can still see some of the early brick and cobblestone sidewalks and roads. Several of the streets have retained much of their former character, and there are still beautiful gardens, though many are tucked behind homes and walls, out of public view. Every spring people come from as far away as Japan for the Beacon Hill Garden Club's annual tour, an event that began in 1925.[12] The community also continues to house a number of descendants of Boston's "first families."

The power of the Brahmins to influence political decisions in Boston was clearly reflected in the way in which they developed Beacon Hill. Encountering only token opposition along the way, the Brahmins were able to establish conditions that facilitated the development. Relying on connections they had made in other Boston land speculations, they were able to obtain building permits quickly and easily. When road improvements were needed to continue Beacon Hill's development, the projects were given priority and paid for by the City of Boston. With the increase in construction, land values on the hill were rising, but property on the hill was kept undervalued on City tax rolls. Beacon Hill's location near the center of Boston's financial and retail centers and historical icons such as the Boston Common and Old State House made it attractive to people outside the elite enclave who wanted to develop the area commercially; but in response, the City of Boston enacted new zoning laws and reinterpreted old ones to protect Beacon Hill from unwanted commercial enterprises that would have detracted from its residential desirability.[13]

This closeness to the center of Boston has been associated in more recent times with an increase in muggings, break-ins, and other crimes in Beacon Hill. Whenever it appears that the enclave is experiencing a crime wave, however, the residents have been able to pressure the City of Boston

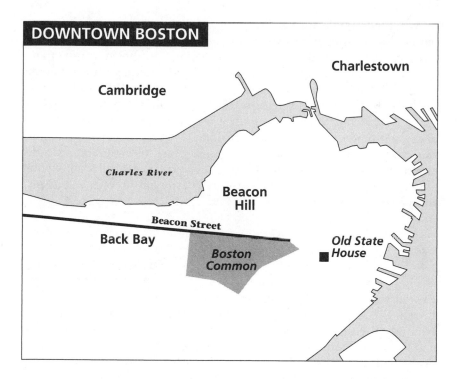

to increase the number of police assigned to Beacon Hill and/or to increase the number of police patrols. Criminals are then pushed to other communities, and Beacon Hill continues to have the lowest crime rate in Boston.[14]

Power and Resistance

The power of the Brahmins to develop Beacon Hill to their liking would not have been surprising to Weber. He viewed power as the influence exerted by "parties"—permanent or temporary associations voluntarily formed by people in order to pursue their interests in opposition to other organized groups. According to Weber, the objectives of parties could pertain primarily to values and lifestyles, to economic interests, or to a combination of the two. The most powerful parties are formed by people who by virtue of their high status in society possess great moral authority or who by virtue of their position in the marketplace possess great financial resources. Either wealth or status or a combination thereof can be translated into power once parties are formed for the purpose of exerting influence. The Brahmins who set out to develop Beacon Hill had both.

Weber recognized differences in the contexts in which power could be exercised and variations in the form it might take, but his emphasis was always on power in the face of opposition. That is, he focused on situations in which there were competing parties, each trying to influence decisions that would affect all. Thus he defined power as the probability that a party or a person "will be in a position to carry out his own will despite resistance."[15]

Parks for Whom?

One of the ways in which the interests of the upper-class residents of Beacon Hill directly opposed those of other Bostonians involved the people's use of the Boston Commons, a large park just across Beacon Street, and the smaller, private parks throughout the enclave on the hill. Because of the density and crowding in ethnic working-class communities in the late nineteenth century, working-class residents looked to parks for unrestricted recreation. To the upper class, however, the key issue was how parks could contribute to a genteel lifestyle. What they had in mind was parks with manicured lawns and a quiet atmosphere, in which nurses wearing white caps and aprons could stroll with baby carriages. Almost all of the uses to which the working-class immigrants wanted to put the parks were at odds with this upper-class conception. But even though the ethnic working class far outnumbered the elite throughout New England cities during the last quarter of the nineteenth century, control over the park system (as with the rest of City government) tended to be in the hands of upper-class Yankee natives.

The activities of the working class, who viewed parks as places where they could engage in activities not possible in or around their cramped lodgings, were offensive to upper-class tastes. The elite considered working-class people to be dirty and unkempt people who had messy picnics in the parks, drunks who were using the park to "sleep it off," roughnecks who were trampling the grass with their ball games, or immoral adolescents who were thought to be seeking sexual orgies in dark parks at night. Park commissioners tended to comply with the elite's wishes and tried to control park uses in a variety of ways, such as posting "keep off the grass" signs, enforcing vagrancy laws, and erecting lights.[16]

The demands both for more parks and for the freedom to use them fully were issues that eventually transcended particular neighborhoods and ethnic groups. Parks became objects of class conflict transcending ethnic differences among the working-class immigrants, who banded together in opposition to the city's elite and the city government, which the elite controlled. The conflict was initially resolved in terms highly favorable to the upper class, namely, the creation of a two-tiered system of separate and unequal parks: elaborate floral gardens in sedate settings in the elite enclaves and little more than open dumps in the working-class enclaves.

During the early years of the twentieth century, the class conflict was redefined in the writings of social reformers who urged investments in parks and playgrounds in all neighborhoods. They specifically argued that supervised play could be used to socialize working-class children into more responsible, harder-working adults. For the upper class, who owned the factories in which these children would eventually work, the arguments of the reformers justified support for public park systems. Across the country, a movement began that would lead to the formation of a National Playground Association in 1906. The association's efforts were initially directed at improving facilities for boys only. It was not until nearly 1920, in conjunction with efforts to extend women's rights to participate in many realms, that a "play-for-all" drive was extended to include improvements in girls' recreational facilities as well.[17]

Ecological Power

Weber's writings on power and opposition have proven to be very influential. It may also be helpful, however, particularly in talking about the power of elites, to recognize a more indirect kind of power involving an ability to arrange the conditions under which people interact. Political scientist Clarence N. Stone calls this capacity ecological power and notes that it can be the most efficient type of power. As Weber's notion implies, it may be very difficult or very expensive or require a continuous struggle for a party to control others. But if a party can institutionalize the advantages it seeks, Stone writes, opposition may become muted, and it may be possible to circumvent many confrontations. If minority political action groups in a city are able to get affirmative-action plans written into law, for example, they can forestall arguments about hiring plans for each construction project that arises. In addition, when such rules become institutionalized, they are more difficult for other parties to challenge. Thus the difficulty or expense of maintaining any political advantage is lessened if it comes to be regarded as part of the established structure within which people must interact.[18]

By focusing on the rules that govern the terms of social interaction, parties can even avoid or minimize initial opposition to their goals. More specifically, if a group has the resources to define situations, it may be able to convince local officials to reach decisions that favor them without appearing to be detrimental to the interests of other parties. Opposing groups will not form then, and the difficulty of the struggle is minimized. For example, a hundred years after Beacon Hill's founding, its wealthy residents were able to obtain property tax reductions for the "historic preservation" of their neighborhood. They convinced local government officials to support their request by passing legislation in the name of preservation, and their gain was apparent. The loss of revenue to the City of Boston or the consequences of such a diminution may not even have been recognized by potential antagonists. However, if the issue had been expressed in terms of a tax break rather than historic preservation, other parties would have been more likely to band together in opposition to it. Thus one very important type of power can lie in the ability simply to decide what to call something.

It is the elite—whether their positions are based on status, wealth, or a combination of the two—that are most likely to have the capacity to structure the social and physical environment in a way that suits their interests without provoking opposition. They wielded this ecological power to establish and maintain elite enclaves in several American cities.

Other Elite Enclaves

Similar elite enclaves were begun in the early and middle 1800s in other Eastern cities and in the late 1800s in Western cities. In Philadelphia at the turn of the nineteenth century, for example, an elite enclave was formed on Chestnut Hill. Known for its chestnut trees, this hill was the highest point between Trenton, New Jersey, and Bryn Mawr, Pennsylvania. Like Beacon Hill in Boston, Chestnut Hill did not simply form unplanned. Its major period of growth, during the late nineteenth century, was directed by Henry Howard Houston, whose wealth came from oil investments, the railroad, and other land speculation in Philadelphia. He obtained permits, got the city to build roads, commissioned architects, and oversaw the building of approximately one hundred mansions. His efforts turned Chestnut Hill into what was then called "Philadelphia's prettiest suburb."[19]

This Philadelphia neighborhood, like Beacon Hill, historically has contained the highest proportion of "Social Register" families in the Philadelphia metropolitan area. Also like Beacon Hill, it had its private schools and clubs and an unwelcoming attitude toward newcomers. Baltzell described Chestnut Hill as parochial and ethnocentric, with "all the qualities of the small village: the social life is inbred . . . everyone knows everyone else; gossip travels very fast.[20]

Distinguished lineages and homes in the proper neighborhoods were strongly correlated. In combination, they constituted a virtually impenetrable barrier to those outside the social and geographic inner circle. One very wealthy young man, who was excluded from Philadelphia's elite because his father's family's money was too recently acquired, explained that his mother, who came from old money, had "married across the tracks." His father's father had been poor and worked in a butcher shop. He (the grandfather) later became fabulously wealthy and built a fine mansion, but not in the elite enclave. Therefore, he said, it was "in Nobody's Land—socially." Despite the family's wealth, his grandson complained, "society called him and his sons *nouveau riche*."[21]

The growth of San Francisco's Nob Hill during the 1870s was in part a replay of the development of the elite enclaves in other sections of the country. There were differences, however, associated with the region and its later development: Mining was creating enormous fortunes overnight; more of the upper-class population of Western cities was composed of recent migrants; and improved modes of intracity transportation, such as cable cars, were facilitating movement out from the center of the city. All of these factors came together to influence the development of the legendary Nob Hill.

In 1870, Rincon Hill was probably the most fashionable residential area in San Francisco. The established old-money families of Rincon Hill did not welcome as neighbors the people with newer money made from mining and land speculation. However, the cable car had made the summit of Russian Hill, to the north, accessible, and the newer-moneyed people and newer arrivals to San Francisco moved there. The Higgins mansion (Mrs. Higgins was the daughter of the attorney general of Kentucky) was the first to be built, in 1872. It contained sixty rooms with high ceilings, marble steps, and enormous bay windows overlooking the Golden Gate. The second home was built by Mr. Higgins's brother-in-law, and then others followed, each more lavish than the last. Most employed a full housekeeping staff, including chefs, and contained splendid ballrooms and gardens in which to entertain families from neighboring estates or other comparable enclaves in the city. The tendency of these people to "hob-nob" with each other led to the summit of Russian Hill becoming known as Nob Hill.[22]

Preserving Beacon Hill

From their initial development in the early 1800s through roughly the middle of the twentieth century, the greatest threats to the continuation of specific elite enclaves came in the form of competition from newer residential areas. Automobiles and commuter trains facilitated travel, leading to the development of fashionable new residential areas that could sometimes offer more land and hence larger homes, bigger gardens, and more privacy. And if some outsiders had managed to "infiltrate" over the years, then starting a new enclave somewhere else could seem desirable to many wealthy families. However in a number of cases, the original enclaves remained in what is at least to some degree recognizable form. Beacon Hill again provides an interesting case study, but it is exceptional in its success in retaining Boston's elite. This success has not been fully matched by the enclaves in other cities that were its contemporaries.

In Boston in the early 1900s, a new area called Back Bay was developed. An elegant community adjacent to Beacon Hill, it came to be defined as "Boston's most fashionable," and a number of the old families left the hill. As they left, the profile of Beacon Hill changed. Mansions were converted into rooming houses, and a new class of people moved in, along with a plethora of commercial shops. Property values began to fall, permitting still further invasions, pushing more families off the hill, and so on in a continuing cycle. For over a decade, the number of Boston's Social Register families living on Beacon Hill declined, while there was a corresponding increase in Back Bay.[23]

However, Beacon Hill still had a rich, long-standing, symbolic value for Boston's elite, and when they banded together, their wealth and power were substantial. They outbid the competition for available mansions, which they collectively purchased, modernizing the interiors and then selling them to individual families. Apartment-hotels and various specialty shops were then denied access to locations on the hill. Further attrition of elite families from the hill was reduced, and there was a return flow. By the 1940s, Beacon Hill's percentage of Boston's Social Register families was actually twice its pre-1900 figure.

Until the 1950s each parcel of land that became available triggered a competition between elite families who wanted the hill to retain its status as a residential area and the commercial interests that would have liked to exploit its proximity to the center of Boston. In the late 1950s, the Beacon Hill Civic Association was able to get the hill designated as a historical district, and a board was established to review all restoration and renovation plans. Zoning ordinances were also passed to promote the hill's use as a distinguished residential area. Thus, using Stone's terms as introduced earlier, the ecological power of the elite provided them with the capacity to reshape the environment without a series of continuing confrontations. Their wealth, contacts, and prestige and their ability to appeal to preservationist values furnished the elite the power institutionally to structure arrangements rather than a power over any specific group.

Stability and Change

Every formerly elite enclave, including Beacon Hill, has been transformed to some degree. Some have not managed to survive at all, and many others are barely recognizable in comparison with their earlier forms. Beacon Hill no longer has as many families connected to each other through marriage, for example, and social life on the hill has many fewer formal balls. On the other hand, recognizable traditions have persisted. In the weeks before Christmas, residents continue to decorate lampposts with green garlands and red bows, and carolers with hand-rung bells stroll the hill's streets. (These traditions are 150 years old.[24]) The Beacon Hill Civic Association continues to advocate actively for the community's interests, including preservation of its traditional brick sidewalks.

Among elite enclaves in general, their upper-class cores tend to be small in size, and the homogeneity of the residents has declined in terms both of residents' characteristics and of diversity of land uses. There has also been a marked decline in the degree to which a range of social activities important to upper-class life has continued to occur within the enclave.

There are a number of reasons for these changes in elite enclaves. We have already noted one: the fact that the expansion of cities, facilitated by modern modes of transportation, resulted in greater dispersal of all segments of the population. From just a few centrally located neighborhoods, the cities' upper classes have moved to many more dispersed city and suburban communities, resulting in less concentrated numbers in each of those communities.

The solidarity of upper-class enclaves has also been diminished by changes in marriage and divorce patterns. As was previously discussed, upper-class culture in American cities was very clannish. High rates of marriage within the local upper class provided important bonds among people in these enclaves. Divorce was almost unheard-of; thus there were few messy divorces and remarriages to complicate relationships among people who worked together, lived together, and belonged to the same clubs.

Baltzell states that the threat of informal sanctions imposed by the family was very strong when divorce was contemplated by people in upper-class enclaves. The Episcopal Church, to which most of the urban elite belonged, was closer to Catholicism on this issue than most other Protestant denominations; it did not recognize the remarriage of divorced persons. In addition to the sanctions of family and Church, divorced persons were automatically excluded from important upper-class social functions such as assembly balls (which were near the apex of local social activities). As late as 1940, Baltzell reports, less than 1 percent of the persons listed in Philadelphia's *Who's Who* were then divorced.[25]

From Local to National Elites

During the twentieth century the scene of the action changed from local cities to the nation and the world. Corporations spanned the entire United States rather than being confined to local markets, and ownership of these giant corporations typically moved from families to institutional stockholders. Corporations began to recruit their elites more from across the nation and the world than from among members of an owning family. Even so, the new recruits to the boardroom frequently came from the same distinguished private universities, were often members of the same private clubs, and regularly sat together on the boards of many other corporations. Thus they were similar in terms of background, lifestyle, and social contacts and they formed a social network but were not bound to each other by kinship or by a tie to one particular place.[26]

In a contemporary study of upper-class women in a Midwestern city, sociologist Susan A. Ostrander's subjects commented on birthrights and birthplaces. The women continued, like their nineteenth-century counterparts, to emphasize the importance their circle placed on being well-born or from an old-line family. However, those who were fourth- and fifth-generation members of their city's elite were also aware that they were starting to be outnumbered by people who were not natives: upper-class newcomers from other cities.[27]

Despite the partial fusing of local and national upper classes, many of the local civic concerns of the old-money elite continue to set the agenda for the class. For example, groups comprising both national and local elites from business, politics, and the arts undertake to support specific cities' museums, symphonies, and libraries. Large contributions from people of high class standing enable them to "buy" status through the association of their names with visible philanthropic or cultural activities; and the special balls and opening nights sponsored by the beneficiary institutions are important places to be seen if one wants to be considered as someone socially important. However, the elite patrons are no longer drawn exclusively from the city that houses the particular cultural entity.

To sum up, the elite enclaves that have persisted until the end of the twentieth century are typically very small. The upper class of cities now lives in more dispersed locations and contains a mixture of natives and migrants from other cities. In contemporary cities there is also more mixing of old and new money. Perhaps because nuances regarding family background are less well known to people raised in different cities, the boundaries of the upper class appear to be more penetrable than they were one hundred years ago. With respect to upper-class clubs, for example, Ostrander reports that membership continues to require the same values, attitudes, and lifestyle, helping to ensure that the class will not dramatically change. However, the gradual absorption of "a few carefully selected 'new' persons of wealth, status, and power . . . protects the class from complete stagnation."[28]

Notes

1. Max Weber, *The Theory of Social and Economic Organization,* trans. A. M. Henderson and Talcott Parsons, New York: Oxford University Press, 1947.
2. Alice Giodano, "Community Profile," *Boston Globe,* March 2, 2002, p. E1.

3. See the introduction in Nelson W. Aldrich, Jr., *Old Money*, New York: Alfred A. Knopf, 1988.

4. Aldrich, op. cit., p. 51.

5. Paul DiMaggio and John Mohr, "Cultural Capital, Educational Attainment, and Marital Selection," *American Journal of Sociology* 90, 1985, pp. 1231–1261.

6. E. Digby Baltzell, *The Philadelphia Gentlemen*, New Brunswick, NJ: Transaction Books, 1989, p. 31, first edition published 1958. Baltzell argues that Bostonians went back more generations than Philadelphians, and that the latter were more concerned with purely economic accomplishments. However, generalization about the importance of ancestry seems to hold for the elite in all cities. See also E. Digby Baltzell, *Puritan Boston and Quaker Philadelphia*, New York: Free Press, 1979.

7. Frederic C. Jaher, *The Urban Establishment*, Urbana: University of Illinois Press, 1982.

8. There were similar concentrations of upper-status African Americans in a number of cities in the late nineteenth century, but their communities were usually not true enclaves. See, e.g., the discussion of the upper-status African-American near-enclave in Detroit in Chapter Four.

9. Elizabeth R. Ameisen, "Exclusivity in an Ethnic Elite," in Philip L. Kilbride, et. al. (Eds.), *Encounters with American Ethnic Cultures*, Tuscaloosa: University of Alabama Press, 1990, p. 76.

10. William H. Fowler, Jr., *The Baron of Beacon Hill*, Boston: Houghton Mifflin, 1980.

11. For further discussion of the development of Beacon Hill, and numerous photographs of the community, see Moying Li-Marcus, *Beacon Hill*, Boston: Northeastern University Press, 2002.

12. Rosemary Herbert, "Gardening," *Boston Herald*, May 12, 2002, p. 54.

13. Jaher, op. cit.

14. For example, in 2001 and 2002, there was an increase in prostitution occurring in Beacon Hill, followed by an increase in police presence until the prostitution declined. Sarah Schweitzer, "Crime Creeps Up Beacon Hill," *Boston Globe*, April 1, 2002, p. B1.

15. Weber, op. cit., p. 152.

16. See the description of class conflict over parks in Worcester, Massachusetts, in Roy Rosenzweig, *Eight Hours for What We Will*, Cambridge, UK: Cambridge University Press, 1983.

17. Karla A. Henderson, "A Feminist Analysis of Selected Professional Recreational Literature about Girls/Women from 1907–1990," *Journal of Leisure Research* 25, 1993.

18. Clarence N. Stone, "Power and Social Complexity," in Robert J. Waste (Ed.), *Community Power*, Beverly Hills, CA: Sage, 1986. A similar view

of power within cities is presented by John R. Logan and Harvey L. Molotch, *Urban Fortunes,* Berkeley: University of California Press, 1987.

19. Richard Webster, *Philadelphia Preserved,* Philadelphia, PA: Temple University Press, 1976.
20. Baltzell, *Philadelphia Gentlemen,* op. cit., p. 165.
21. Ibid., p. 205.
22. Julia C. Altrocchi, *The Spectacular San Franciscans,* New York: E. P. Dutton, 1949, p. 101.
23. Walter Firey, "Sentiment and Symbolism as Ecological Variables," *American Sociological Review* 10, 1945.
24. The history of many of these practices is described in Li-Marcus, op. cit.
25. Baltzell, *Philadelphia Gentlemen,* op. cit. His figure refers to those currently (i.e., 1940) divorced and not remarried, rather than the sum of all those persons who had ever been divorced; but it is clear that the latter number was also extremely low in comparison with today's figures.
26. See Donald A. Palmer and Roger Friedland, "Corporation, Class and City System," in Mark S. Mizruchi and Michael Schwartz (Eds.), *Intercorporate Relations,* Cambridge, UK: Cambridge University Press, 1987. See also Michael Useem, *The Inner Circle,* New York: Oxford University Press, 1984.
27. Susan A. Ostrander, *Women of the Upper Class,* Philadelphia, PA: Temple University Press, 1984.
28. Ibid., p. 110.

"Back of the Yards"

Chicago and Other Working-Class Enclaves

In most American cities during the early 1800s, there was little separation between the locations of work and residence. Shoemakers made shoes in the front rooms of their homes; small groups of men rolled cigars in the local tobacco store while the proprietor's family lived upstairs. Carpet weaving premises and small machine shops sat among row houses and tenements. A few small manufacturing concentrations—textiles, woodworking, leather goods, meatpacking houses—were also just beginning to appear in areas immediately surrounding the financial and retail centers of the downtowns.[1]

The invention of various machines in the middle of the century gradually facilitated larger concentrations of labor. Manufacturing moved from homes to factories, and production came to rely on a larger and more complex division of labor. Because the work was mechanized, the biggest demand was for unskilled labor, and a ready supply was provided by the European immigrants who began flooding into America during the last half of the nineteenth century. The unskilled workers and their families tended to concentrate around the large factories that employed them, which resulted in working-class enclaves. Because immigrants from a given country tended to cluster in a particular industry, many of the working-class enclaves were composed largely of people from the same country of origin.

Chicago's rapid growth during the middle of the nineteenth century was in large part a result of the railroad and westward expansion. Almost every rail line in the nation west of Lake Michigan was linked to Chicago. By 1860, these tracks resembled the spokes of a wheel, dividing the western region into pie-shaped wedges, each of which was linked to Chicago.[2] Hogs, sheep, cows, and other livestock were increasingly shipped by rail to packinghouses on the southwest side of Chicago, about five miles from the downtown. In 1865 all the packing operations were consolidated when Union Stock Yards was opened. The subsequent development of refrigerated railcars and improvements in canning made it increasingly practical to slaughter livestock in a single location. Swift, Armour, and other major meatpackers located their facilities nearby, and by 1910 the complex, which included rail lines, slaughterhouses, and packing and canning houses, covered five hundred acres and had its own power station.

Working conditions in all of the plants and factories in Back of the Yards were dreadful. Those fortunate enough to have jobs were pushed by supervisors to keep working as fast as possible under unsafe and unsanitary conditions, and their wages were barely sufficient to cover the minimal essentials.[3] One of the main reasons the owners were able to keep people working under these conditions was their deliberate manipulation of the "army of the unemployed." Karl Marx had described this practice in European factories in the mid-nineteenth century.[4] In Chicago fifty years later, it worked the same way. The owners (*bourgeoisie,* in Marx's terms) kept the unemployed work-seekers hanging around outside the factories so they would be visible to everyone working inside. Because the workers (*the proletariat,* in Marx's terms) realized they would be very easy to replace, and they had no safety net—unemployment compensation, welfare, or the like—to fall back upon, the owners had tremendous leverage.

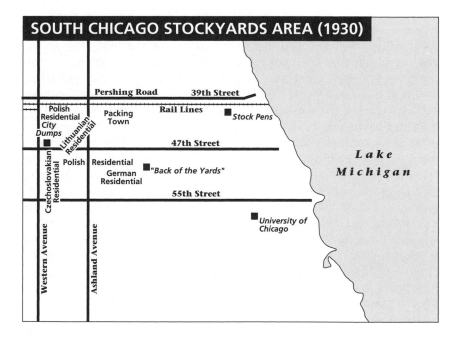

SOUTH CHICAGO STOCKYARDS AREA (1930)

Living Conditions

Residential construction followed the growth of employment in the Yards. Some homes were built by residents on land owned by meatpacking companies, a few areas were developed by Armour and other meatpacking companies specifically for employees, some private developers built subdivisions, and some residential areas just sprang up in a jumble on land adjacent to the Yards. The typical home was a small, two-story, wooden frame house that covered about 60 percent of its lot. The amount of open space this left between cottages partly concealed the actual degree of crowding in the neighborhood.[5]

Crowded was the word that best described living conditions in Back of the Yards at the turn of the twentieth century. Most of the Catholic immigrants who lived in the Yards had very large families, a fact that by itself would have been sufficient to create crowded conditions in the small housing units. Even so, many owners and primary tenants also took in boarders. Over one quarter of the entire Back of the Yards population lived as boarders with other families, and that figure would be substantially higher if one looked only at adults. In 1908, Milton B. Hunt, an early social researcher, canvassed thirteen blocks in the stockyards district and found that 213 families did not have lodgers but over four hundred did. Of those who did, approximately 40 percent had three or more lodgers. Each lodger's rent included meal preparation but not food. The housekeeper typically kept a separate grocery ledger for each boarder and at mealtimes would serve each boarder exactly the food that had been purchased on his or her behalf.[6] One can imagine how awkward some of the meals must have been, given variations in the quality and quantity of food being eaten at the same time by people at the same table.

At night, lodgers typically slept in the same rooms as family members, often in the same beds! Some slept in a bedroom, and others slept in the kitchen, which in many homes served as an additional bedroom at night. As a result of the crowding it was very difficult for married couples to obtain any kind of privacy. Arranging for sexual relations, personal family discussions, and childbirth required delicate negotiations. One woman who was raised in the Yards remembers when her mother went into labor with a younger sibling. The boarder told her to go outside and watch the chimney: "Any minute the stork's going to fly over." She waited for about four hours, heard an infant's cries, then went back into the house confused. "Somehow you missed him," the boarder explained.[7]

For some families, taking in a boarder was probably a matter of choice—to supplement family income or temporarily accommodate a relative or friend. For many families, however, it was a matter of necessity. A paying boarder was the only way they could make monthly payments. Rents were high relative to factory wages, and landlords justified this fact by pointing to the presence of boarders who were paying the primary tenants. So the landlords raised the rents further, which led residents to seek additional boarders, which landlords felt justified further rent increases, and so on.

Located near the outskirts of the Yards were some once-fashionable homes that had been converted into rooming houses. This was a common practice in American cities at the turn of the twentieth century, when growth and expansion led to the decline of many residential areas. Some reasonably large single-family homes were deserted by residents who wanted to move farther away from encroaching immigrant settlements or smelly factories. The conversion of these homes into rooming houses provided a major addition to the housing stock of the period. The rooms attracted a diverse and colorful assortment of occupants. A canvass of people living in furnished rooms in Chicago at this time disclosed a great number of single men, many of whom found occasional work in factories and were described as having drinking and/or gambling problems. The investigators also reported such room occupants as a husband and wife, both of whom were heavy drinkers, in a single room with seven children whom they regularly sent out begging; and a woman with four children who cleaned offices at night and liked living in a rooming house because her children would be around other people while she was away.[8]

Descriptions of physical conditions in the Back of the Yards area painted a dismal picture. Smoke from factories and wood stoves fouled the air and produced high rates of lung disease. Rats the size of cats ran down the poorly paved streets at night, and there were swarms of flies in the filthy alleys where the children played. The smells of rotten meat, fumes from fertilizer factories, the nearby city dump, and poor sewerage facilities pervaded the air. One company regularly left an open wagon filled with bits of meat and globs of fat sitting out in the sun every day. The stench reached across the neighborhood and sickened riders in nearby streetcars. One visitor to the area later recalled getting off one streetcar and onto another because when the first streetcar approached the Yards a passenger boarded, and she mistakenly associated that passenger with the sickening odor. In addition to the foul air and odors, the Yards' residents had to contend with the screeching and puffing of locomotives, constant bells signaling the stops and starts of streetcars, noisy trucks, and loud whistles from the factories.[9]

Death rates from some childhood diseases were two to five times higher in the Back of the Yards than in other Chicago communities. Physical conditions contributed to this problem, as did the limited medical care received by Back of the Yards families. Physicians were never engaged short of serious emergencies, because of their cost and most families' skeptical views of the medical profession. Neighborhood midwives assisted with births, and mothers tried various home remedies with sick children. If their concoctions of soap and herbs and plants did not work, the next step typically was to consult the local pharmacist. Most pharmacies contained eight to ten chairs for customers waiting for a consultation. After listening to the symptoms, the pharmacist prepared an appropriate medicine and charged only for its cost.[10]

Other explanations at the time for the Yards' high child mortality rates were interesting, if one can indulge a little levity in a matter of such gravity. For example, Charles Bushnell completed one of the first doctoral dissertations in sociology at the University of Chicago in 1901. He studied living conditions in the Back of the Yards community and seems to have been one of the first scholars to condemn the evils of junk food. In summarizing his findings, he presented various child mortality rates that he related to the general health conditions of the district, citing inadequate sewerage, the squalor and dirt of the neighborhood—and the children's nonnutritious diet. "A mere glance into the lunch boxes of school children," he wrote, "shows . . . cakes, jellies and unwholesome pastry" for which the children "seem to have almost a special craving."[11]

During the 1920s and 1930s, many of the graduate students of Robert Park and other professors at the University of Chicago continued the research previously begun by Bushnell. At that time the Polish enclave in the Yards was especially large, and it was the subject of several studies on family life and adolescence. According to the researchers, these studies showed that family disorganization, delinquency, alcoholism, and other social problems were a result of the general processes of acculturation and social change that all immigrants go through, and were not caused by any intrinsic aspect of Polish culture or personality. However, community cooperation with these sociological studies eventually became problematic because many Poles resented public discussions of their drinking and delinquency, so they regarded the studies as slanderously anti-Polish.[12]

Separate Ethnic Villages

The residential area known as Back of the Yards had reasonably distinct geographic boundaries and its residents shared similar lifestyles, but it actually comprised a number of separate enclaves at the turn of the twentieth century. Each enclave consisted of core groups of fifty to one hundred people bonded by kinship who were tied to other core groups of people of the same nationality. Common language and culture and the same churches and church-related organizations forged core groups into what have been called "old-world villages." Because the Yards contained a number of such ethnic "villages," it was not, circa 1900, a single community. It was, Slayton writes, "an industrial neighborhood dominated by one form of community structure of which there were numerous examples."[13]

The first large ethnic group to move to the Yards area was Irish, and the packinghouse area initially had a strong Irish identity. (As explained in Chapter One, for an area to have an ethnic identity it is not necessary for a majority of its residents to be of that background. A relatively small percentage can appear to dominate if the group's institutions and stores are conspicuously placed and no other sizeable group is present.) The Irish influence was evident when a large meatpacking warehouse was christened "Castle Garden," after the name of New York's port of entry, because Irish immigrants were said to go immediately to the Yards in Chicago after docking in New York. They established a parish, Saint Rose of Lima, which along with its school was a focal institution for the immigrants. By 1900 Saint Rose's membership had risen to seven hundred Irish families, and the area in which the Irish predominated was known as Roseville. During the same period, a large number of German families moved into another Back of the Yards area, one developed by a German entrepreneur. They also established distinctive communities with their own churches and schools, but in each area there was some intermingling and overlap of groups. The next large groups to move into the Yards were Polish, Lithuanian, Italian, and in the 1930s, African American.

Each of the early-arriving nationality groups established its own parish churches and schools as well as its own distinctive restaurants and retail shops. For example, in the Polish area near the stockyards, saloons with Polish bartenders and clienteles proliferated. If a German or other outsider came in, a fistfight was likely to occur. Around 1910, a survey disclosed an average of three saloons per block in the Polish sections of the Yards. They served as social centers, as informal employment bureaus where people found out about job opportunities, and as "banks" that would cash checks for the immigrant Poles.[14]

The re-created villages of each ethnic group were also served by separate neighborhood food stores. By the 1920s there were over five hundred corner grocery stores serving the 75,000 people living in the Yards area, each operated by a shopkeeper of the same nationality as the local residents who shopped in the store. Store owners knew almost all of their customers by name, and relations were very personal. They gave pieces of candy to customers' children, bones to shoppers who planned to make soup that day, and waste products from the back of the store to customers they knew had pets. If a religious holiday or cultural celebration was coming, store owners of the same ethnicity could be counted on to provide the special items, such as hams, sausages, or candles, that their customers would need.[15]

Movies and Dances

By current standards, recreational opportunities were limited in Back of the Yards. Social-athletic clubs organized baseball and other sports on local streets and fields. Diverse social and religious activities were conducted in churches. There were also a number of neighborhood theaters; in fact, four movie theaters were competing with each other in the Yards by 1910. Some of the local theaters were actually grand emporiums, with padded chairs, smoking rooms, and spittoons. Each tried to attract customers by offering complete shows, which often included a double feature; a vaudeville show, usually featuring comedians; and for the kids, on Saturdays a serial—an adventure series shown in ten- to fifteen-minute episodes that continued over several weeks. All the theaters had a posted charge of 5 cents, but one owner used to stand in front of his theater and ask kids going by how much money they had with them. Even if they had as little as 2 cents, he would say, "Gimme it," then let them in.[16]

During the early decades of the twentieth century, the major recreational activity for young adults in Back of the Yards was dancing. Local high schools and churches regularly sponsored dances, and almost every neighborhood tavern had a dance hall behind it. A few large ballrooms attracted young people from across the entire city of Chicago, but the dance craze was largely a local neighborhood phenomenon. Most of the dances in the Yards were organized by the young men's social-athletic clubs. A club would rent a hall and hire a band, and members acted as hosts and bartenders. Sometimes members of the club would arrange a formal entrance for themselves, and, with a tumultuous fanfare from the band, the group members would march around the perimeter of the dance floor. Fights among the men were common; sometimes they were over a woman at the dance and sometimes they resulted from ongoing bad feelings between members of different local clubs. The young women made lengthy preparations for these dances. For example, a typical way to do one's own hair was to roll wet hair around small rolled pieces of newspaper, then tie long strips of cloth through the paper and around the head. When the hair dried and the paper came out, the young woman had a head of curls—an early permanent.[17]

In working-class neighborhoods of large cities across the United States, essentially the same types of locally organized dances were the major form of recreation during the first quarter of the twentieth century. The dances, historian Kathy Peiss notes, were highly provocative for the time, especially in New York, but in Chicago and other cities as well. In working-class dance halls around 1900, youths were "pivoting," performing a parody of the stiffly controlled upper-class waltz. The woman stood erect, the man slouched over her, and each put their chins on the other's shoulder. Then they would spin around crazily in tiny circles, in close physical contact, often shouting and singing. Later, working-class youths engaged in "tough dancing": A couple faced each other with pelvises shaking, lowering hands from shoulders to hips and moving closer and closer to each other.[18]

In order to understand fully the place of these dances in enclave social life, let us put the situation of young working-class people from 1910 to 1920 into perspective. Some schooling was valued by immigrant parents, but not necessarily to the point of graduation. In places like Back of the Yards, children as young as eleven years old got jobs in the meatpacking factories or railroad shops. Their strength was more important to employers than their intelligence, and their financial contributions to the household were needed. Parents attempted to control the activities of their working youngsters and tended to be especially watchful of their daughters whenever a situation even hinted at the possibility of sexual contact. And in the small, closely knit communities in which they lived, where everyone knew everyone else, one's conduct was almost always subject to surveillance.

Prior to marriage, working-class youths usually lived at home. Neither they nor their parents could afford for them to live in a separate residence, and going off to college was not an alternative. Marriage thus became one of the best means of "liberation." Until at least the late 1950s, many working-class youths, women in particular, married to escape from the watchful eyes of parents. This escape theme dominated the replies given by working-class women to Mirra Komarovsky's question, "How does marriage change a woman's life?" When many of her respondents described living in their parents' home, they said it had been "like prison" or stated that they had felt "all cooped up." One woman who had married at the age of sixteen offered an additional reason: she wanted to marry to have her own room. She was tired of waiting for her brothers' friends to go home so she could get into her bed, which was in the parlor.[19]

Unmarried women also faced more serious financial problems than men. They earned less on average from paid employment, and those who lived at home ordinarily received less than men in the form of parental "allowances." Almost all young working men and women turned their paychecks over to their parents, and parents in turn gave them some spending money. For women who lived at home, this allowance was typically not enough to pay for much in the way of recreation. An extreme but interesting illustration was provided by W. I. Thomas, a famous member of the old Chicago School of Sociology. One day around 1920, he was collecting information for his research in Chicago's juvenile court when a young girl was brought in for shoplifting. Prior to having stolen some beads and mirrors from a department store, she had worked for two years in a factory. She testified that she had faithfully given her entire $9-per-week pay to her mother, and her mother returned only 10 cents for the girl's own use. Her mother confirmed these facts, which led the judge to resolve the case by directing the mother to increase her daughter's allowance to 25 cents per week.[20]

Women who did not live at home and were self-supporting usually lived in furnished rooms. After paying for room and board, they also had little left over for recreational spending. They often walked to work to save money so they could pay the admission to a dance. It was worth it; a dance was the best place to find excitement and perhaps even meet a prospective husband.

Young men and women typically went to the dance hall with friends of the same sex. Some mixed-sex couples came together on "dates," but that was more common in middle-class circles. When the band began to play, women would often dance with each other. The men would look them over and engage in a practice called "breaking women": Two men would walk up to a pair of dancing women and, with no introductions, separate them, and each man would then dance off with one of the women. The couples might stay together for one dance or for the rest of the evening.[21]

A lot of alcoholic beverages were consumed at the dances. Men drank nickel beers, and a number of cocktails were offered, mostly for the women. The popularity of women in working-class dance halls in Chicago and elsewhere was frequently tied to the amount of alcohol they consumed. Abstainers were ostracized and sometimes asked to leave, whereas those who drank the most were given prizes. Drinking like this could become expensive, and, as already noted, the women had little money. So a woman would hope to find a man who would treat her to drinks. Finding such a man accorded a woman very high status among her peers. In return for treating, however, men ordinarily expected sexual intimacy. It was an arrangement some viewed as bordering on prostitution. From his studies in Chicago, Thomas described these women as an "equivocal class of girls who participate in prostitution without becoming definitely identified with it. The . . . line between the professional and the amateur . . . has become vague."[22]

The habitues of working-class dance halls were often called "charity girls" to differentiate them from prostitutes, who explicitly exchanged sexual participation for money. One New York City vice investigator (in 1917) concluded that the women who regularly frequented certain dance halls were not prostitutes in a legal sense, and he offered the following generalization: "Most . . . are working girls, they smoke cigarettes, drink liquers and dance disorderly dances, and stay out late . . . with any man that pick(s) them up."[23]

Class Solidarity and Ethnic Subenclaves

Through the first decades of the twentieth century, communities of working-class families were expanding across large sections of cities. In Back of the Yards, for example, employment in meatpacking continued to grow, and with the discoveries that waste parts of the slaughtered animals could be used to make a variety of products such as soap and glue, other industries crowded into the Yards. The residential areas housing factory workers grew as a result, producing giant factory towns in the midst of cities. By 1920, Back of the Yards had a population of over 75,000 people, and it blended in with working-class communities of several hundred thousand people on the southwest side of Chicago. Similar working-class aggregations had also formed at the same time in cities such as St. Louis, Philadelphia, and Cleveland.

Even as the spread of the automobile during the 1920s and 1930s made commuting possible for greater numbers of people, factory workers continued to cluster in working-class enclaves. Less-expensive housing was certainly one attraction. Proximity to social-athletic clubs, churches, old friends, and extended families was another. In addition, strong ties between work and community persisted, so people who lived near the factories, whether in Chicago or elsewhere, continued to benefit. In northeast Philadelphia in 1930, for example, there were several hundred thousand people and over two thousand factories. The largest industries, textiles and metalwork, tended to have seasonal variations in the size of the workforce they needed. Workers who were temporarily laid off would seek fill-in jobs at plants that were hiring, but success required personal contacts and knowledge of openings. It depended on "tavern friendships and gossip. . . . Most workers got their jobs because someone they knew [spoke for them] or told them on what day to apply at the . . . gate."[24]

During the Great Depression of the 1930s, such contacts were even more important as people struggled to survive. The problems of the entire nation were mirrored in the Back of the Yards: all types of neighborhood retail stores went out of business, all four banks serving the Yards closed at least for a period at one time or another, and many people lost their life savings. Many families had just enough bread and potatoes to eat to stay alive. People foraged for loose boards from railroad tracks that they could burn in their homes as heating fuel.[25] Traditional, community-based forms of informal charity to help people who were temporarily out of work were simply overwhelmed by the sheer number of people who were unemployed. In 1932, almost one fourth of the civilian labor force was estimated to be unemployed. With homeless people sleeping on courthouse stairs and children starving, such news headlines as "Girls in High School Bake Cookies for Red Cross Relief" were beginning to look a bit foolish.[26]

Within working-class enclaves, there tended to be an ambivalent attitude toward unions. The Congress of Industrial Organizations (C.I.O.) unions that were organizing workers in the meatpacking, textile, automobile, steel, and other industries tended to be militant and advocate the interests of the workers as a social class. Although only a minority of union leaders were avowed Marxists seeking revolutionary changes, many others held with a Marxist-inspired view that emphasized the similarities among all wageworkers in their relations to the means of production. Many of the workers, however, were first- and second-generation immigrants "who remained embedded in a culture defined by traditional ties to family, kinship, church, and neighborhood club or tavern."[27] In other words, their identities were bound up in their ties to neighborhood institutions more than in membership in a broader, more inclusive class as advocated by unions.

In addition, different ethnic groups were often in competition with each other over the same factory jobs and places to live. They focused their efforts on keeping members of other ethnic groups out of their jobs and their neighborhoods. This competition reinforced interethnic hostilities. During the 1930s, when jobs were particularly scarce, there were growing numbers of blacks, migrants from the rural south, seeking jobs in the Yards. The competition and antagonism between them and white ethnics was often intense. The growth of the union movement, on the other hand, required that workers regard class struggle as more important than their interethnic conflicts.[28]

The hardships of the Great Depression slowly led many blue-collar workers to conclude that their traditional relationship with industry, which did not include unions, could no longer be sustained. In addition to the workers' shift in attitude, and to substantial long-term effect, leaders of the trade union movement realized that the success of the movement depended on unions' ability to forge links to local working-class enclaves. They recognized that community support was critical to a union's chances of organizing workers. Thus, in Back of the Yards during the 1930s, the Packinghouse Workers Unions engaged in such activities as raising funds for local orphanages and sponsoring youth activities, and union leaders attended neighborhood housing meetings. The union also forged a delicate unity across racial lines, adopting antidiscrimination policies and including both blacks and whites in union leadership positions.[29]

It was in conjunction with initial efforts to combat juvenile delinquency in the Yards that local church and union leadership created the Back of the Yards Neighborhood Council in 1939. The council firmly linked factory, union, and community. Its very first resolution called on the Armour meatpacking company to meet union demands in order to avert a strike that would harm the community. Later, it urged all union members to shop exclusively at stores within the Yards.[30]

By the middle of the twentieth century the Neighborhood Council and the unions had slowly enveloped most of the different enclaves within Back of the Yards, forging ties across different ethnic groups and church organizations. The Yards became more of a single community centering around a common class and less a series of separate ethnic villages, although many remnants of the latter remained. In sum, working-class identity and union membership transcended, without replacing, ethnic boundaries. The ethnic enclaves that persisted might better be described as subenclaves.

The Decline of Working-Class Enclaves

The trend toward more inclusive communities based on class rather than ethnicity was paradoxically occurring at the same time that factories started to move out of established working-class communities. In Chicago, most of the major meatpackers began to leave the stockyards area during the 1950s and were gone within a decade. Like most U.S. factories involved in the same kind of exodus, they moved from North to South, from East to West, from cities to small towns, and sometimes completely out of the country.

For a variety of reasons, working-class enclaves have not typically formed around the relocated factories. The work force of IBP Inc., a major food-processing company, is illustrative. In 1980, IBP moved to Garden City, a small town in southwest Kansas. Over the next decade the company hired nearly three thousand people. Some workers came from the area, others came from Iowa and Nebraska, but the bulk of the workforce now consists of relatively new immigrants from Asia or South America.

Garden City is not the initial (or final) destination of these immigrants. They move to Garden City from Los Angeles and other large Western cities in response to work opportunities and a chance for a better life. They do not, however, typically remain in Garden City for very long. They accumulate a little money, then head for Texas or Louisiana in search of other kinds of work or to start their own businesses. They do not form enclaves, as we have employed the term, for a variety of reasons, beginning with the fact that they have a very weak place attachment. The outlook of Bob Ma, a Vietnamese refugee, is illustrative. He met his Chicana wife in Los Angeles, where he had made a marginal living in construction. After moving to Kansas and working for six months at IBP, Inc., he and his wife bought a trailer to live in. He explains, "Over there, in L.A., it's too wild and expensive. Over here, it's boring, but it's better. And you don't got to stay forever. You can save up and move on."[31]

The working-class enclaves of the Northern cities deserted by factories have suffered a number of different fates. Many became slums very quickly, as homeowners who feared for the future of their neighborhoods were panicked into selling their houses for whatever they could get. Land speculators bought the homes and converted them to accommodate multiple families. Housing prices then fell further, there was more panic selling, and the spiral continued. This familiar process of deterioration was at work in Back of the Yards when the Neighborhood Council (which had survived the exodus of the factories) succeeded in getting banks to invest in the area, in encouraging families who remained to remodel their homes, and in sponsoring a new housing development that succeeded in attracting new families. By the late 1960s, housing values in the Yards actually began to increase, and portions of the Yards were preserved as part of a stable residential area.[32]

With the stockyards gone, Back of the Yards became a less meaningful geographic area. Today this historic area is often considered a part of adjacent neighborhoods from which it had historically been separate. Almost all of the factories once found in this community and much of the way of life that had evolved around them are gone. The ethnic and racial composition has also changed. According to the 2000 Census, the two largest ethnic-racial groups in Back of the Yards were Hispanic and Black. Less than 15 percent of the Yard's residents were non-Hispanic whites. Most of the Yard's once large Polish population spread to the outskirts of the community and into adjacent neighborhoods.[33]

Within the Yards today, there is more commercial activity across ethnic groups. For example, doctors and dentists, supermarkets and Realtors, all tend to emphasize their multilingual capacities when they advertise in local community newspapers (e.g., "We speak Polish, Spanish and Chinese").[34] In addition, while ethnic life continue to be focused around local parishes, these parishes are less closed to outsiders than they used to be. To illustrate, they actually compete with each other to attract people from the extended community to their bingo nights.

There also remains a mixture of ethnic animosity and working-class solidarity in the community that mirrors its past. On the one hand, apparently concerned with increasing numbers of people of color in the neighborhood, one conspicuously Polish writer took out an advertisement in the community newspaper condemning the government's laxity in enforcing immigration laws. He claimed the cost of supporting illegals in U.S. prisons to be $800 million yearly and urged readers to write their representatives. On the other hand, issues such as trade and tariff agreements with other nations tend to transcend differences in race and ethnicity, inspiring working-class cohesion. Chicago factory workers who have kept their jobs or are trying to replace jobs they have lost emphasize class considerations in discussing such issues. For example, one referred to the people who preferred free trade with Mexico and Canada as "fancy pants elites" who do not care about American workers' jobs. He concluded, "I guess when you live up on a hill, you just don't see the people in the valley."[35]

The people who remain in working-class enclaves or subenclaves after the factories leave obviously have to find other kinds of employment, and this is both practically and emotionally difficult. In ethnic and working-class South Philadelphia, for example, nearly fifty thousand people were once employed as welders, installers, and other such workers at the Naval Shipyard before it closed in 2000. With the Philadelphia area losing over 7,500 manufacturing jobs yearly, it was unlikely that many in this community would ever find similar kinds of new jobs.

As part of a federal retraining program, thousands of shipyard workers were trained to be respiratory therapists, hairdressers, medical technicians, real estate agents, and paralegals. Even when they remained in the shipyard area, however, the nature of the residential community would not be the same. As one long-time resident explained, "When you talk about the shipyard you're not just talking about a job, you're talking about a choice of life."[36]

Notes

1. For a detailed description of Philadelphia during this period, see Sam B. Warner, Jr., *The Private City*, Philadelphia: University of Pennsylvania Press, 1968.
2. William Cronon, *Nature's Metropolis*, New York: W. W. Norton, 1991.
3. The working conditions and the demoralization they produced were best described in a 1906 novel by Upton Sinclair, *The Jungle*. It was an indictment of the meatpacking industry in Chicago, and it led to a number of government regulations. The novel has recently been reprinted with substantial background comments. See *The Jungle*, edited by Claire V. Eby, New York: Norton, 2003.
4. For further discussion, see Karl Marx and Friedrich Engels, *Manifesto of the Communist Party*, New York: International Publishers, 1848.
5. Dominic A. Pacyga, *Polish Immigrants and Industrial Chicago*, Columbus: Ohio State University Press, 1991.
6. Milton B. Hunt, "The Housing of Non-Family Groups of Men in Chicago," *American Journal of Sociology* 16, 1910.
7. Robert A. Slayton, *Back of the Yards*, Chicago: University of Chicago Press, 1986, p. 74.
8. Sophonisba P. Breckinridge and Edith Abbott, "Chicago's Housing Problem: Families in Furnished Rooms," *American Journal of Sociology* 16, 1910.
9. Thomas J. Jablonsky, *Pride in the Jungle*, Baltimore, MD: Johns Hopkins University Press, 1993.
10. Slayton, op. cit.
11. Charles J. Bushnell, "Some Social Aspects of the Chicago Stock Yards," *American Journal of Sociology* 7, 1901, p. 301. For more examples of the humanitarian and welfare emphasis of many of the Chicago dissertations of this time, see Robert E. L. Faris, *Chicago Sociology*, San Francisco: Chandler, 1967.
12. Pacyga, op. cit.
13. Slayton, op. cit., p. 112.

14. Pacyga, op. cit.
15. Slayton, op. cit.
16. Ibid., p. 59.
17. Ibid., p. 61.
18. Kathy Peiss, "Dance Madness: New York City Dance Halls and Working-Class Sexuality, 1900–1920," in Charles Stephenson and Robert Asher (Eds.), *Life and Labor: Dimensions of American Working-Class History,* Albany: State University of New York Press, 1986.
19. Mirra Komarovsky, *Blue Collar World,* New Haven, CT: Yale University Press, 1987, originally published 1962.
20. W. I. Thomas, *The Unadjusted Girl,* New York: Harper & Row, 1967, p. 108, originally published 1923.
21. Peiss, op. cit.
22. Thomas, op. cit., p. 119.
23. Peiss, op. cit., p. 187.
24. Warner, op. cit., p. 181.
25. Slayton, op. cit.
26. Robert S. Lynd and Helen M. Lynd, *Middletown in Transition,* New York: Harcourt, Brace, 1937, p. 106.
27. Melvyn Dubofsky, "Not So 'Turbulent Years': A New Look at the 1930s," in Stephenson and Asher, op. cit.
28. For further discussion, see Suzan Olzak, "Labor Unrest, Immigration, and Ethnic Conflict in America, 1880–1914," *American Journal of Sociology* 94, 1989.
29. Rick Halpern, *Down on the Killing Floor,* Urbana, IL: University of Illinois Press, 1997.
30. Slayton, op. cit.
31. Quoted in *New York Times,* October 18, 1993, p. B7.
32. Slayton, op. cit.
33. For additional data on Chicago neighborhoods, see "European Ethnic Makeup Changes in Neighborhoods," *Chicago Sun-Times,* August 21, 2002, p. 9.
34. At least until 2003, advertisements of this type regularly appeared in the *Back of the Yards Journal,* and *Brighton Park and McKinley Park Life.*
35. Quoted in *New York Times,* November 14, 1993, p. 16.
36. Quoted in *New York Times,* October 17, 1993, p. 18.

African Americans in Detroit

On the east side of Detroit's downtown waterfront stands the Renaissance Center (locally called the "RenCen"). Built in 1971 by Henry Ford II, after rioting burnt down much of the inner city in 1967, RenCen contains a modern, seventy-three-story Marriott hotel, office tower, and convention center as well as a shopping mall with four movie theaters and thirteen restaurants. For those who come by car, the RenCen is highly accessible, although newcomers are usually a bit overwhelmed when they first enter the building and confront a battery of elevators, escalators, and spiral staircases. For those who have business to transact, the center offers cushioned seats by ponds and waterfalls and cocktail lounges with dangling greenery. In its lobbies are well-dressed conventioneers, local businesspeople, and a Kinko's.

Just a few blocks away is grimy, inner-city Detroit. The area contains block after block of abandoned, burned cottages on weedy plots, gutted apartment buildings, and boarded-up little stores. On a windy day, dirt and discarded newspapers swirl down deserted streets. Interspersed among the abandoned structures are dilapidated but occupied houses where groups of young children play on broken-down porches. There are a few large public housing projects and here and there an empty factory, a reminder of the city that Detroit used to be.[1]

A busy expressway is a barrier to anyone in the inner city who might want to walk over to the RenCen. For local residents who manage to cross the expressway, access is also discouraged by an entrance that is surprisingly difficult for pedestrians to see because it is recessed and largely hidden behind a concrete rampart. In addition, a very large and visible security staff patrols the entire complex and monitors its entrance, discouraging neighborhood visitors.

When it was twenty-five years old and suffering from high vacancy rates, the RenCen was sold to General Motors. In 1999, the corporation made RenCen its global headquarters and began a multimillion-dollar renovation of all the buildings. Between 1999 and 2003 General Motors also moved thousands of its employees from suburban offices to the RenCen. That served to attract several other smaller corporations to the area and led to some new street openings.[2] Development may eventually spread to the rest of the inner east side of Detroit, but it has not done so yet. The inner east side remains a deteriorated area that people in Detroit's suburbs fear. To illustrate, a trolley covers a one-mile route from the RenCen through downtown, and passengers who wish to can get off near park benches that mark the end of the line. Two elderly women, visitors from Detroit's suburbs, got off one day. As the trolley left, they looked fearfully at the empty buildings and deserted streets at the edge of the downtown area. A professor from nearby Wayne State University happened to walk by, and one of the women asked him what he thought they should do. He suggested they walk around or sit on the benches and wait for the trolley to return. "But won't we be killed?" she asked.[3]

Some of the burned and deserted buildings in the city's inner east side are remnants of the uncontrolled fires in the rioting of 1967. At the same time, there were also large-scale inner-city riots in many other cities with large African-American populations, including New York, Chicago, Cleveland, and Los Angeles. The largest of those riots was in Detroit, where police and federal troops engaged in sporadic gun battles with armed residents over the period of a week. Meanwhile, arsonists and looters celebrated in the streets in the light of huge fires that gutted hundreds of stores and shops. When it was over, many sections of the inner city resembled a devastated war zone.[4]

Around Halloween, the destruction of inner-city stores and buildings that began in the 1967 riot continued to the mid-1990s. The night before Halloween came to be known locally as "Devil's Night" and was celebrated by burning dozens of structures, mostly in the inner city. The tradition peaked in the late 1980s when one Devil's Night spectator recalled that the scent of burning wood and the sight of large fires surrounded by hundreds of onlookers initially reminded him of a college homecoming rally. However, that lighthearted impression vanished when he noticed the grim looks on the faces of residents, mostly older African Americans, who stood in front of their homes with coats over their bathrobes. They held shotguns and garden hoses to protect their property, while the police guarded the overextended fire fighters.[5]

Between the mid-1980s and the mid-1990s there were typically over 350 fires in Detroit during the three-day Halloween period. Then Detroit's civic leaders pushed to change the name from Devil's Night to "Angels' Night," acknowledging the contributions of volunteers (called "angels") who were recruited to patrol the city streets. In the last few years, the number of volunteers has grown to between 35,000 and 40,000. Their patrols, combined with a "porch light" program, a curfew—and the fact that there were few structures left to burn in many areas—reduced the number of fires during the Halloween period to about one hundred to 125, close to the typical number that occurred in Detroit during any three-day period.[6]

While the destruction associated with Devil's Night was peaking in Detroit, shootings among its citizens were becoming an everyday event. The city's rising rate of violent crime led the state legislature to consider gun control proposals; but Coleman Young, then Detroit's mayor and an African American, refused to support any measure that would impose gun control in the city. He said he did not want to "disarm Detroit" as long as the city was surrounded by "hostile suburbs" and armed Ku Klux Klan "vigilantes."[7] To people unfamiliar with race relations in Detroit, Mayor Young's position may have been impossible to understand, but it stemmed from the fact that African Americans in Detroit have frequently been victimized.[8]

Early History

It was around 1850 that Detroit changed from a small frontier town to a manufacturing center. During the following decades, the city grew as Southerners and European immigrants came to find work. Shipbuilding and other types of manufacturing used the Detroit River, and because most people had to walk to work, the areas closest to the river grew first.

The unpaved streets of the east riverfront were home to a dense mixture of stores, factories, and the one- and two-story frame houses of immigrants. Around 1860, estimates indicated that Detroit's African-American population had increased to over one thousand persons, 80 percent of whom were clustered among immigrant populations on Detroit's near east side. The streets with higher concentrations of African Americans tended to be referred to as "Negro areas," but analysis of city directories suggests that there was no one street in the city on which African Americans comprised 50 percent or more of the residents. Most African Americans lived in areas with mixed immigrant populations, though they tended to live in the oldest, smallest apartments.[9]

Because blacks, Southern whites, and European immigrants competed for jobs and for housing, relations between these groups were often particularly hostile. The crowded, integrated, near east side "erupted" in 1863 when an African American man was accused of sexually assaulting two nine-year-old girls, one black and the other white. The girls later confessed they had made up the entire story, but not before the man was found guilty and sentenced to life in prison. As soldiers were escorting him to the prison, a crowd of African Americans threw stones and bricks at them and tried to seize the prisoner. The soldiers fired several volleys, wounding and killing some in the crowd. The soldiers were then able to move the prisoner into the jail, and they returned to their barracks, thinking the incident over. However, a white mob, comprised mostly of immigrants, then formed and went on a haphazard spree, setting fire to the homes of African Americans. Following the rules set by the Detroit fire marshal, only when white homes were accidentally set ablaze did the fire department turn on their hoses. They ignored fires in black-owned homes. Shouting "Kill the nigger!" white men and boys also clubbed and beat any blacks they happened to find on the street.[10]

Within a period of about six months, in the spring and summer of 1863, white mobs went on similar rampages in other Northern cities. Competition among groups living in crowded, integrated communities was the common underlying cause. In New York, for example, drunken immigrants stormed into the city's African-American sections, burning homes, looting stores, and hanging people from lampposts.[11]

When electric streetcars were installed in Detroit in the 1880s, they enabled people to commute to work from longer distances, and the city's growing white population expanded outward. However, the growing African-American population remained mostly concentrated in the near east side. Between 1880 and 1910 the city of Detroit grew from just over 100,000 persons to nearly half a million. The African-American population doubled during this period, reaching a total of nearly six thousand persons. Throughout these decades, about 85 percent of the city's African-American population lived in the near east side, and it was here that Detroit's most complete African-American enclave formed in the early twentieth century.

At the same time, other ethnic groups were moving into Detroit— German, Irish, Polish—and they also formed enclaves in the near east side. Particularly sizable in the late nineteenth century was a German concentration called "Little Berlin." When the Germans moved out of their near east side enclave they were replaced by Greek immigrants. They too have since left, though a small area locally referred to as "Greektown" remains, consisting of a couple of blocks of Greek restaurants, coffee shops, and boutiques that cater to tourists (along with a casino that opened in 2001). The Greek restaurants and shops are the near east side's last remnant of the former European immigrants' enclaves.[12]

The Near East Side Enclave

Let us begin our examination of the near east side by placing it in relation to the rest of Detroit. The city's southern boundary is the Detroit River. The main north-south thoroughfare is Woodward Avenue. It runs from just north of the river to the city's suburbs and divides Detroit into east and west sides. In the late nineteenth century it was a wide boulevard lined with trees and private homes. When electric streetcars (in the 1880s) enabled the city to expand northward, some of the largest suburban-type residential concentrations remained near Woodward. The other principal street that provided a boundary for the near east side was Gratiot Avenue. It began at Woodward, just north of the river, and angled diagonally to the north and east. The near east side refers to an almost pie-shaped sector east of Woodward between Gratiot and the river.

In Detroit's near east side around 1910, there were variations in the wealth of African Americans that correlated with how recently they had moved to Detroit and where in the near east side they lived. The immediate waterfront area contained rooming houses that were home to the poor and disabled, the disreputable (such as criminals and alcoholics), and young newcomers to Detroit. At the opposite, northern, end of the near east side, close to Gratiot, was situated a small African-American middle and upper class, composed of owners of small shops, salesmen, and the like. Most lived in small cottages that they owned.

A majority of the African-American families in the near east side were, both physically and socially, between the two extremes. They lived in apartments that varied from poor to horrible. There were a large number of one- and two-story wooden frame homes, sometimes separate and sometimes built in rows. Each floor was subdivided into a number of small apartments, but because African Americans paid a premium for any kind of housing, they were under pressure to sublet some of their already limited space to other tenants. Thus these old, deteriorating cottages were very crowded. A number of African-American families also lived in the upper floors of three-story brick buildings, above barbershops, saloons, drugstores, or restaurants. Rear entrances led to these upstairs apartments, which were very small and dark. (The sides of the buildings had no windows so that new buildings could easily be attached to them.) Many of the poorest black families lived in alleys in sheds and stables that had been converted to rows of family dwellings. Alleys had been built behind the streets in the near east side originally to provide access to stables and for sewerage systems, later for use as garbage-dumping grounds. Naturally,

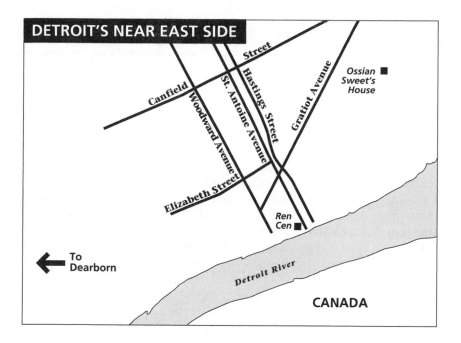

DETROIT'S NEAR EAST SIDE

they presented serious health hazards for residents. Most of the alley dwellings were unpainted wooden units less than six feet wide, but many of the people who lived in them still took in boarders.[13]

A majority of the African-American families in the near east side could probably best be described as struggling members of the lower working class. Most took whatever kind of work they could find, but they often could not find enough to be continuously employed. Their ongoing job searches, and the African American newcomers' ignorance of city ways, led to a good deal of harassment by whites in the guise of humor. For example, pranksters gave bogus work orders for day labor to black men, who would show up for work at the designated place only to discover that the contractor did not exist.

Commerce and Entertainment

White-owned stores outside the area frequently refused service to African-American customers or tried to discourage their business. Many middle-class, white-owned restaurants and hotels employed African Americans but, even so, refused to serve them or required that they pay double if they insisted on going where they were not wanted. White barbers typically refused to cut the hair of African Americans, citing fear that it would drive away their white customers. Ironically, many African-American barbers with white clienteles expressed the same fear and refused to cut the hair of other African Americans. Thus blacks who opened restaurants, barbershops, drugstores, funeral parlors, taverns, and pool-halls in the near east side found a concentrated number of ready patrons. By 1910, St. Antoine, a north-south street near the eastern edge of the African-American community, became its commercial center.

The funds for this commerce came in large part from real estate and related investments. There were a number of free blacks who had migrated from Virginia to Detroit before the Civil War, and they had brought with them funds that they used to buy a good deal of land. That land lay in what later became the downtown business district and in the near east side. Later, other African-American businessmen and professionals also invested in land, mostly in the near east side. Then, as the black business district expanded northward up St. Antoine, the value of real estate holdings increased dramatically, producing capital for further commercial and residential expansion. In addition, some rental housing in the near east side was owned by African Americans, and there were several prominent African-American real estate agents and promoters. The African-American landowners and promoters helped their white counterparts to maintain the east-of-Woodward color line because they benefited economically from keeping the growing black population in the crowded near east side.[14]

The St. Antoine commercial district was a place in which African Americans were welcome as customers. Leaders of their community urged them to patronize African-American businesses as a matter of racial pride. It was also the area in which goods and services distinctively associated with the African-American community were readily available: products for straightening hair and whitening skin; "soul food" such as fatback, collards, and chitterlings; and newspapers published by African Americans that focused on issues of interest to African-American readers. The shared cultural traditions of those who had come to Detroit from the South were also kept alive in "back-alley jukes" behind Hastings Street, in the center of the enclave near the river, and in waterfront saloons where African-American musicians played and sang the blues. These were mostly small, raucous nightclubs that featured the blues and bawdy humor and sometimes had brothels and gambling as well. Some clubs had an almost exclusively black, male, laborer clientele from the immediate area; others catered to more varied audiences.

One of the better-known performers in Hastings Street clubs around 1910 was Speckled Red, later known as Detroit Red. He performed in

African-American clubs in cities throughout the Midwest and in traveling medicine shows throughout the South. Red's most famous song, "The Dirty Dozens," was originally a rhyme used to teach children the biblical creation story. As a blues number, it evolved into an obscene series of verbal insults, culminating in the accusation, explicitly stated, that a man had had intercourse with his own mother.[15] The strong language and graphic sexual descriptions of these early black performers were a precursor to contemporary hip-hop and rap, an African-American cultural form initially limited primarily to inner-city neighborhoods.[16]

Most of the blues as played and sung in these clubs was created by African Americans to make sense out of lives and events that often made no sense. It was a musical form that provided an emotional commentary on the misfortunes of people living poor and black. "Going Down the Road, Feelin' Bad," for example, recounts the days of the "man snatchers" in the old South. These were agents employed by cotton farmers or railroad supervisors who needed laborers. The man snatchers would get African-American men drunk and cart them off. The hijacked men would then find themselves miles from home with no alternative to working as laborers. When they finished working, however, there would usually be no pay, and they had to trudge back home empty-handed.[17]

Churches

Churches were a major institution in the cultural life of the near east side. In the rural South, family and church had been the primary institutions, and African Americans' reverence for them was carried to the Northern cities. Outside of the home, the church was the only place where blacks had status and were not subordinate to whites. The pastor/preacher/minister was the leading figure in, and the church was the organizational center for, the African-American community. Newcomers to the city often first turned to the older, established Baptist and Methodist churches in Detroit for help in finding work and shelter. However, they often encountered discrimination from white congregants, pressuring them to organize new churches. Particularly noteworthy was the Second Baptist Church of Detroit, built in 1852 when former slaves left the white-controlled First Baptist Church. It grew into a large and very active congregation aiding escaped slaves from the South prior to the Civil War and petitioning the state government for "Negro suffrage." It is one of the few structures remaining from the near east side enclave, though its main building was rebuilt after a fire in 1914, and there were several later additions to the building.[18]

During the first decades of the twentieth century, the number of Southern black migrants began to increase dramatically; they overwhelmed the traditional churches' capacities, and a large number of new African-American churches were born in the crowded streets of Detroit's near east side. A few were large, having been explicitly built as churches, and attracted citywide followings. Most, however, were small—converted storefronts and residences—and they served a very local area, mirroring the small and intimate African-American church of the South. A typical example was the Holiness Church of Living God, founded by "Bishop" J. B. C. Cummings. He began organizing his "brethren and sistern" in the near east side, and in 1909 he bought a small frame house in the center of the community, put up a banner, and his "temple" was in operation.[19]

This proliferation of local congregations was an attempt to establish within the enclave the kind of institution with which the recent migrants were familiar. They were comfortable with a church in which if someone were not in their usual seat on a Sunday, the pastor would come to his or her home to find out what was wrong. By contrast, the large denominational churches were bureaucratic and impersonal, and in the white denominational churches, blacks were relegated to the rear. The small storefront churches also offered forms of worship the migrants were accustomed to: familiar spirituals and hymns, singing, shouting, dancing, and other forms of free religious expression.[20]

Of particular significance in Detroit and elsewhere during the early decades of the twentieth century was the Black Spiritual Movement. Many of its congregations were nominally identified as Baptist but were actually amalgams of diverse practices and beliefs, with elements taken from Catholicism, Pentacostalism, Spiritualism, Judaism, and Voodoo. For example, the leader of the Spiritual Israel Church in Detroit had the title of bishop, was regarded by members as "king of Israel," and was addressed as "holy father." In addition to the minister (or king or queen), many spiritual churches included the following roles:

Missionaries: women who said a prayer or gave a short sermon during Sunday services and helped the sick or needy during the week.

Mothers: older women who assisted in the service and were accorded a place of honor in a reserved section of pews.

Mediums: men or women believed to have the gift of prophecy who were also known as prophets or spiritual advisors. During services they provided "messages" to many congregants and in private they offered advice about everyday life, sometimes suggesting what numbers a person should bet on in policy games or lotteries. Many were also believed to be healers.

Nurses: usually women dressed like hospital nurses, stationed throughout the sanctuary. During services they looked after congregants who
collapsed or fell into trances.[21]

Enclave Summary

In summation, let us consider the degree to which the African-American
population of Detroit's near east side constituted an enclave. The primary
question is whether a distinct group occupied a clearly defined area. While
the near east side was also home to nonblacks, the sheer presence of outsiders does not negate a racial or ethnic group's enclave. The crux of the
matter is whether the concentration was sufficient for it to be locally regarded as an African-American area—and it was. It is also apparent that
the group's distinct way of life was supported by specialized local institutions and commercial activities.

The enclave criterion we know least about concerns whether the African-
American residents felt a sufficient attachment to the near east side; but
most probably did. It housed the churches, clubs, stores, family, and friends
that were integral to their collective lives. Further, people tend to judge
their experiences in relative terms, so while housing was usually inadequate, employment opportunities were often limited, and blacks were sub-
jected to harassment in the near east side, all of these conditions were
worse in the South they had left behind. Thus, around 1910 in Detroit's
near east side, the concentration of African Americans probably qualified
as an enclave. In this regard it differs from contemporary African-American ghettos in Detroit and elsewhere. Some of the differences and their
implications are discussed at the end of this chapter.

A Suburban-Type Near-Enclave

An African-American upper class, living in mansions located in predominantly white areas or in distinct sections of larger black areas, emerged after about 1880 in Detroit as well as in other cities, including Boston,
Chicago, and New Orleans. A large percentage of the African-American upper class in Detroit were offspring of the prominent "free black" (nonslave)
families that had migrated to Detroit from Virginia before the Civil War.

Many of these original families were well educated by the standards of their day, and they brought business skills, capital, and a strong work ethic with them to Detroit. Only about 10 percent of all blacks were free prior to the Civil War, but the material and nonmaterial advantages of this group continued to be transmitted from generation to generation. One hundred years after the Civil War, for example, over 50 percent of black professionals surveyed were still found to be descendants of free African-American ancestors.[22]

Along with a few relative newcomers to Detroit, the grown children of the free blacks from Virginia formed an exclusive social clique initially consisting of forty families, which they called the "cultured, colored forty." Between 1900 and 1910 the aristocratic group actually grew to include fifty-one families that constituted the core of the African-American upper class in Detroit, but their original name remained. Within this clique were six physicians, seven attorneys, and three dentists, many of whom had substantial white clienteles. Nonprofessionals were also included among the city's black elite if they had family ties to members of the aristocracy or had substantial wealth, typically gained from inner-city real estate investments.

Formal social activities such as dances, dinners, and teas were usually held in the large and well-furnished homes of members of this elite group. Only other clique members were regularly included on guest lists. (There were a number of other upper-status African-American families, a little less prominent or a little less rich, that were included only periodically.) Except for the summer months, when the families vacationed in Saratoga Springs, their social calendars were full. Teenage children were included in the formal activities of Detroit's upper-class African Americans. The youngsters mingled, their parents nearby to serve as chaperons, and gradually learned the genteel ways of behaving expected in "polite society."[23]

A majority of the upper-class African-American families lived between Woodward and St. Antoine, on the east side but north of Gratiot, hence north of the larger African-American enclave. It was along Woodward that streetcars had facilitated the development of suburban-type residential areas in the city. Here the elite black families lived on tree-lined streets in well-tended three-story homes bordered by privet hedges. A few upper-class African-American families lived in mansions west of Woodward, where they were the only black families in their neighborhoods.

The most important associations and institutions of the upper class tended to be located near the area of its greatest residential concentration. For example, the Phillis Wheatley Association was an organization of elite African-American women whose major charitable activity was the Home for Aged Colored Ladies. This voluntary association's headquarters was an eleven-room house on Elizabeth, a street that ran for about half a mile beginning at Woodward and going east. It was a few blocks north of Gratiot. Also on Elizabeth was the St. Matthew's Protestant Episcopal Mission, the church to which nearly two thirds of the fifty-one most elite African American families belonged, and they provided the church's governing core.[24]

When St. Matthew's was first established in 1846, it was the first black Episcopal church west of the Alleghenies. In those early years, however, it was too small to be viable, and a decade later black Episcopalians sought baptisms and confirmations in white churches. In 1883 a new building was erected on Elizabeth Street, and the pulpit was given over to a succession of mostly white ministers. After 1890, a series of distinguished African-American clergy was brought in, and the parish grew to over five hundred communicants by 1920.[25] Unlike other African-American churches in Detroit, St. Matthew's recruited a lot of its membership from beyond its immediate neighborhood. Even so, the church's pew rental policy kept out poor newcomers, who probably would not have been attracted to its dignified and reserved services in any case. To most of the church's elite membership, it seemed entirely reasonable for poor blacks to worship in separate churches. Rich and poor blacks, they believed, were two groups that had "nothing in common."[26]

Questions about the proper relationship between the small African-American upper class and the much larger African-American lower class were frequently raised in response to the upper-class women's "self-culture" clubs. In cities across the country, upper-class African-American women met regularly to study literature, art, and music. Their highly restrictive clubs emulated those of the white upper class and were designed to help mold the "ideal lady": cultured, fashionable, confident. It is easy to understand why such women might have seemed haughty and their concern with matters of style absurd to lower-class African Americans. At the same time, the women's clubs did periodically involve themselves in some matters of more general racial concern, such as antilynching crusades and support for local orphanages. At any rate, not all upper-class women, black or white, subscribed to this notion of the "ideal lady." Some pursued professions and were highly successful. Meta Pelham, for example, ran a family-owned newspaper, and a number of other women's club members served actively on a variety of Detroit's civic boards.[27]

Members of the African-American elite were also divided on questions of racial integration. Those who believed a clear separation between themselves and poor African Americans was justified tended to see integration as the ideal and were confident that it was attainable. This segment of the elite included physicians and lawyers with predominantly white clienteles and others who participated in elite black clubs while belonging to predominantly white churches.

Enclave Summary

In evaluating this group on its enclave characteristics, one notes first that the African-American upper class was a distinctive group whose lifestyle was supported by special institutions. However, even though most of the elite families lived in an eastern, streetcar, suburban-type neighborhood with local organizations and associations, they were too small a part of the overall area to give it an African-American identity. Furthermore, if the area *were* predominantly African American, regardless of class, it is not clear that most of the black elite would have felt the same degree of attachment to the place. Thus the term "near-enclave" fits best because although the African-American upper class was a very distinctive group and most of its members lived in the same area, neither racial nor territorial identities seemed sufficiently strong to warrant the enclave label.

Over the next few decades, most of this near-enclave disappeared. The traditional, distinctively local upper classes in most American cities were declining, among both African Americans and whites, as described in Chapter Two. In addition, and more specific to Detroit, some of the elite African-American families were childless. The offspring of other families moved to cities such as Chicago and Washington, where the African-American upper class was considerably larger. So Detroit's African-American elite, small to begin with, became too small to constitute even a near-enclave.

What became of the larger enclave in the near east side is a more complex story. Despite the fact that the poor black population continued to grow and remained segregated from whites, that enclave also disappeared. We close this chapter with an examination of how the enclave eventually became the victim of a redevelopment plan, and why a new enclave did not form in its place.

More Growth, More Segregation

During the first half of the twentieth century, there was a steady stream of migration into Detroit from several southern states—Arkansas, Kentucky, Alabama, and Tennessee—where job opportunities were very limited.

Around America's entry into both world wars (1917 and 1941), an increase in Detroit's job creation in relation to war-related factory production led to peaks in the migration rates. In both instances, the influx of job-seeking migrants overwhelmed the supply of housing, competition for housing between whites and blacks intensified, and blacks were left more segregated than before. Several dramatic confrontations symbolized the degree of white opposition to integration.

During the first peak, what had been a small Ku Klux Klan chapter in Detroit grew as a result of both the influx of Southern whites and a national "Klan fever" following the success of the 1915 film *The Birth of a Nation*. That movie presented a sympathetic portrayal of the Klansman as a noble white hero and led to popular emulation of Klan dress, at costume parties, for example.[28] A rejuvenated Klan in Detroit reached out to the white immigrant Europeans, teaching them whom Americans were supposed to hate. "Using the odious term 'niggers' gave the foreign-born worker (mainly Polish) a sense of identity with white society."[29]

Even high-status African Americans found it difficult to find suitable places to live, because most of the white population was disinclined to make socioeconomic distinctions among African Americans. The case of Ossian Sweet, a physician, is illustrative. In 1925, when Dr. Sweet and his wife (also a college graduate) bought a home in a formerly all-white neighborhood, the Klan in Detroit organized opposition. The police ignored groups of whites who milled nightly across the street, throwing stones at the Sweets' house. One night someone in the home shot into the crowd, killing one white man and injuring another. Then the police responded, arresting the Sweets along with Mr. Sweet's brother (a dentist) and several other family members who were in the home at the time. A long series of trials began, during which time Klan membership and influence increased. The mayor, who was considered liberal and had strong African-American backing, nevertheless condemned the Sweets and others who would follow in their footsteps. In his open letter to a Detroit newspaper in 1925, he wrote, "I must say that I depreciate most strongly the moving of Negroes or other persons into districts in which they know their presence may cause riots of bloodshed."[30]

Over the next decades, Detroit's growing African-American population continued, for the most part, to reside in terribly substandard housing on the east side. When migration dramatically accelerated around 1940, though, the housing problem became too serious to ignore. In order to house war workers, agencies of the federal government decided in 1941 to fund two projects through the Detroit Housing Commission. The commission planned to build one housing project of several hundred units for blacks on the east side (named Sojourner Truth Homes after the Civil War preacher and orator) and one for whites in a white area. The site for the proposed African-American project was later moved west to a white area, despite protests from the local residents. After the project was completed and leases were signed, the Ku Klux Klan organized picket lines of more than one thousand men, many of whom were armed, to prevent the new tenants from actually entering. For several days at the end of February 1942, small groups of African Americans tried to drive through the barricade but were forced to retreat under a barrage of bricks. On March 1 the fighting escalated, and about twenty people, black and white, required hospitalization to treat wounds caused by knives, bullets, and flying bricks. Police subsequently arrested participants on such charges as inciting to riot, assault, and carrying concealed weapons. Of the 104 arrested, 102 were black.[31]

In the postwar years the suburbs outside Detroit grew rapidly, but African Americans were largely excluded from them. The most violence tended to occur when African Americans tried to integrate ethnic, blue-collar suburbs such as Dearborn. In this suburb just west of the city near Ford's River Rouge plant, there were a number of mob actions during the 1950s and 1960s. The regularly reelected mayor of Dearborn, Orville Hubbard, opposed integration on the grounds that it would lead to racial intermarriage and "mongrelization." The Dearborn police made a house call to any African-American family that moved into town and suggested they move out as quickly as possible. When they stayed and white mobs threw bottles and bricks, the Dearborn police failed to take any action.[32] In upper-class suburbs, in contrast, African Americans were typically excluded by more subtle means, because white homeowners feared that violent demonstrations would harm neighborhood reputations and therefore property values.

During the period of Detroit's rapid suburban growth, roughly from 1950 to 1980, fifty incorporated communities were added to the metropolitan area. These villages and townships, which became the new suburbs, contained a total of nearly three quarters of a million white people and fewer than five thousand African Americans. Less than 1 percent of the population of the new suburbs were African American.[33] Among large U.S. metropolitan areas, Detroit has consistently been the most racially segregated.[34]

When African Americans did move out of the city, it was usually into older suburban areas. Realtors regularly profited from this movement by "block busting." Using fear of invasion by blacks to spur white residents to sell at any price, realtors would buy property cheap, then sell it at high prices to black families or partition it into smaller units for rent.

Meanwhile, white neighbors were stampeded into selling at further-reduced prices, and agents made off with the bargains. One block at a time, the African-American ghetto spread, following on the heels of middle-class African Americans trying to move up and out. One long-term consequence is that among African Americans in Detroit there is almost no correlation between their social class and the racial segregation of their neighborhoods. To be specific, African Americans in Detroit making over $50,000 per year are about as segregated as those making less than $2,500; both live in almost totally segregated areas. In contrast, as the income level of Asians or Hispanics rises, their levels of segregation from whites drop by about 25 percent.[35]

The Demise of the Enclave

By the middle of the twentieth century, parts of the inner cores of many industrial cities, including Detroit, were so old and deteriorated that their market values had steeply declined. The low value of inner-city parcels of land made redevelopment, or "slum clearance" attractive to entrepreneurs. City officials were often convinced to take the side of the entrepreneurs by the belief that redevelopment would lower crime or increase tax revenues. For these postwar redevelopment plans to be eligible for federal funds, though, the city had to provide other housing for the people who were displaced. Beginning around 1950, public housing projects were touted as the answer. In principle, they were cost-effective ways to address the housing shortage and meet federal requirements. In reality, however, they almost never fully replaced the lost housing and they produced some highly undesirable consequences that were not recognized at the time.

Urban renewal, sociologist Gerald Suttles argues, has generally tended to proceed like a successful "confidence game." Announcement of the plan is usually made in a setting that commands attention, such as the mayor's office or a penthouse executive suite. Scale models are presented to give the public the sense that the project is solid, real. It is often claimed that the improvements will occur at no cost to the city; funds will come only from the private sector or the federal government. Furthermore, if the project is begun at once, a representative promises, jobs will be created and the neighborhood will receive, as an additional free gift, a park or a plaza.

Any delays, on the other hand, could result in cost overruns that would jeopardize the entire project. Thus the plan moves forward like a steam-roller over the objections of residents who do not wish to be displaced.[36]

The first and largest site selected for redevelopment in Detroit was a de-teriorated 129-acre site near the center of the 1910 enclave. The announced beginning of the Gratiot project occurred during the early 1950s, when hundreds of resident families were forced to vacate their dwellings after receiving official notification that demolition was imminent; it did not ac-tually begin for ten more years, though. Most resettled close to their orig-inal homes while the city's plans were debated over the next decade. Low-income (replacement) housing was eventually built in the original enclave area and just to the east of it, forcing many of these families to move again.[37] Then one high-rise project after another was built in the inner city.

Building public housing projects near the center of an African-Ameri-can population, as Detroit did in the Gratiot redevelopment project, con-tributed to the concentration and isolation of poor African Americans. Higher-status African Americans, who could have served as role models, were missing from the area. (Even if middle-class people had wanted to live in public housing, they would not have qualified because of income restrictions.) Neighborhood life suffered when homogeneously poor peo-ple were moved into these high-density housing projects, because the res-idents did not feel connected to any neighborhood, and few participated in community affairs.[38]

At the same time as it was experiencing a proliferation of public hous-ing projects, Detroit began to lose manufacturing jobs. (Recall that these were the jobs that traditionally lured African Americans from the South.) To be specific, during the 1960s and 1970s Detroit lost an average of about seven thousand factory jobs per year as factories moved to distant suburbs, to Southern and Western cities, and to industrializing nations in Asia and Latin America. Many of the blue-collar jobs that were lost were eventually replaced by white-collar jobs in finance and technology, but these new jobs required substantially more formal education than that obtained by most inner-city residents in Detroit (or other cities). This mismatch be-tween skills required and skills possessed resulted in soaring unemploy-ment and no expectations of ever finding work, especially among African-American males without high school diplomas.[39]

With the reduced ability of black males to find jobs, rates of marriage fell in the black community, and rates of nonmarital births increased.[40] The poor single mothers, whose births were generally unplanned, typically lacked social and economic resources. So just when there was the most pronounced need for neighborly help—because of the large number of single-parent families living in poverty—that help and support was not available because of the way public housing weakened community involvement. Neighbors did not trust each other, the community lacked the means to control teenagers, and crime, drugs and gangs, truancy, welfare dependency, and other social problems plagued the tenants of public housing.

Once many of these problems reach a certain threshold, they are worsened by self-perpetuating processes. For example, among those not directly involved, each crime that occurs encourages a "psychic withdrawal" from community life. Vigilance declines, the possibility of collective action is reduced, and crime is likely to increase further. Similarly, once any resident fails to maintain a home or apartment properly, the unsightliness reduces the incentive of neighbors to invest time or money in the upkeep of their own places.[41] In the public housing projects, the capacity of residents to pursue their interests collectively has been so weakened that drug dealers and gangs have been able to impose reigns of terror over tenants.[42]

Danger so suffuses everyday ghetto life that it creates an oppressive climate of fear that, along with the poverty of the area, results in widespread institutional withdrawal. Hospitals and public health facilities minimize their community involvement or move out of the area; the police and courts are overwhelmed; public schools, libraries, and youth clubs lack facilities and limit their functions.[43] No one in the community has the funds to open stores or start newspapers or other activities that could lead residents to feel positive about their neighborhood. There are no enclave-like qualities. People remain in such places not because of any attachment but only because they have nowhere else to go.

Notes

1. For further description of the contrast between the RenCen and East Detroit, see B. J. Widick, *Detroit: City of Race and Class Violence,* Detroit: Wayne State University Press, 1989; and Wolf Von Eckardt, "Renaissance and Risorgimento," in Wilma W. Henrickson (Ed.), *Detroit Perspectives,* Detroit: Wayne State University Press, 1991.
2. For a recent history of the RenCen, see Andrew Dietderich, "If You Build It," *Crain's Detroit Business,* June 1, 2003, p. 68.
3. Jerry Herron, *AfterCulture: Detroit and the Humiliation of History,* Detroit: Wayne State University Press, 1993, p. 133.
4. See Widick, op. cit.
5. Ze'ev Chaffets, *Devil's Night,* New York: Random House, 1990.

6. Associated Press, "'Angel's Night' Volunteers Take to Detroit's Streets." October 30, 2002.

7. Quoted in Widick, op. cit., p. 233.

8. For an analysis of historic racial differences in employment, housing, political treatment, and so on, see Heather A. Thompson, *Whose Detroit?* Ithaca, NY: Cornell University Press, 2004.

9. David M. Katzman, *Before the Ghetto*, Urbana: University of Illinois Press, 1973.

10. For further details, see NAACP, *Anti-Negro Riots in the North, 1863*, New York: Arno Press and The New York Times, 1969.

11. Ibid.

12. For a history of the European enclaves in Detroit, see part two in Tamar Jacoby, *Someone Else's House*, New York: Basic Books, 2000.

13. Katzman, op. cit.

14. Ibid.

15. Arnold Shaw, *Honkers and Shouters*, New York: Collier, 1978.

16. Michael E. Dyson, *Reflecting Black*, Minneapolis: University of Minnesota Press, 1993. See also Amy Binder, "Reflecting Racial Rhetoric," *American Sociological Review* 58, 1993.

17. Philip H. Enis, *The Seventh Stream*, Hanover, NH: University Press of America, 1992. The "man snatcher" was one of the historical figures that combined with legendary figures to produce widespread beliefs among African Americans that "white demons" were trying to capture, burn, or otherwise destroy their bodies. This theme persists in inner-city rumors such as those that the twenty-eight African-American children murdered in Atlanta were victims of the FBI, who wanted their bodies for research; and that the Church's Fried Chicken franchise is owned by the Klan, and they put something in the chicken to make African-American men sterile. See Patricia A. Turner, *I Heard It through the Grapevine*, Berkeley: University of California Press, 1993.

18. Additional history of the Second Baptist Church, the oldest African-American church in the Midwest, is in Cheri Y. Gay, *Detroit Then and Now*, Berkeley, CA: Thunder Bay Press, 2001.

19. Katzman, op. cit.

20. E. Franklin Frazier, *The Negro Church in America*, New York: Schocken, 1974.

21. Hans A. Baer, *The Black Spiritual Movement*, Knoxville: University of Tennessee Press, 1984.

22. For a review of these studies, see Richard A. Davis, *The Black Family in a Changing Black Community*, New York: Garland Publishing, 1993. An examination of their descendants in New York is in John Hewett, *Protest and Progress*, New York: Garland Publishing, 2000.

23. Willard B. Gatewood, *Aristocrats of Color,* Bloomington, IN: Indiana University Press, 1990.
24. Katzman, op. cit.
25. George F. Bragg, *History of the Afro-American Group of the Episcopal Church,* Baltimore, MD: Church Advocate Press, 1922, repr. Johnson Reprint Corporation, New York, 1968.
26. Gatewood, op. cit., p. 126.
27. Ibid.
28. Wyn Craig Wade, *The Fiery Cross,* New York: Touchstone Books, 1987.
29. Widick, op. cit., p. 28.
30. *Detroit Free Press,* September 13, 1925, quoted in Henrickson, op. cit.
31. Betty S. Jenkins, "Sojourner Truth Housing Riots," in ibid.
32. David L. Good, *Orvie: The Dictator of Dearborn,* Detroit, MI: Wayne State University Press, 1989.
33. Joe T. Darden, et al., *Detroit,* Philadelphia, PA: Temple University Press, 1987.
34. Reynolds Farley, Sheldon Danziger, and Harry J. Holzer, *Detroit Divided,* New York: Russell Sage Foundation, 2002.
35. Douglas S. Massey and Nancy A. Denton, *American Apartheid,* Cambridge, MA: Harvard University Press, 1993.
36. Gerald D. Suttles, *The Man-Made City,* Chicago: University of Chicago Press, 1990.
37. Darden, et al., op. cit.
38. On the general relationship between concentrated poverty and African-American community participation, see Bruce Rankin and James Quane, "Neighborhood Poverty and the Social Isolation of Inner-City African American Families," *Social Forces* 79, 2000.
39. William J. Wilson, *When Work Disappears,* New York: Knopf, 1996.
40. The nonmarital births that increase in relation to male joblessness tend to involve young mothers and unplanned births. For further discussion, see Mark Abrahamson, *Out-of-Wedlock Births,* Westport, CT: Praeger, 1998.
41. Jonathan Crane, "The Epidemic Theory of Ghettos and Neighborhood Effects on Dropping Out and Teenage Childbearing," *American Journal of Sociology* 96, 1991.
42. Langley C. Keyes, *Strategies and Saints,* Washington, DC: Urban Institute Press, 1992.
43. Loic J. D. Wacquant, "Dangerous Places," in William J. Wilson (Ed.), *Urban Poverty and Family Life in Chicago's Inner City,* New York: Oxford University Press, 1994.

Germans in Southern Brazil

For a period of about one hundred years between the 1830s and the 1930s, Brazil's southern tip was the destination of several hundred thousand German immigrants. They clustered in a few cities, which they dominated with their language, culture, and traditions. Around the turn of the twentieth century, they also established manufacturing firms that became global in their reach, often beginning with a connection to firms in Germany. Today their descendants manage these companies, which are among the largest employers in southern Brazil.

In this chapter we will focus upon "Teuto-Brazilians" (i.e., Brazilians of German descent) in two places that they once dominated: Blumenau, a city of about one-quarter million persons in the state of Santa Catarina; and São Leopoldo, a city almost as large as Blumenau but now a satellite, or suburb, of Pôrto Alegre in the state of Rio Grande do Sul. German traditions and culture appear to be somewhat more salient in Blumenau, probably due to the fact it has remained more of a separate and distinctive place than São Leopoldo. As discussed in the introductory chapter, ethnic identities tend to be stronger when they are linked to a specific place that the ethnic group considers its own.

The Impetus to German Immigration

Shortly before Brazil gained independence from Portugal in 1822, the crown prince of Portugal married the Hapsburg (Germany) archduchess. The royal match stimulated each nation's interest in the other. German banks, trading companies, and shipping lines began to pursue commercial possibilities in Portugal and in its largest colony, Brazil. The goal of the

German trading houses was to establish outposts in Brazil and then induce German workers to emigrate. Most of those who boarded ships for
South America were responding to problems in Germany, notably famines,
unemployment, and revolutionary unrest. Brazil's southernmost areas were
a logical destination because they were then very sparsely populated. This
territory, which was later divided into several states, was regarded as having little commercial value, and in the early nineteenth century was essentially available for the taking. Possession (i.e., squatting) was the most
common way of acquiring land by those who were able successfully to survive in the wilderness and fight off the native Indian tribes.[1] As an inducement, Brazil offered free land, two years worth of supplies, and ex-
emption from both military service and (for ten years) taxes.

Brazil encouraged these southern settlements to support its claim against
Argentina for this land. In addition, within Brazil there was demand for
European labor to replace slaves brought from Africa. As early as the 1820s,
Brazil considered the abolition of slavery due primarily to slave unrest and
rebellion which made slavery less profitable. In addition, the outbreak of
several deadly epidemics was popularly associated with the slave trade and
prompted public outcries against slavery. Although emancipation was not
fully and legally in place until 1888, slaveholding declined throughout the
nineteenth century, and Brazil's elite wanted to replace African slaves with
white, European workers.[2] Between 1825 and 1828, the Brazilian government established three German settlements and gave subsidies to the Hamburg (Germany) merchant and shipping interests to transport immigrants
to these settlements.

During the second half of the nineteenth century, German immigration to Brazil increased primarily because of high unemployment in Germany. Economic problems often led inhabitants of entire villages to sell
all of their property and belongings to raise funds for a fresh start and,
with their clergy, to emigrate en masse. In Brazil, they largely recreated
their German villages, with most people, at least initially, remaining in
the same occupations.[3] There were also some immigrants who left Germany for religious or political reasons and saw Brazil as offering more
freedom.

The large-scale emigration to Brazil was encouraged by the German government as part of a set of practices described as *informal imperialism:* utilizing immigration to establish not actual colonies under German rule but
commercial contacts that Germany could dominate.[4] The term *informal
imperialism* distinguishes Germany's emigration practices from the formal
colonial administrations established by Britain, Spain, and Portugal. Germany's elite wanted a place to send the unemployed to reduce social

unrest. They were also concerned with a reduction in domestic demand for German products, which they attributed to high unemployment. Government and industry leaders advocated foreign settlements comprised of German immigrants as the solution to all of the nation's economic problems: emigration would reduce unemployment, and as the colonies of German immigrants grew, they would (it was hoped) expand local German influence, thereby providing new markets for German products.

By the close of the nineteenth century, an estimated 200,000 Germans had emigrated to the state of Rio Grande do Sul, concentrating around Pôrto Alegre and São Leopoldo; and 100,000 had emigrated to the state of Santa Catarina, clustering particularly around Blumenau and Joinvile.[5] The continued "Germanness" of the region seemed certain. One influential German traveler writing in 1903 stated: "Surely to us belongs the future in this part of the world. . . . Here indeed in south Brazil is a land where the German emigrant may retain his nationality."[6]

German immigration to Brazil, especially southern Brazil, remained brisk up to the outbreak in 1914 of World War I. However, when Brazil joined the allies fighting against Germany and Brazil's conspicuous German enclaves became targets of violent demonstrations, German immigration ended until after the war. Then, improved relations between Brazil and Germany, combined with a severe depression in Germany, led to the last sizable immigration from Germany to Brazil's southern states between the early 1920s and the early 1930s. Brazil's census figures for this period are not very reliable, but according to estimates by population experts, in the early 1930s there were approximately one million people living in the state of Rio Grande do Sul, and about one-half of them were German. The total population of the state of Santa Catarina was about 360,000, and about two thirds of them were German.[7]

Adolf Hitler's Nazi Party took control of depression-ravaged Germany in 1933 and viewed commercial exchanges with Brazil (and other nations) as an important way to improve the Reich's economic position. The two nations signed a number of extensive trade agreements, and with government encouragement, German airlines established regular flights to Brazil and German banks opened offices in several Brazilian cities.[8] However, by the late 1930s Brazil was slowly edging toward the Allies in their war against Germany, and immigration again stopped.

Since the middle of the twentieth century there has been little German immigration to anywhere in Brazil, but the southern cities have grown substantially. As a result, the Teuto-Brazilians are not as dominant in most of the southern cities, and that has been associated with a general diminution of German language and culture. However, as we shall describe, they did not completely lose their German roots or identities.

A Virtual Tour

Brazil and the United States share some geographical similarities: the total land area of each is almost the same, and many of the largest cities in
each are on the Atlantic seaboard. However, Brazil is shaped roughly like
an upside-down triangle and is divided into twenty-six rather than fifty
states. This chapter focuses upon cities in two states near the bottom of
the "triangle" in southeastern Brazil.

Step one in any tour is to book an international flight to Brazil. One
might choose to fly on Varig, Brazil's leading carrier. It was founded in
the 1920s by Otto Ernest Meyer, who left Germany to settle in southern
Brazil in precisely the area we will be examining. Meyer received assistance
from a German airline, and his initially small fleet consisted of a few
German-made aircraft, German pilots, and German-trained technicians. In
the early days of Varig's existence, it flew between only a few of the larger
cities in southern Brazil; however, these were the first commercial flights
by any Brazilian-based carrier and they facilitated the growth of the German firms in Brazil's southern states.[9]

The international airport closest to southeastern Brazil is in São Paulo,
the nation's leading industrial center. Varig offers dozens of flights to São
Paulo from New York, Los Angeles, and other major world cities. Leaving
the São Paulo airport and driving through the city, one is struck by con-
trasts. The new high-rise office buildings in the downtown financial center epitomize the modern metropolis, and the city's more fashionable shopping areas rival those of any city in the world. At the same time, however,
there are miles of tiny, makeshift shacks housing families in primitive conditions and hundreds of homeless children begging on the streets, which
are crowded with cars and buses barely moving at any hour of the day.[10]

Our virtual tour is now going to head south, out of the city (and state
of) São Paulo. We shall follow highways that are close to the eastern edge
of Brazil, near the Atlantic Ocean, because most of southern Brazil's German enclaves formed near the country's east coast. After several hours of
driving, we reach the state of Santa Catarina.[11] About four hundred miles
from São Paulo, near the center of Santa Catarina's east coast, we approach
Blumenau, a city of nearly a quarter-million people. The billboards on the
roadside are dominated by German-sounding names: they advertise Rot-
tweilers from the Borstadt kennels, schnitzel and strudel at the Frohsinn
restaurant, and the Oktoberfest—proudly billed as the largest beer festival
in the world outside Germany. Actually, apart from the subtropical heat,
visitors to Blumenau might believe they had arrived in the Black Forest

rather than a city in Brazil.[12] Much of the architecture in the city is also conspicuously German, involving half-timbered chalet-style homes and businesses.

After we describe Blumenau we shall move a couple of hundred miles further south to where German immigration to Brazil began in Rio Grande do Sul, Brazil's southernmost state. (Uruguay is on its southern border.) Walking down the street or rummaging through the *Yellow Pages* in several of the Rio Grande do Sul cities, one is immediately struck by the Germanic names of people and businesses; also by the Germanic names of the cities, themselves: Novo Hamburgo, Hamburger Berg, São Leopoldo, and so on.

Blumenau

The first German settlements in the state of Santa Catarina were rural villages established in the 1820s. They were very small and separated from each other by rivers and ridges, therefore relatively self-contained. They consisted primarily of the families of farmers, ranchers, and craftsmen who consumed most of the textiles, beer, sugar, coffee, tobacco, and dairy products that they collectively produced. A small portion of their total production went to Brazilian cities to the north, and a little was exported. However, there was little contact, commercial or otherwise, between or among individual settlements. The German communities were, with respect to their relative isolation and self-containment, typical of most settlements in Santa Catarina during the first half of the nineteenth century.[13]

The first sizable German settlement in Santa Catarina was at the site of the current city of Blumenau. This settlement began in 1850 when a German physician, Dr. Hermann Blumenau, led a group of followers to the site. (His mausoleum is now a museum in the city.) Dr. Blumenau's first visit to the area was in 1848, and he later explained how its forests, valleys, and rivers reminded him of forested areas around the Rhine River in Germany. He bought land at a subsidized price with the assistance of the Brazilian Consul, and each of his followers received a small plot. In order to plant crops and graze cattle, they cleared the forests in a manner later described as "swift and violent" because they showed little regard for the long-term ecology of the area.[14] They simply burnt acres of forest, gathered turtle eggs, shot egrets, and so on. After clearing the land, the settlers—most of whom were from Pomerania, then a province in Northeastern Germany—built their homes in the traditional Pomeranian design: brick construction with outside beams.[15] This housing style has continued to predominate in Blumenau.

The early days were extremely difficult for the Germans who settled in Blumenau. Malaria caused a lot of deaths, and there were recurrent confrontations with the Shokleng Indians, who considered the area around Blumenau to be within their hunting territory. Nevertheless, by 1870 the town had grown to about six thousand people due to some additional German immigration and extremely high fertility rates among the immigrants. The early settlers averaged nearly five children per family. By 1870 they owned an estimated 27,000 domestic animals and had built a twenty-mile network of wagon roads connecting them to other towns in the region. During the first decades of its existence, the town of Blumenau devoted roughly two thirds of its total revenue to building roads and bridges, improving travel within the town and between it and nearby towns. At the time these German colonies were described as having the finest roads in all of Brazil.[16] As the colony grew and expanded, and as commercial travel from Blumenau into an extended region increased, the settlers invaded more of the Indian's hunting territory. When skirmishes became commonplace, the settlers hired professional killers who nearly exterminated the Indians, and they ceased to be an obstacle to the colony's expansion.[17]

The German settlers were joined by other German-speaking immigrants from Austria and Switzerland, and there were also some Italian and Portuguese émigrés. However, in the 1880s about three quarters of Blumenau's growing population was still almost exclusively German-speaking.[18] Two of the immigrants who arrived in the 1880s, the Hering brothers, had special significance for the future of the city. Their family had been involved in textile manufacturing in Germany since the late eighteenth century, and when they arrived in Blumenau they became the founders of the Hering Company (Cia Hering). This Blumenau clothing firm, now run by their descendants, manufactures every type of clothing for men, women, and children and sells its products through more than a hundred franchised stores, mostly in South America. It also distributes other licensed brand-named apparel, such as Disney shirts and pajamas, across both South America and Europe. For many years, Cia Hering has been the largest employer in Blumenau.[19]

The majority of the German immigrants had only their labor to sell and initially worked for the most part in agricultural settlements. When they acquired a little money, they often moved to nearby towns to work as artisans or small merchants. This type of outflow from Blumenau was important to the initial growth of several towns in the region, beginning with Joinvile. From its inception, Joinvile was more urban and less agricultural than Blumenau, and this made it a desirable initial destination for some of the later-arriving German immigrants who had business or professional backgrounds and wanted a more urban life. In the 1920s, Joinvile was described as an "idyllic German village," parklike, with plants and shrubs surrounding timber-framed houses with German-style folding windows. In many of the homes a small shop or restaurant occupied one side, the dwelling the other.[20]

The Teuto-Brazilians in Blumenau, as in other such communities in southern Brazil, built their own distinctive churches and schools, supported an active German-language press—consisting of daily, weekly, and monthly publications—and established a variety of clubs and organizations. The latter were recreations of associations and activities that had been commonplace in Germany and included rifle clubs, complete with hunting jackets and caps, charitable societies, library associations, and bowling clubs.[21]

Churches and Schools

Religion probably provided the most integral institutions in Teuto-Brazilian communities. The immigrants were both Catholic and Protestant, and members of each religious denomination built their own churches. The significance of organized religion to the settlers was indicated by the fact that the émigrés brought their own clergy with them. However, in Blumenau, as in other towns in southern Brazil, the Catholics and Protestants actually formed separate and different subcommunities. They tended to differ from each other in attitudes toward Brazil and Germany, the associations they joined, which of the German-language newspapers they read, and so on.

Because Brazil was (and is) predominantly and officially a Catholic country, the German Catholics shared an important feature with the Luso-Brazilians. Although they retained aspects of German culture, their religious identity probably came to supersede their ethnic identity. Thinking of themselves more as Catholics than Germans, they tended to be better integrated into Brazilian society than German Protestants. For example, later generations descending from German Catholics were less likely than their Protestant counterparts to speak German.[22] In addition, while both Protestant and Catholic families typically sent their children to private German schools, this was especially true for the Protestants, who feared that Catholicism would creep into the curriculum of public schools.

The Protestant immigrants received help from missionary societies in Germany that provided funds for the construction of schools as well as churches. They also sent pastors and teachers to work in the colonies, and they were supplemented by untrained immigrants. Professional and lay personnel were alike, however, in speaking very little Portuguese—the nation's dominant and official language. Thus, particularly for the Protestants, schools and churches became important institutions for maintaining German language and culture. One Evangelical pastor unabashedly explained that the German cultural heritage of his church was, "a God-given gift to be held in honor and nourished in church and school. . . . The German Evangelical church in Brazil therefore wears its German dress consciously and proudly."[23]

Given that no governmental unit in Brazil initially took responsibility for schools in the German districts of the south, the immigrants necessarily established their own, modeled after those in Germany. Even after public schools were instituted, however, families in Blumenau (and other towns with large German populations) continued to prefer their own private schools. Around 1910, there were ten state-run schools in Blumenau with a total enrollment of just over five hundred children. However, more than one hundred private schools served the German community, and their total enrollments were in excess of five thousand. Instruction in these latter schools was, of course, exclusively in German. Printed on the cover of each child's notebook in the German-run schools throughout Santa Catarina was the admonition: "Remember that you are German!"[24]

There was a tendency, especially in the Protestant community, to look down upon the Luso-Brazilians and to regard them as lazy, stupid spendthrifts, in contrast to the Germans themselves, whom they viewed as smart, industrious, and frugal. They saw themselves as colonists who transformed a forest of Indians and wild beasts into a modern society. Most wanted to remain aloof from the non-Germans who surrounded them, and the Protestant clergy opposed marriage between Teuto- and Luso-Brazilians in order to maintain their separateness. Even many second-generation Germans in Blumenau refused to learn Portuguese, and as previously noted, it was the German Protestants who were especially likely to avoid learning Portuguese. By contrast, many non-German Brazilians working in Blumenau and other German-dominated towns in Santa Catarina had to learn to speak German as the language of commerce and industry.[25] They found this ironic reversal in their own homeland a source of resentment. The Luso-Brazilians in Blumenau, Joinvile, and other towns also envied the quality of the German homes and schools.

Because of the Germans' success and aloofness, laws aimed at controlling the German communities became politically popular in Santa Catarina. In 1911 the state asserted that all private schools operating within Santa Catarina must observe Brazil's national holidays. The specific targets of this ruling were the Protestant schools, which had frequently ignored these events. In addition, any institution that accepted any government funds was required to utilize Portuguese as the language of instruction.[26] Neither of these rulings had a dramatic effect upon the schools and churches in the German community because few received any government funds, but more severe restrictions were coming with World War I.

When the war began in 1914, the major Portuguese-language newspapers in Brazil tended to support the Allies (England and France, later joined by the United States). At the opposite pole, the German-language newspapers that served Protestant communities generally expressed support for Germany. The German-Brazilian Catholic press was in between the extremes. However, within Blumenau, both Catholics and Protestants were supportive of the German cause, if to varying degrees. Within the enclave the war was an energizing event. Religious congregations raised funds for the German Red Cross, they purchased German war bonds, and they celebrated reports of German battle victories by singing the German national anthem. One leading Protestant pastor who was also a newspaper publisher urged Teuto-Brazilians to boycott businesses whose owners were Allied sympathizers. Some of the more extreme members argued that the southern states should secede from Brazil. One prominent Portuguese-language newspaper, in a somewhat exaggerated report, warned its readers that there were forty German rifle clubs in Blumenau that were really paramilitary societies ready to fight for southern Brazil's right to link to Germany.[27]

Brazil officially declared its neutrality when the war first broke out, but after a German submarine sunk a Brazilian freighter in 1917, Brazil joined the Allies, and there was a burst of flag-waving nationalism among the Luso-Brazilians. They turned in anger against the German enclaves as visible symbols of their enemy. Throughout southern Brazil, stone-throwing crowds vandalized, burned, and looted many German schools, churches, and businesses, especially those linked to the Protestant community. The rioting was more limited in Santa Catarina because German descendants were well represented among the state's political leaders. However, the Santa Catarina legislature did respond to the public's anti-German sentiments by requiring that *all* (public and private) schools in the state teach Brazilian history and geography.

The federal government went further, banning the publication of German-language books and newspapers. Some publishers went out of business, others tried to adjust to the new situation. Two German newspapers in Blumenau decided to try to publish in Portuguese and began by changing their names: The *Urwaldsbote* ("messenger") became the *Commercio do Blumenau,* and The *Blumenauer Zeitung* ("newspaper") became the *Gazeta Blumenauense.* In their Portuguese editions, they urged more assimilation and less stereotyping of the Luso-Brazilians by their German readers.[28]

The federal government finally required that all schools not teaching in Portuguese be closed. In Blumenau, crash courses in Portuguese were offered to German-speaking teachers, but few were able to meet all of the new requirements. Some of the schools were able to adjust, but the problems were insurmountable, especially for many of the Protestant private schools, and they were forced to close. Some parents found that there was no room for their children in local public schools, others refused to send their children to them. As a result, thousands of Teuto-Brazilian children in Blumenau and other Santa Catarina towns did not attend school for most of the war.[29]

When Germany surrendered in 1918 to end World War I, many of Blumenau's residents were stunned and depressed. It took weeks for some to believe what had happened to the fatherland. As the shock wore off, most expected life to return to "normal," that is, as it had been prior to the war. However, Santa Catarina continued to demand that all schools in the state provide Portuguese language instruction and teach Brazilian history, geography, civics, and so on. None of these regulations were repealed until 1921, but by then a number of German schools had permanently closed, and the continuation of some pro-Portuguese, pro-Brazil regulations discouraged new German schools from opening. In addition, the private schools that survived had substantially different curricula. Similarly, German publications were not the same after the war as before. Many newspapers and other periodicals failed to survive the war, and most of those that did returned to the German language slowly; but even the Protestant-German press tended to express less opposition to assimilation than it had before the war.

Sizable German immigration to Brazil resumed in the early 1920s, and much of it continued to destinations in the southern states. Over the next decade, the Teuto-Brazilians in Blumenau, Joinvile, and other historically German towns continued to exceed two thirds of the population.[30] Their symbolic attachments to Germany remained strong, though not quite as strong as they had been before the war.

When Adolf Hitler and the Nazi Party took control in Germany in 1933, some in the Teuto-Brazilian community found that Hitler's great plans for the fatherland rekindled their German pride and identity. An estimated five thousand Brazilians, mostly in the southern states, joined the Nazi Party. In Blumenau, where these attachments were especially strong, local party members paraded with swastikas through the streets of the town.[31] In 1938, security-conscious Brazilian Army officials became concerned about the potential influence of this foreign political entity, and they banned the party. Nevertheless, more indirect and hidden support for the Nazis continued in Blumenau and southern Brazil. Some in the community feared that these actions would eventually bring World War I–type reprisals. They were right.

As in World War I, Brazil initially tried to maintain neutrality, but again German naval vessels (U-boats this time) sank Brazilian merchant ships, and in 1942 Brazil joined the Allies in the war against Germany. Once again, angry mobs of Luso-Brazilians stoned and burned churches and stores that they associated with local German communities. The federal government jailed Nazi sympathizers and those suspected of being sympathizers, and in some cases did not release them until several years after the war ended in 1945. Officials also instituted a "Brazilianization" campaign designed to promote assimilation by all groups throughout the country. One aspect of this campaign that particularly targeted Teuto-Brazilians in the south was a prohibition on instruction in German in any school, even the private schools affiliated with the German communities.[32]

Assimilation

After World War II, German immigration again trickled into Brazil, though it never reached the consequential prewar levels. The continuing growth of cities in the south—such as Blumenau's, whose population reached one-quarter-million persons in 2000, and Joinvile, which approached one-half-million—was primarily due to migration *within* Brazil. Between roughly 1950 and 1965, north-to-south movement within Brazil was particularly pronounced. Between about 1965 and 2000, the rural-to-urban migration was especially dramatic.[33] Both trends led to a reduction in the German majority in most of the southern cities and towns. In addition to the changing demographics, there was also the slow loss of the German language among later generations of Teuto-Brazilians, who did not learn it in school. In addition, their socialization experiences in public schools and most churches placed more emphasis upon being Brazilian than on being German.

A number of other events that occurred in the middle of the twentieth century also contributed to a weakening of German identities by strengthening Brazilian identities, even among the Teuto-Brazilians in the south. Brazil instituted a national radio network that attracted a mass audience after World War II and exposed everyone to the same popular culture (in Portuguese, of course). At the same time, the growth of the domestic movie industry in Rio de Janeiro produced films that presented more authentic views of Brazilians than did those made in Europe or the United States and thereby contributed to a sense of nationhood. Professional soccer leagues were also established across Brazil, further reinforcing the idea that Brazil was a single nation, and fanaticism for the national soccer team became a shared passion that transcended ethnic lines.[34]

Regardless of how they thought of themselves, the youngsters growing up in the German enclaves had numerous advantages relative to Luso-Brazilians: higher rates of literacy, greater wealth, a tradition that placed more stress upon ambition and enterprise, and more familial connections to modern commercial and industrial firms. In Blumenau and across southern Brazil, German immigrants had established firms, such as Cia Hering, that grew into some of the largest and most successful in the nation. In many cases, much of these companies' ownership and management continued to be drawn from the Teuto-Brazilian community. These firms benefited from support by the German government via German chambers of commerce and industry in Brazil's southern states. The chambers' primary objective has been to promote bilateral trade between Germany and Brazil, but these efforts simultaneously helped to tie Brazilian firms to the global economy.

The leaders of the German-founded firms, often direct descendants of the immigrants who founded them, became segments of Brazil's new social elite, nudging aside many of the large landowners who once dominated Brazil's hereditary aristocracy. By about 1970, even though German descendants made up only 2 percent of Brazil's population, they comprised between about 10 percent and 15 percent of Brazil's elite. To be specific, they were substantially overrepresented among the most socially exclusive *Who's Who* families in Brazil and in the ranks of colonels and generals in the army officer corps, then the most important indicator of political power in Brazil.[35] A degree of assimilation was required for the German descendants to attain this upward mobility into the ranks of Brazil's elite, and that mobility, in turn, promoted further assimilation.

Another important variable promoting German Brazilians' assimilation was racial polarization. Historically, many Luso-Brazilians considered their culture a mixture of European, Indian, and African influences. In the 1960s, however, more attention was focused upon racial *differences*. Culturally, this entailed recognizing that it was the African-Brazilians who had the strongest link to African music, art, and religion while "white" Brazilians were more attached to European culture. Socially, it involved awareness of the degree to which Brazilians of European descent exceeded African Brazilians in education, income, political representation, and so on. In this more racially polarized context, the German Brazilians' similarities to Brazilians of Portuguese, Italian, and other European descents led the Germans to more panethnic European identities.

Finally, even the Protestantism of many of the Teuto-Brazilians became less distinguishing. As late as 1950, only 4 percent of Brazil's population was Protestant, and most of them were German. (Almost all of the rest of the nation was Catholic.) By 2000, an estimated 15 percent of the population was Protestant.[36] The Protestant denominations that grew did so by recruiting non-Germans, primarily the urban poor who were attracted to Pentecostal groups. So while Brazil remained very much a Catholic country, the substantial increase in the number and diversity of Protestants made German Protestants less distinctive. Being Protestant no longer implied that one was German.

At the same time, many of the descendants of German immigrants living in Blumenau did not discard all of their German traditions. For example, at least into the early years of this century, some residents continued to speak perfect German. One prominent example was the great-grandson of the Hering brothers who had originally founded the dominant company in the city. He was the honorary German consul in Blumenau and in 2001 he described one of his major tasks as involving translating Portuguese into German—a service that was sometimes in great demand because many of the Teuto-Brazilians living in Blumenau wanted German names for their businesses but were no longer literate in German. Their motives were varied. German names had nostalgic value for some residents, while other people thought they might be of help in doing business with the large German-run firms that dominated the area. Some Teuto-

Brazilians in Blumenau were able to accomplish this objective simply by utilizing their surnames, for example, the Schmidt Porcelain Company. Others wanted to select an appropriate German name for their product or service; for example, Blumenau's butcher shop is called "Fleischhaus" (i.e., meat house). When a local real estate broker decided to name his business "Freudenhaus," however, Consul Hering warned him off because that German word translates into "brothel."[37]

"Selling" a distinctive culture, as long as it appears to be "authentic," also has commercial value. In a multicultural society, such as Brazil or the United States, people are interested in distinctive local cultures, especially if they seem to be genuinely attached to a place. Thus it would be difficult to "sell" tourists or shoppers on a Chinatown in Blumenau, but a German historical presence seems legitimate.[38] That probably accounts, at least in part, for the success of Blumenau's annual Oktoberfest, the largest German folk festival in Brazil and the nation's second largest festival of any kind.

It is also important to recognize that to promote a culture commercially also requires some degree of attention to cultural history. People who have forgotten their roots are at a disadvantage. Blumenau's Oktoberfest is notable as a continuing expression of the city's (and the region's) German identity. Dressed in ancestral German clothing, bands from Blumenau and throughout the region play traditional German folk songs. Youngsters who also dress in historic costumes perform German dances, and through the main street there are floats featuring people dressed like the original German settlers standing in front of primitive houses, waiving to onlookers. And of course there are the giant beer halls featuring many types of German beer.[39]

São Leopoldo/Pôrto Alegre

The earliest German settlements in Brazil were in the nation's southernmost state, Rio Grande do Sul, near the Atlantic coast. The very first colony, in 1824 or 1825 (accounts differ), was in São Leopoldo. Other German colonies in this same area soon followed in Pôrto Alegre, Montenegro, Novo Hamburgo, and others. Today, São Leopoldo is a small city of approximately 200,000 persons with its own AM and FM radio stations. However, like the other former German colonies in this area, it is also a suburb of metropolitan Pôrto Alegre, the state capital, which, with its metropolitan population of about three million, is the largest urban area in southern Brazil. The integration of São Leopoldo into the Pôrto Alegre metropolitan area has numerous indicators: São Leopoldo is served by Pôrto Alegre's airport and harbor, its television stations, professional sports teams, and so on. And at night São Leopoldo's streets and sidewalks are crowded with young people from throughout the Pôrto Alegre metropolitan area. They are attracted to the suburb's clubs and bars and especially the "Beer Factory," with its diverse selection of German beer.[40]

In the following pages we shall focus primarily upon the history of Brazil's first German settlement in São Leopoldo. However, given its proximity to Pôrto Alegre and the fact it later became part of the Pôrto Alegre metropolitan area, we shall examine both the city and the metropolitan area. We shall pay little attention to developments within São Leopoldo and Pôrto Alegre that essentially duplicated those previously described in the section on Blumenau.

The first German settlers in São Leopoldo were thirty-nine farmers from Germany's northern provinces near Hamburg. All of them were Catholic— as the Brazilian government then required—and they were all from Germany's lower classes, having been serfs or hired workers on Prussian manors. Using primitive equipment, they began by planting traditional German crops, such as rye and potatoes, then added some indigenous crops, such as maize.

The founders of the colony began by making a straight cut through the forest to provide a road. Along the road settlers received small plots of land on which they built simple farmhouses. A row of this type constituted a rural village. As more settlers arrived, a new road was built connecting to the earlier one, and a new village formed.[41] Throughout much of Rio Grande do Sul, clusters of such villages formed a colony. In the center of colonies, such as São Leopoldo, settlers from all of the villages built a church and school, a few stores, and a mill. Within five years, the industrious colonists in São Leopoldo had added a soap factory, locksmiths, cabinetmakers, tailors, and seven more grain mills.[42]

High status in Brazilian society at the time of the first German settlements was based upon owning large amounts of property and slaves. Manual work was held in very low esteem. Therefore the immigrant German farmers, despite their commercial successes, initially occupied a very low place in the Brazilian social hierarchy. They looked up to the "gauchos" whose culture dominated the region. Like North American "cowboys," the gauchos were gun-carrying, horse-riding men who wore wide-brimmed hats, neckerchiefs, and leather boots. They greatly valued bravery, a readiness to defend one's honor, and fast horses. Their almost immediate influence upon the former German peasants was apparent. An upper-status visitor from Germany who visited the São Leopoldo settlement in 1827 wrote that he was surprised to find that "There are few children who know how to read and write while all the time possible they ride on horseback . . . and practice the throwing of the lasso . . . used to catch cattle."[43] Riding horses, throwing lassos, and the like were all activities that had been totally unknown to German peasants.

In São Leopoldo, like other German colonies, there were also ample signs of the immigrants' European past. Their houses were distinctive: clean wooden chalets with curtains and vases of flowers in the windows, surrounded by well-kept gardens. Inside, they continued such German traditions as displaying bunnies at Easter, and at Christmas they took out little trees covered with fake snow and images of "Hans" with fake cotton whiskers, dressed in a long red nightshirt.[44]

With primitive living conditions and extensive deaths due to various epidemics, the colony at São Leopoldo grew slowly during the early-to-middle part of the nineteenth century. An 1859 census estimated that there were only about twenty thousand Germans in the entire state of Rio Grande do Sul. Over the next fifty years, however, their number increased tenfold due to high birthrates among the German immigrants and continued German immigration.[45] This period of high emigration in the closing decades of the nineteenth century was also characterized by changes in immigrant composition. The early German settlers were necessarily all Catholics, given Brazil's immigration rules. This restriction was relaxed later in the nineteenth century, and then there were more Protestant than Catholic émigrés. By the early twentieth century, the population of São Leopoldo and other German communities in the Pôrto Alegre area was estimated to have somewhat more Protestants (among whom Lutherans predominated) than Catholics.[46] The late-nineteenth- and early-twentieth-century German immigrants were also better educated than their predecessors and more likely to be artisans, industrial workers, and entrepreneurs.

Among this later group of immigrants were a number of people who established firms, often with links to Germany, that subsequently grew into large, modern corporations. A noteworthy example is provided by João Gerdau, a German immigrant, who in 1901 purchased a small nail factory in Pôrto Alegre. It grew slowly at first, acquiring the plants of small competitors, then later buying up larger ones. The founding family's ties to German companies and banks provided the firm with "an international mentality" from its inception, according to one of Gerdau's four great-grandsons who currently run the company. Metallurgica Gerdau S.A., as it is now known, is still headquartered in Pôrto Alegre, owns manufacturing facilities in Argentina, Canada and the United States, and is the twenty-fifth largest steel producer in the world.[47]

There were also a number of firms begun by German immigrants in São Leopoldo, Novo Hamburgo, and other towns in the region that grew and then moved to Pôrto Alegre because it offered more supporting business services and its port provided the best site for shipping. By the middle of the twentieth century, people of German descent came to dominate Pôrto Alegre's import and export businesses.[48]

The influx of German immigrants to São Leopoldo/Pôrto Alegre was halted by World War I. While visible symbols of the German community in Blumenau and other German-dominated towns in Santa Catarina were attacked by patriotic crowds when the war broke out, the destruction was far worse in the Pôrto Alegre area. Part of the difference was due to an initial confrontation at the Hotel Schmidt. As reported in the *Deutsche Post* of São Leopoldo, on April 24, 1917, a mob passed by the hotel, a well-known German inn. The owner, Friedrich Schmidt, his son, and two associates anticipated them and erected a barricade in front of the hotel. They were armed with pistols—the gaucho influence?—and from behind the bulwark they fired into the crowd. The mob overcame them, smashed every window in the hotel, set it on fire, and over the next three days proceeded to vandalize São Leopoldo and Pôrte Alegre's German-language newspapers, pharmacies, beer halls, and so on. Newspapers and churches associated with German Catholics were generally targeted less than those of Protestants (as in Blumenau).[49]

The extraordinary destruction around Pôrto Alegre probably had two causes: first, the Hotel Schmidt confrontation, which acted like an incendiary agent; and second, tepid protection of the Teuto-Brazilians by state and local officials. Especially by comparison to the strong political representation of Blumenau's German community in Santa Catarina, there were very few prominent German-Brazilians in Rio Grande do Sul state politics.

After the war, German immigration to towns in the Pôrto Alegre area resumed, and the wartime restrictions on Teuto-Brazilians gradually declined. The growing German enclave in São Leopoldo exhibited many traditional German influences, though fewer than in Blumenau. One visitor during the 1920s noted that while most of the architecture and landscaping did not appear particularly German, the streets and homes of São Leopoldo did look "German-like" in that they were very clean and well kept. Signs above a few of the stores were in German, and the language of immigrants and their descendants continued to be almost exclusively German. Local Luso-Brazilian informants told one visitor in the 1920s that Germans "own all the land" and whenever he saw children of the "well-to-do class" they were fair-skinned (i.e., German, rather than darker-skinned Luso-Brazilians) and their language was German.[50] The blond, light-skinned, freckle-faced Germans stood out even though they were wearing ponchos and boots, carrying guns, and riding horses.

On the other hand, even though the gauchos were not particularly industrious, the Germans continued to emulate them. Riding horses, betting on horse races, and carrying guns—all aspects of traditional gaucho culture—continued to be important aspects of life in the German enclave. One local citizen in 1930 complained about the role guns had come to play. As soon as they leave school, he claimed, "almost all boys have their guns hanging at the belt. . . . Even in the church . . . I have seen people kneeling . . . with guns at their belts."[51]

Conclusions

German identities continue to have some salience for Teuto-Brazilians in São Leopoldo and other Pôrto Alegre towns. Helping to maintain this identity are a number of large firms with conspicuously German-Brazilian ownership, many with strong commercial ties to Germany. Thus having a German background can be a business asset. In addition, as in Blumenau, traditional German culture can be commercially exploited. São Leopoldo's museum of historical German immigration, for example, continues to draw tourists. Outside of the commercial realm, having a German surname can also be an asset. As his name implies, the city's mayor in 2002, Waldir Schmidt, was from the Teuto-Brazilian community. Even São Leopoldo's official motto, "Faith, Culture and Work," is clearly an expression of its German Protestant (rather than Portuguese Catholic) origins. And there are strong pockets in which a point of view persists that is sympathetic to Germany: nearly one-half a century after the end of World War II, some publications in Pôrto Alegre continued to deny that the Holocaust ever occurred.[52]

The Teuto-Brazilians in São Leopoldo appear to be less German and more Brazilian than their Blumenau counterparts, though. One reason probably has to do with the strength of gaucho culture in Rio Grande do Sul when the early Germans immigrated. It almost immediately provided another set of cultural representations to mix with traditional German. By contrast, while the gauchos were present as far north as Santa Catarina, they were much less dominant cultural figures there. Thus the early German settlers in the sparsely settled hills and ridges of Santa Catarina did not confront as strong a local culture into which they could be absorbed.

In addition, Blumenau remains a distinct place: a city in which Germans historically dominated. The Web site of Santa Catarina cities still lists Blumenau as *Mein Blumenau* (German for "My Blumenau"). For Teuto-

Brazilians from Blumenau, the city has intrinsic German connotations; that is, what it means to be from Blumenau is to be German (or German-Brazilian). As one fourth-generation descendant of German immigrants to Brazil put it in 1990: "If there is a holy city for those who cling to the old Germanism . . . it is Blumenau."[53] By contrast, São Leopoldo is a less distinct place. Though it was as German as Blumenau, it is now part of metropolitan Pôrto Alegre, and while there has been a historically strong German presence in Pôrto Alegre, both the city and the metropolitan area involve a much more diverse mix of people. Thus being from Pôrto Alegre does not imply any specific ethnicity; being from São Leopoldo could, but given the social and economic integration of São Leopoldo and Pôrto Alegre, it is more difficult to think about São Leopoldo as a distinct place.

Notes

1. Emile Viotti Da Costa, *The Brazilian Empire,* Chapel Hill, NC: University of North Carolina Press, 2000.
2. Joseph Smith, *A History of Brazil,* London: Pearson Education Publishing, 2002.
3. Marion K. Pinsdorf, *German-Speaking Entrepreneurs,* New York: Peter Lang, 1990.
4. Ian L. Forbes, "German Informal Imperialism in South America Before 1914," *Economic History Review* 31, 3, 1978, pp. 383–398.
5. Pinsdorf, op. cit.
6. Quoted in Stephan Bonsal, "Greater Germany in South America," *North American Review* January 1903, p. 58.
7. See the table on p. 531 in Leo Waibel, "European Colonization in Southern Brazil," *Geographical Review* 40, 4, 1950.
8. Stanley E. Hilton, *Brazil and the Great Powers, 1930–1939,* Austin: University of Texas Press, 1975.
9. Pinsdorf, op. cit.
10. Some of the neighborhoods in São Paulo historically attracted very large numbers of German immigrants, but Germans did not tend to dominate in São Paulo as they did further to the south. São Paulo's mix of immigrants included large numbers of Italians, Poles, and others.
11. Leaving São Paulo the next state is Paraná, but our virtual tour will not make any stops here because the German influence in this state

is not significant. Some Germans did emigrate to Paraná during the mid-nineteenth century and tried but failed to cultivate wheat. Most then moved on to Argentina or the United States.

12. That observation was offered by Tony Smith, Associated Press writer, in a story distributed by the AP on July 15, 2001.

13. Bertha K. Becker and Claudio A. G. Egler, *Brazil: A New Regional Power in the World-Economy,* Cambridge, UK: Cambridge University Press, 1992.

14. Pinsdorf, op. cit., p. 118.

15. James, op. cit.

16. Pinsdorf, op. cit. In fact, the Germans in southern Brazil introduced almost every form of transportation to the entire nation. They were the first to organize wagon transport for both freight and passengers. They later introduced automobiles and, as previously noted, airline travel as well.

17. Greg Urban, "Interpretations of Inter-Cultural Contact," *Ethnohistory* 32, 3, 1985, pp. 224–244.

18. James, op. cit.

19. For further information on the history of Cia Hering, see the company's Web site: http://www.hering.com.br/.

20. Mark Jefferson, "Pictures from Southern Brazil," *Geographic Review* 16, 4, 1926, pp. 533–552.

21. Bowling, for example, had been a popular sport in Germany since the Middle Ages. Some trace the history of modern bowling to Germany in the third century, when most German peasants carried a club (called a *Kegel*). In many churches, parishioners would raise their kegels as targets, representing the heavens. Then they would roll a stone, attempting to knock down the kegel, and if they succeeded, they would be considered free of sin. The Germans eventually moved the game out of the church and played it as a secular club sport. For further information on the history of German bowling, see http://www. hickoksports.com.

22. Frederick C. Luebke, *Germans in Brazil,* Baton Rouge, LA: Louisiana State University Press, 1987.

23. Quoted in ibid., pp. 43–44.

24. Ibid., p. 78.

25. Pinsdorf, op. cit.

26. Luebke, op. cit.

27. Ibid.

28. Ibid.

29. Ibid.

30. Waibel, op. cit.

31. Tony Smith, op. cit.
32. Hilton, op. cit.
33. Joseph Smith, op. cit.
34. Ibid.
35. Glenn A. Nichols and Philip S. Snyder, "Brazilian Elites and the Descendants of the German, Italian and Japanese Immigrants," *Journal of Interamerican Studies and World Affairs* 23, 3, 1981, pp. 321–343.
36. Joseph Smith, op. cit.
37. Tony Smith, op. cit.
38. For further discussion, see Mark Goodwin, "The City as Commodity," in Gary Kearns and Chris Philo (Eds.), *Selling Places,* Oxford, UK: Pergamon, 1993, pp. 145–162; and Miriam Greenberg, "Branding Cities," *Urban Affairs Review* 36, 2000, pp. 228–263.
39. Pictures taken at recent Oktoberfests are available online at http://www.Santa-Catarina.net.
40. "History of the City of São Leopoldo," available at http://www.sindileo.com.
41. Luebke, op. cit.
42. Pinsdorf, op. cit.
43. Emilio Willems, "Acculturation and the Horse Complex Among German-Brazilians," *American Anthropologist* 46, 2, 1944, pp. 153–163.
44. Pinsdorf, op. cit.
45. Preston E. James, "The Expanding Settlements of Southern Brazil," *Geographical Review* 30, 4, 1940, pp. 603–629.
46. Jefferson, op. cit.
47. Larry Rohter, "From Brazil, An Emerging Steel Giant," *New York Times,* August 30, 2001, p. C1.
48. Ibid.
49. Luebke, op. cit.
50. Ibid., p. 536.
51. Willems, op. cit., p. 157.
52. Jeffrey Lesser, *Welcoming the Undesirables,* Berkeley: University of California Press, 1995.
53. Pinsdorf, op. cit., p. 113.

Chinatown in San Francisco and Little Taipei in Suburban Los Angeles

In 1965, the U.S. Congress passed an immigration act that changed quotas limiting the national origins of immigrants and opened the United States to a different stream of newcomers, particularly from Asia and South America. Many in the post-1965 stream were professionals or had operated businesses in their homelands. They were generally much more advantaged economically than the immigrants that preceded them, though this was not true of all of them.

Differences in the economic resources of immigrants are associated with enclaves of two distinctly different types: the older enclaves with predominantly poor residents that were almost always in the center of cities, and the more recently formed enclaves with sizable middle and upper classes that tend to be located in suburban areas.[1] In addition to variations in socioeconomic status, the population of newer enclaves tends to be younger and more politically active, and differences in the roles of women are especially pronounced. Nowhere are the differences between these two types of enclaves more vividly illustrated than in two Chinese communities in California: the old Chinatown in the heart of San Francisco and the new enclave, Little Taipei, in suburban Los Angeles.

Chinatown

Of all of the nation's Chinatowns, the oldest and probably best known is San Francisco's. It was erected on the ashes of the Chinese Quarter, which was destroyed by fire following a massive earthquake in 1906. Until its destruction, the Quarter was the point of entry for Chinese immigrants going anywhere in the United States. The core of Chinatown is an old seventeen-block area densely packed with apartment buildings and housing projects, banks, markets, schools, cultural associations, restaurants, and professional offices. Huddled around park benches, groups of elderly Chinese men play cards and checkers, speaking only in their native language. Many of them share small apartments, so public squares serve as "community living rooms."[2] Almost all of Chinatown's nearly fifteen thousand residents and proprietors are Chinese. Many are also elderly, relatively poor, and foreign-born. Their origins have changed dramatically in recent years, though. Most of the recent immigrants have come from mainland China, where Mandarin is spoken, and it is now heard nearly as often in Chinatown as the Cantonese dialect of earlier arrivals. This is a big change. In 2003, Rose Pak remembered speaking Mandarin thirty years earlier, when she first arrived in Chinatown, and people quietly muttered that she was a "Chinese person who didn't speak Chinese."[3]

CENTER CITY SAN FRANCISCO

PACIFIC OCEAN

San Francisco Bay

Chinatown

Sacramento Street   Nob
                     Hill
                         Financial
                         District

Market Street

To the north and west of the core is a Greater Chinatown which is several times larger than the core. This is a newer and less crowded area that contains approximately fifteen thousand additional Chinese residents. They are still a plurality in Greater Chinatown, but its store owners and residents are a mixed population. Farther to the west lie Nob Hill and Russian Hill, described in Chapter Two. Although neither area still houses an elite enclave, the mansions of the area stand in marked contrast to the small shops and apartments of Chinatown. To the south and east, Chinatown abuts San Francisco's main financial district, whose skyscrapers, including the pyramid-shaped Transamerica Building, provide Chinatown with another dramatic boundary.

Chinatown is several times more densely populated than the remainder of San Francisco, and a steady influx of tourists and shoppers can make it difficult even to walk down the streets. The human congestion is made worse by the fact that meat and fish markets sometimes leave their refuse on pedestrian thoroughfares when they close their stores at night. Buses and cars compete for insufficient space on narrow streets, and there is frequent gridlock. As one might expect, surveys have indicated that a large proportion of Chinatown's residents dislike its noise, its filth, and its crowding.[4]

Over the past few decades there have been mostly piecemeal efforts to improve living conditions in the core of Chinatown. This has entailed replacing old, cramped rooming houses with more spacious apartment buildings, adding lights and trees to alleyways, paving old brick roadways with concrete, and so on. However, there is little that can be done about crowded, narrow streets and walkways without dramatically altering historic Chinatown, and its preservation has been emphasized by local advocates and city planners. The city adopted a master plan for Chinatown in 1987 that was designed to promote the community as both a residential enclave and a tourist site, but those two objectives proved to be very difficult to balance.

Some protection against change might be afforded if Chinatown were officially certified by the city's Board of Supervisors as a historic district. Chinatown's property owners have resisted, though, claiming it would create obstacles to renovation or sales. Preservationist organizations disagree and decry the slow loss of some of Chinatown's traditional architecture. One activist, walking down a main artery in Chinatown, fretted over the steel and glass that have replaced many of the ninety-year-old wood-frame doors and windows. "I call this the Hong Kong mall-ization look," she said.[5] Above street level, however, many ornate balconies and cornices remain; there are a number of pagoda-style buildings in red, yellow, and green, symbolizing good luck or good health; and the entrance to the enclave on Grant, the oldest street in San Francisco, still has a dragon-crested gate.

Given the conflicting interests, there is little reason to believe that the crowded, noisy conditions of San Francisco's Chinatown will markedly improve any time soon. So why do the residents stay? Many remain because they are old and poor and have nowhere else to go. One older man who left China for America as a teenager is typical of this group. He traveled around the country searching for work and finally settled in San Francisco's Chinatown. "I go all around the country, like a hobo I am," he said and laughed. After a stroke, however, he became unable to take care of himself and moved into one of Chinatown's many senior centers. "I never thought of spending my life here," he said, motioning to his small room in the center. "I got bad luck."[6]

Other residents could, of course, leave Chinatown if they wished. What do they like about living there? Their answers focus on factors that are the advantages of any enclave. They like having daily newspapers in their native language. They like being close to the Chinese restaurants and shops where they can obtain the goods and services available nowhere else. They also like the proximity to their relatives and friends and are comfortable living in a relatively homogeneous community. Older residents in particular are likely to explain their attraction to the neighborhood with such comments as "Since I don't speak English, it's better for me to live here," or "I want to be close with my people."[7] For younger residents of both the core and noncore areas, closeness to place of work is another important part of neighborhood satisfaction. Chinatown is, for them, a place of residence and of work.

Working within the Enclave

Over the last few decades, Chinese-owned firms have increased more rapidly than any other, minority or majority, and they tend to have more employees than other minority-owned businesses.[8] Thus they offer a lot of jobs. However, while it is clear that Chinatowns generally and San Francisco's specifically continue to provide employment for many Chinese Americans, there is some argument as to how much the employees benefit from this arrangement. On the one hand, studies in San Francisco have shown that Chinese Americans who work outside the enclave in Anglo-owned companies receive better wages on average, even when the comparison holds constant such factors as the industrial sector, type of job, and the workers' educational levels.[9] The thousands of illegal immigrants who take jobs in Chinatown's factories, stores, and restaurants no doubt drive down wages within the enclave. They are typically willing to work long hours under difficult conditions and accept less than minimum wages but, lacking working papers, they have no real alternatives. In addition to paying low wages, because many enclave businesses are poorly capitalized and operate in highly competitive markets, they often demand much of their poorly paid employees. One immigrant man, typical of many others, finally returned to China disgusted after seven years of feeling exploited at work: "Get up. Work for 16 hours. Go to bed. Get up again. I was a fool. A machine."[10]

Comparing wages inside and outside the enclave may not be entirely meaningful, though. To circumvent record-keeping, the owners of enclave businesses sometimes pay in cash, which means that the workers have no medical, retirement, or other benefits. One man begged his boss, the owner of a dry-cleaning store in San Francisco's Chinatown, to put his entire salary on the books. He had been receiving one-half of his salary under the table so that the owner could pay less in mandatory contributions and taxes; but with only one-half of his salary on the books, the employee could not qualify for a mortgage. His boss not only refused the request, he replaced the employee with an undocumented immigrant who made no such demands.[11]

Furthermore, there are probably advantages to working in an enclave that are difficult to detect in a conventional analysis of wages. For instance, stores in the enclave may be willing to hire poorly prepared workers who would not be considered employable outside the enclave. There may be less racial harassment. Employment in enclave firms may also offer opportunities to learn a business and acquire the "social capital" necessary to be a business owner-entrepreneur. Chinese workers employed outside the enclave by people who are not coethnics are probably much less likely to acquire these skills or be given opportunities to become co-owners.[12]

The Beginning: The Chinese '49ers

In order to understand the origins of San Francisco's Chinatown, it is best to begin with the California gold rush of 1849. It attracted people from around the country and from around the world. Facing widespread famine in China, thousands of Cantonese peasants risked dangerous trips across the ocean to get to San Francisco and then to the gold mines. Most traveled on a credit system: merchant brokers paid their passage in return for promise of repayment with hefty interest from their future earnings. Ticket in hand, they were packed into ships like "herrings in a box."[13] Some of the immigrants wound up settling close to the San Francisco wharf where they landed. In 1850, a stretch of five blocks along Sacramento Street was called Tong Yen Gai ("Street of the Chinese People"). Within ten years it had doubled in size, had become known as the Chinese Quarter, and served as a provisional stop for Chinese prospectors. It later served the same role for Chinese immigrant railroad laborers and agricultural workers.

The Chinese prospectors, like the German, Irish, and others, moved across California, Nevada, and other Western states as word of big gold strikes spread. Life in these mining towns was rough-and-tumble, without much recourse to law, especially for the Chinese. Their baggy pants, pigtails, and "strange" eating habits set them apart, and they were robbed, beaten, and murdered with impunity. State laws also discriminated against them. In California, for example, the state legislature passed a law that required only "nonwhites" (of which there were then sizable numbers of two types, Chinese and Mexicans) to pay a prohibitive tax for mining. The Chinese also lacked fundamental rights, such as being able to testify in murder trials. When a white man, George Hall, shot a Chinese miner, he was initially found guilty of murder, but on appeal the California Supreme Court released Hall because the testimony against him all came from Chinese witnesses.[14]

In the mining towns that boomed after the discovery of gold or silver, the Chinese population was usually highly segregated as a result of prejudice reinforced by local ordinances. In Virginia City, Nevada, for example, white citizens could have a Chinese residence or business removed from their neighborhood simply by petitioning the board of aldermen. In the center of Virginia City was a "bawdy district," composed of saloons, boardinghouses, and flimsy dwellings in which prostitutes worked in small cubicles containing a bed, a chair, and a basin. At the northern edge of the bawdy district were the small dwellings and mud streets of Virginia City's Chinatown. In 1875 it was home to every Chinese resident: 1,254 men and eighty-four women, seventy-five of whom were prostitutes.[15]

Most of the small Chinatowns that formed in Western towns during the latter part of the nineteenth century disappeared. News of a distant gold strike could send everyone packing in a hurry. Some gradually became too small to sustain a distinctive Chinese way of life. For example, by 1880, only about twenty Chinese women, all prostitutes, and six hundred Chinese men remained in Virginia City; the rest had moved on. To find suitable marriage partners for their children, Chinese parents were forced to look in larger Chinatowns, the net effect being a population redistribution favoring the already larger enclaves such as San Francisco's. In addition, the only work for many of the men, according to sociologist

Rose Hum Lee, was "women's work, i.e., cooking, washing, and domestic service," and there tended to be more demand for these services in larger cities.[16]

The Vice Quarter

As the gold fever of 1849 gradually dissipated, many of the Chinese prospectors turned for employment to the railroads being constructed across the West. Along with new Chinese immigrants to the United States, these Chinese men found jobs cooking and cleaning for the railroad laborers. However, by the 1870s, most of the work on the railroad was completed. Thousands of Chinese men then returned to their original U.S. embarkation point, San Francisco.

In the relative safety of the Chinese Quarter, they took whatever jobs they could find in small factories, laundries, and restaurants. The men, desperate for work, were regarded by whites as causing lower wages by their willingness to work cheaply, and in retribution they were harassed in the streets and the courts. In San Francisco during the last decades of the nineteenth century, "anti-coolie clubs" formed in every ward of the city to discourage employment for unskilled Chinese men. A "pole ordinance" prohibited carrying vegetables and clothes on poles while walking on sidewalks. The Chinese were the only ones who used such poles, so the objective of the law was clear.[17] Chinese salesmen and others who dared to venture outside the Chinese Quarter were regularly "found strung by their pigtails to lampposts."[18] So the enclave grew during the late nineteenth century because Chinese immigrants were not welcome and did not feel safe anywhere else. It is clear that the enclave did not grow because it was a physically attractive place. Firsthand accounts of late-nineteenth-century Chinatown described it as comprising "rat-infested . . . narrow alleys and underground cellars and secret passages, more like a warren of burrowing animals than a human city. . . . And Chinatown was accounted vicious because it was the haunt of gambling . . . and prostitution.[19]

Prostitution was historically associated with most Chinatowns because of the scarcity of Chinese women in America until after World War II. Almost all of the early Chinese immigrants were men traveling alone who intended to make their fortunes, then return to China and their wives or parents or else send for them. In conformity with Chinese tradition, wives remained with their husbands' families when the men left. However, in

1884 the U.S. Congress ruled that the Chinese Exclusion Act of 1882 prohibited the wives and families of Chinese laborers from entering the country. This act remained in effect until 1943.

At the turn of the twentieth century, there were hundreds of Chinese males for every Chinese female in the United States. Among all of the immigrants coming to America at this time there was a surplus of males to females, but the ratio was not nearly as lopsided among other nationalities as it was among the Chinese. The solitary Chinese males had limited heterosexual alternatives. Intimate relations with white women were hardly possible given the low standing of the Chinese. Marriages between whites and Chinese were prohibited by miscegenation laws in many states. Even white prostitutes were generally unwilling to engage in sexual relations with Chinese men. The answer was brothels staffed with young Chinese girls who were kidnapped from their villages in China, tricked into coming to California, ostensibly for an arranged marriage, or sold into slavery by destitute parents. Those who could provide women made enormous profits. A woman who was sold for $400 in Hong Kong in 1880 was worth $1,800 in gold in San Francisco.[20]

Gambling of various sorts has a long tradition in Chinese culture, so the appearance of faro, fan-tan, and other games of chance in Chinatowns was hardly surprising. The immigrant workmen who did not have families to go home to were looking for recreation within the enclave, creating a demand for places to gamble as well as for prostitution. Estimates are that around 1885, San Francisco's Chinatown had about seventy brothels, 150 gambling establishments, and an unknown number of opium dens.[21] The clientele was mixed, consisting of enclave residents, Chinese from the hinterlands, and non-Chinese tourists. The mainstream media exaggerated the role of drugs and prostitution in its depictions of Chinatown, conveying the image of a vice-dominated community.[22] That image attracted thrill-seeking tourists, and to ensure that they did not leave Chinatown disappointed, enterprising guides sometimes staged arrests or planted suspicious-looking people in alleyways.

The gambling, opium, and prostitution were operated under the authorization and protection of secret criminal organizations which have a long history in Chinese communities, both in China and the United States. In Chinatown beginning in the late nineteenth century, the organizations were typically called "tongs." In 1900, there were an estimated thirty tongs in San Francisco's Chinatown, each of which claimed a monopoly on the brothels, gambling joints, and opium dens in its territory. These illegal activities persisted as a result of police complicity and the strength of the tongs, which rivaled that of any Mafia anywhere. The tong gunmen effectively protected member businesses and killed witnesses who might be a threat to their activities. Although the gangs concentrated on China-town, they sometimes had an extensive reach. The prostitution in Virginia City's Chinatown, for example, was controlled by tongs in San Francisco's Chinatown.[23]

Intermittent periods of peace and war characterized relations among San Francisco's tongs until the great earthquake and subsequent fire of 1906 destroyed most of the Chinese Quarter. The fire swept through the flimsily built enclave, scattering the residents: "Out of the narrow alley-ways and streets they swarmed. . . . With bundles swung on poles across their shoulders, they retreated. . . . Smoke rose thousands of feet in the air."[24] The brothels and the opium and gambling dens that were the core of the tongs' operations were wiped out along with everything else. During the ensuing discussions on whether to rebuild the Chinese Quarter and where to put it, much of the tong leadership in San Francisco either retired or moved to other Chinatowns. The weakened gangs then fought each other in the streets of Chinatown during the 1920s. The violence of these "tong wars" was difficult for police to ignore, and there were more arrests than before, though few convictions because witnesses were reluc-tant to testify.

In recent decades the criminal syndicates in Chinatown have been more internationally organized, reaching from Hong Kong to far-flung cities with large Chinese communities, including Amsterdam, London, New York, and San Francisco. These criminal organizations are usually referred to as "tri-ads," and their presence in Chinese communities dates about as far back as the tongs.[25] The major business of the triads include trafficking in weapons and heroin, smuggling illegal immigrants, and Internet pornog-raphy. Peter Chong was alleged to be the long-standing crime boss of Chi-natown and head of a triad based in Hong Kong and San Francisco. Fed-eral officials tried, beginning in 1993, to arrest and prosecute him, and finally in 2003 he was sentenced to fifteen years in prison for racketeer-ing; but his place was likely to be taken by another crime boss.

The New Enclave

The contemporary Chinatown in San Francisco was rebuilt a few years af-ter the fire on top of the site where the old quarter had lain in smoking rubble. It continued to attract newly arriving Chinese immigrants and other Chinese who had initially settled elsewhere in the United States.

Essentially the same forces that had led to the growth of the earlier Chinese Quarter now led to the development of Chinatown. It again became a bustling and crowded residential and commercial area. However, Chinatown never again contained a proliferation of vice resorts like the old quarter because of a number of social changes that were occurring during the early twentieth century. There was, as noted, the disassembling of the tongs that had organized vice in the pre-fire Quarter. In addition, opium use in the United States was down dramatically, discouraging anyone from rebuilding opium dens. Finally, as a result of high birthrates and a decline in male-dominated immigration, the ratio of women to men began to approach parity, leading to a decline in the demand for prostitutes. The Chinese responded to these changes by replacing brothels and gambling dens with restaurants and nightclubs.

The success of the Chinese in making this transition where other groups had failed was the result of their ability to make middle-class tourists feel secure in their enclave. In order to be successful, most nightclubs and restaurants must cater to middle-class couples. Attracting this clientele requires a higher level of security in the streets than attracting single men to a red-light district. Making the streets reasonably safe requires the kind of community organization that was present in Chinatown. Particularly notable were the associations created primarily by well-to-do merchants. These associations, corresponding with the founders' native districts in China, were designed to assist newcomers, to help people from "home" remain in contact with each other, and to represent them in community affairs. During the mid-nineteenth century, six of the associations formed an umbrella organization, the Chinese Six Companies. For the past 150 years, this organization has exerted powerful control over many aspects of life in Chinatown; for example, its resistance to designating Chinatown a historic district has been crucial.

The transformation of Chinatown was also aided, according to Ivan Light, by the past unbalance in the sex ratio because its low birthrate resulted in a community with a relatively small number of adolescent males. (It is adolescent males who are most likely to commit street crimes.) It was possible for the well-organized Chinese to control the small number of youths who had the highest potential of committing robberies and muggings. By keeping the streets safe, Chinatown's business sector successfully converted to a general tourist base, while other ethnic and racial enclaves could not maintain sufficient control to make the transformation.[26]

Ironically, the low status of the Chinese may also have been an asset in the growth of Chinese restaurants—restaurants being the heart of any tourist trade. Sociologists Gaye Tuchman and Henry Levine argue that European immigrants were the most avid patrons of Chinese restaurants.

Even though most groups favored the eating establishments of their co-ethnics and worried about acceptance in those of other ethnic groups, everyone could "eat Chinese." There was no need to fear that one was overstepping some boundary, because the status of the Chinese was so low that no one felt threatened in their establishments. Customers could even make derogatory racial comments about Chinese waiters, and they would accept the insults without comment.[27]

Like any enclave, contemporary Chinatown is partly a product of the immigrants who first populated it. The Chinese immigrants who got off the boat on San Francisco's wharf and settled in nearby Chinatown were generally very poor. They came to the United States to seek wealth, but they had few skills to sell. When they arrived they also faced tremendous overt discrimination, which was backed up by government actions. They were pushed and pulled into a poor and crowded enclave, which has over the years retained many of the characteristics of its early residents.

Chinatown, as we have described, was a refuge, and as such people in the community tended not to be actively involved in San Francisco politics. Historically, enclave residents have had low voter turnouts for city elections, and prior to 2003, one of Chinatown's large Chinese-language newspapers, *Sing Tao Daily,* had never endorsed a candidate for city mayor. In recent years, however, the community has become somewhat more engaged in San Francisco politics. During the fall of 2003, a candidates' debate was translated and broadcast on Chinese-language television, and campaign signs in both English and Chinese were placed in many windows across Chinatown.[28] Despite this recent increase, political activity in Chinatown remains well behind that of suburban Chinese communities, and that is another of the defining differences between them.

The Los Angeles Connection

The Chinese immigrants of the last third of the twentieth century were very different from their earlier counterparts. Between 1949 (when the Communist Party took control of mainland China) and 1964 there were only about seventy thousand Chinese immigrants to the United States. After the liberalization of U.S. immigration policy in 1965, there was a dramatic increase in the number of Chinese immigrants: nearly one million entered the United States between 1965 and 2000. Some were political refugees, who tended to come from the ranks of the elite. Others, who were very well trained, came to pursue professional and technical positions which were more available in the United States than in China. Their money and technical and business skills stood in marked contrast to their nineteenth-century counterparts. Some moved to traditional Chinatowns such as the ones in San Francisco or New York, but the suburban Los Angeles area has been the favored destination of the most recent Chinese immigrants.[29]

The current popularity of Los Angeles as a destination for Chinese immigrants is a result of changes in the world system as well as changes in the nature of the immigrants. Most nations have increasingly become part of a world economy in which major decisions are made in the leading global cities. These are cities that house the headquarters of multinational corporations, are centers of finance, investment, and high-level legal and accounting services, contain the entertainment conglomerates, and are major links in global transportation and communication networks. The firms housed within these large and complex cities control and coordinate all kinds of commercial and cultural activities around the world. New York has historically been the preeminent global city in the United States and the nation's principal link to the other leading world cities: London, Paris, and Tokyo.[30] As the United States became more closely tied into the world system, more American cities joined New York as important links in the international network. Los Angeles, of particular importance in this regard, became the second most important global city in the United States.

Los Angeles' global role was enhanced by the economic development of the Pacific Rim nations. During the 1970s, as relations between the United States and the People's Republic of China (PRC) were normalized, many wealthy families in Taiwan feared that their country would be reclaimed by the PRC. This fear prompted a capital outflow from Taiwan to the United States, with the Los Angeles area the favored destination of both capital and immigrants. They were joined by an exodus from PRC, and their combined presence had a dramatic effect upon the Los Angeles area: airlines added numerous nonstop flights from Los Angeles to Taipei (Taiwan's capital city) and Beijing; the PRC opened a consulate general office in Los Angeles to promote trade and cultural exchanges; the number of Chinese-owned banks proliferated; and greater Los Angeles became the U.S. metropolitan area with the largest concentration of Chinese-owned firms.[31]

Many of the more recent Taiwanese immigrants in Los Angeles, as previously noted, had been professionals and executives in Taiwan and had access to substantial capital. Their transitions to lives in America, at least economically, were not difficult. In many less visible cases, however, immigrants made major lifestyle sacrifices in order to escape the communist threat, to offer their children a chance for a better life, or both. Taking part in this exodus out of Taiwan were Mai Lin (a pseudonym) and her family. Mai Lin was ten years old in 1977 when her parents told her they were going to go to America—to California, to Disneyland. Her friends were all excited for her, because everyone in Taiwan knew about Disneyland. Mai Lin's parents left professional jobs in Taipei. He was a newspaper editor; she was a head nurse in a hospital. They could not duplicate their jobs in the United States, though. Mai Lin's mother worked as a waitress in a Chinese restaurant; her father worked nights as a janitor. The blow to his pride temporarily changed Mai Lin's father completely, causing him to become withdrawn and depressed. The parents' lives improved some years later, however, when they were able to buy a small franchise convenience store.[32]

Despite many differences between the earlier and the more contemporary Chinese immigrants, both were alike in that large numbers of each group were attracted to a particular enclave, and that enclave grew with successive immigration. Many of the communities that have recently attracted the greatest numbers of Chinese immigrants are located in east-suburban Los Angeles. In Westminster, for example, a mostly Vietnamese population has established a community now known locally as Little Saigon. Nearly one-quarter-million Vietnamese live in the area around Westminster and are served by the enclave's malls, modern shops, a TV station, and a radio station. It is the largest Vietnamese population in the world outside Vietnam.

Monterey Park: Little Taipei

The first groups of Taiwanese immigrants to arrive in the early 1970s established an enclave in Monterey Park, a suburban area 15 miles east of Los Angeles that is now known as Little Taipei to all its residents.[33] In the early 1970s, Monterey Park was a mostly white residential suburb with Mexican-American, African-American, and Japanese-American minorities. During the 1980s, the community was actively promoted by realtors and developers in Taiwan, who sold it as "the Chinese Beverly Hills." In less than a decade the majority of its population of 62,000 was Asian, with Taiwanese predominating, and the city was visibly Chinese, with Chinese ownership of most of the city's banks, supermarkets, restaurants, and newspapers. They also opened new types of businesses to serve their coethnics.

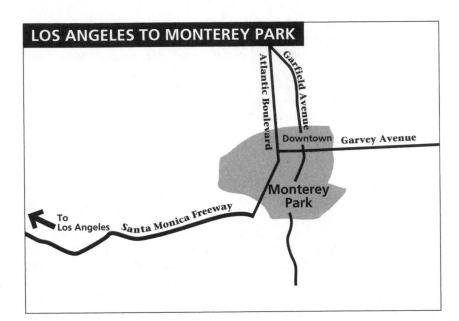

LOS ANGELES TO MONTEREY PARK

For example, the Universal Chung Wah Funeral Home specializes in bringing the ashes of deceased family members from China to Monterey Park.
(Keeping the remains close, according to Chinese tradition, makes it easier for the memory of the deceased to be revered.)

The main commercial thoroughfare of Monterey Park is Atlantic Boulevard. On both sides of the boulevard are retail stores and commercial offices with large, colorful Chinese-language signs. Even though journalist
Timothy Fong was accustomed to seeing Chinese-language signs from visiting his grandparents in San Francisco's Chinatown, his first trip down
Atlantic Boulevard nevertheless made his jaw drop. "It really did feel like
a foreign country," he thought.[34] Just east of Atlantic Boulevard in the
city's original downtown area, Garvey Avenue is lined with Chinese restaurants, bookstores, herb shops, and banks, and again, almost all of the signs
are in Chinese.

One particularly noteworthy store on Garvey Avenue is the 99 Ranch.
Part of a chain of modern supermarkets, most of which are located in California, its name blends traditional Chinese (99 stands for eternity in Chinese numerology) and the American West (the reason ranch was added).
In its wide, brightly lit isles, young families and singles find Gatorade and
Skippy Peanut Butter as well as fungus buns, marinated pigs' ears, white
gourd juice, and tanks of live fish—not the iced headless fish that make

these shoppers uncomfortable. Sho Kang, a thirty-five-year-old electrical engineer, was looking over Taiwanese entertainment magazines when a reporter asked him about people and stores. His answer summarized many of the differences in age, wealth, and lifestyle between residents of the city and suburban enclaves. "Chinatown is for the old immigrant; 99 Ranch is for the new," he answered.[35]

Prior to the influx of immigrants that began in the 1970s, Monterey Park was a sleepy, tree-lined bedroom community of modest, single-family homes. That quickly changed when the Chinese refugees arrived. Using the capital they brought from China or could get from Chinese banks in the Los Angeles area, they began to build malls and condominiums and develop commercial strips. They converted the quiet downtown area into a busy commercial center. They took over many businesses, most of the restaurants, and all but two of the supermarket chains serving Monterey Park: "Bok choy is more common than lettuce in produce departments, and dim sum . . . more readily available than a hamburger . . . in the restaurants.[36] Long-term non-Chinese residents had a feeling of being overwhelmed by a foreign invasion. One elderly white man complained, "Before, immigrants . . . lived in their own neighborhoods and moved into ours after they learned English. . . . Today, the Chinese come right in with their money and their ways. We are the aliens."[37] Another white man sold his home to a Chinese developer because he was disgusted with the changes that had occurred in his neighborhood. When he had moved into the house, the neighborhood had consisted of other individual family homes like his own. Now there were large condominium complexes on both sides of the street filled with large Chinese families living in cramped quarters and speaking little English. "What I might do," he said, "is hang a little American flag on my truck and drive through town on my way out and wave goodbye to all my old friends."[38]

This feeling of being inundated by immigrants is, of course, not unique to the contemporary "natives" of suburban Los Angeles. At the turn of the twentieth century, Americans with Western European roots were expressing similar reactions to the Eastern and Southern European immigrants. To illustrate, the Literary Digest—an amalgam of newspaper and magazine stories from around the country—printed in 1900, "The swelling tide of immigrants from Southern Europe . . . who can not even speak our (language) . . . is a startling national menace that cannot be disregarded with safety."[39] (They were primarily referring to people from Italy, Poland, and Russia.)

During the 1980s, the rapid influx of the Chinese into Monterey Park and the subsequent proliferation of commercial and residential construction changed forever the character of Monterey Park and caused traffic on

its now-crowded streets to grind to a halt. The long-term residents of the city objected to the uncontrolled growth as well as to the feeling of being invaded, and sought to resist further growth and immigration. The city council, dominated by whites, approved a master plan that greatly restricted further commercial development. (Similar growth-control issues have polarized a number of California communities.) Local governments do not generally tend to favor no-growth positions because continued growth fueled by land development enhances the fiscal situation of a local government.[40] Nevertheless, the no-growth policy was endorsed by Monterey Park's white-dominated city council, its intent clearly to inhibit further in-migration of the Chinese.

If there was any doubt about the intent of the no-growth policy, in addition English was declared the official language of Monterey Park. The council member who offered the most xenophobic regulations also tried to promote traditional symbols of patriotism and Anglo domination. In the spring of 1989, for example, he organized street parties in preparation for later Fourth of July celebrations and planned to speak at the one in his neighborhood. He never showed up, but what happened at the May picnic offered a glimpse of the community's multicultural future. The largest group in attendance was made up of elderly Chinese. They sat under a tree on which they had placed a banner with Chinese characters. The main speakers were Latino; they wished everyone a "happy Cinco de Mayo," and one speaker made a point of noting that the Chinese lion dancers had been invited to perform at the main Cinco de Mayo event.[41]

In terms of constituencies, by the 1990s, Monterrey Park consisted of three major groups: white Anglo, Hispanic, and Asian (predominantly Chinese from Taiwan). Decision-making power in the community had historically been in the hands of the Anglos, and the other two groups were slow to organize. However, when Anglo officeholders attempted to pass legislation that was designed to harm the interests of the other two groups, it helped those groups to overcome their initial antagonisms toward each other and pushed them into a coalition that was large enough for them to elect officials and pass legislation.[42]

Asian-American Women

The council member who had organized the xenophobic neighborhood parties was voted out of office in 1990, receiving the fewest votes among the candidates from Anglos as well as from Chinese and Latino voters. The mayoral election was won by Judy Chu, an American-born woman of Chinese descent. As a former council member, she had spoken at length about separating ethnicity and xenophobia from growth policies. Her platform promised growth, but of a managed sort, and cultural diversity. Judy Chu's election as mayor of Monterey Park in 1990 was dramatic in terms of the way it demonstrated not only the shift in power to members of an ethnic enclave but also the changes in the gender roles of Chinese women. Picture her inauguration in front of a packed room: well-dressed Chinese men recording the event on cameras, large baskets of flowers with messages of good luck in red ribbons from Chinese individuals and associations, a gyrating Chinese dragon entertaining council members and visitors.[43] One hundred years earlier, Chinese women were bought and sold on San Francisco's wharves. A potentially good prostitute was worth up to $3,000; a domestic slave unsuitable for brothel work could be bought for as little as $100. A few high-status Chinese prostitutes wore silk and jewels, but most dressed in plain cotton and charged their customers 25 cents. Their only escape from prostitution or slavery was suicide.[44]

Relatively few Chinese women, as noted, came to the United States until after World War II. Many of those who did come earlier came only as a result of being tricked or stolen as youngsters. Because of our interest in the establishment of urban enclaves in this country, we have focused primarily on the migrating males rather than the women they left behind. However, it should be apparent that the women who remained in China were part of the decision-making process. Migration decisions are almost always made at the household level, even when it is primarily men who, at least initially, migrate.

It would be easy to overlook women's contribution to the economic position of their households after the women arrived in this country if one looked solely at their wages for labor outside the home. The Chinese (and other immigrant) women played a central role in maintaining the kinship and friendship ties that connect their households to the ethnic enclave. The various types of informational and economic assistance that coethnics offer each other, from housing to jobs, may be provided to members of one family from another because of kinship and social ties among their women.[45] As Chinese women adjusted to life in America, they slowly encountered a somewhat different set of gender arrangements. Although women did not and have not reached economic parity with men in the United States, Chinese-American women have had more opportunity to participate in the labor force than they had in China, and their relative status has been enhanced by their ability to contribute very directly to household income.[46]

For the women who were raised in the United States, learning how to combine ethnicity and gender in a meaningful way was often stressful.

Mai Lin—who was introduced earlier as a ten-year-old leaving Taiwan for Disneyland—felt that her adolescence was especially difficult. Looking back at the time she was a senior in college, she felt that her adolescence was not just a matter of growing up and choosing what was right and wrong, but of choosing what was right and wrong in each culture. Chinese women are supposed to be submissive, she noted. And although she considers her lifestyle totally American, she also recognizes that she has internalized many Chinese values. So she tries to reconcile the Chinese image of women with an American image in which, it seems to her, women are supposed to be blond, blue-eyed, and fair-skinned. Growing up was a difficult struggle because neither of the cultural images seemed to fit her very well.[47] (As a postscript, Mai Lin graduated with a degree in engineering from M.I.T. in 1989.)

Over time, efforts to improve the conditions of Chinese Americans, male and female, came to include all Asian Americans, rather than just Chinese Americans. This was partly because the differences among Chinese, Koreans, Japanese, and other Asians were starting to blur in response to the tendency of white Americans to include all Asians in a single category. In addition, a wider ethnic alliance provided each group of Asian Americans with more leverage in confronting a system dominated by whites that discriminated against all who were "other."

Some of the initial efforts to improve Asian-American women's roles resulted in the formation of women's caucuses within existing Asian church, civic, and professional associations. However, these organizations tended to be male-dominated and supportive of the status quo with respect to gender. Adherence to the traditional hierarchies of authority put Asian women in a particularly subordinate position to men.[48] On the other hand, feminist organizations dominated by whites had broader agendas that only partly met the needs of Asian women, so as Asian women became more aware of their multiply disadvantaged positions—as females and as racial minorities—they established a number of Asian women's organizations.[49] To illustrate, in cities with large numbers of recent Asian women immigrants, Asian women's centers have been formed specifically to assist Asian women who are victims of domestic violence. Immigration-related stress caused by loss of status or constant encounters with strange customs seems to be a common precursor to domestic violence. The young Asian wife, traditionally subordinate to both her husband and his family, has been a favorite target for abuse in new and stressful settings. These centers have recorded numerous stories of women who have been punched and kicked by husbands and in-laws, sexually attacked, and locked in their rooms indefinitely. Lack of fluency in English and fear of officials in a strange society inhibit many from seeking help. To make matters worse, among South

Asians the woman has traditionally been viewed as the guardian of family honor. If she were to seek outside help for domestic violence, she would be bringing shame on her family.

The first problem faced by a woman whose situation is so bad that she is ready to seek outside help is to know who to call. In large cities, immigrant women's assistance programs have become highly specialized. In New York, for example, the Asian Women's Center operates a telephone help line called Sakhi that specifically targets Indian women. The name means "a woman's friend" in Hindi, Urdu, and Bengali, and a friend is exactly what some of these women desperately need. One woman, after being married in New Delhi, moved to New York with her husband and his family. The husband proceeded to regularly kick her and pull her hair, sometimes in front of his parents. She eventually ran away and contacted Sakhi. "They really understood," she said, adding that "their being Indian really helped."[50]

Banding together has led many Asian-American women to develop a feminist consciousness that helped them to overcome feelings of inadequacy and adjust to a new society. Most importantly, perhaps, they have learned that they can control outcomes in their lives.[51] As they have acquired more positive and more efficacious self-concepts, they have made possible such accomplishments as those of Mayor Judy Chu. She was reelected mayor twice, and in 2001 was elected to the California Assembly, representing Monterey Park and surrounding communities. In this role she has continued to serve the same constituencies. In 2003, for example, after being reelected to the Assembly, she introduced a bill to prevent bait-and-switch practices that victimize consumers with little English comprehension; primarily Spanish- and Asian-language speakers. Assemblywoman Chu said she became interested in the issue after learning of a case in which a car salesman in her district negotiated a lease deal in Mandarin Chinese, then produced a contract in English. The customer signed it, believing he was getting a new Toyota, but the lease stipulated a used Chevrolet![52]

Notes

1. See Richard D. Alba, John R. Logan, Brian J. Stults, Gilbert Marzan, and Wenquan Zhang, "Immigrant Groups in the Suburbs," *American Sociological Review* 64, 1999.

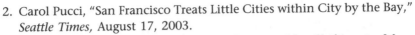
2. Carol Pucci, "San Francisco Treats Little Cities within City by the Bay," *Seattle Times*, August 17, 2003.
3. Deborah Kong, "America's Chinese Communities Shifting to Mandarin," *Seattle Post-Intelligencer*, December 28, 2003.
4. Chalsa M. Loo, *Chinatown*, New York: Praeger, 1991.
5. Gerald D. Adams, "Trying to Save Chinatown's Look," *San Francisco Chronicle*. August 16, 2002.
6. June Namias, *First Generation*, Urbana: University of Illinois Press, 1992, pp. 64–65.
7. Loo, op. cit., pp. 81–82.
8. Alexandro Portes and Min Zhou, "Gaining the Upper Hand," *Ethnic and Racial Studies* 15, 1992.
9. Suzanne Model, "The Ethnic Economy," *Sociological Quarterly* 33, 1992.
10. David W. Chen, "For Many Chinese, America's Lure is Fading," *New York Times*, September 7, 2003, p. 14. See also Victor Nee, Jimy M. Sanders, and Scott Sernau, "Job Transitions in an Immigrant Metropolis," *American Sociological Review* 59, 1994.
11. Reported in *New York Times*, March 12, 1995, p. 40.
12. This issue is discussed in Ivan Light and Steve Gold, *Ethnic Economies*, San Diego, CA: Academic Press, 2000.
13. Loo, op. cit., p. 32.
14. For a review of early laws discriminating against the Chinese in California, see Charles J. McClain, *In Search of Equality*, Berkeley: University of California Press, 1996.
15. Marion S. Goldman, *Gold Diggers and Silver Miners*, Ann Arbor: University of Michigan Press, 1981.
16. Rose Hum Lee, "The Decline of Chinatowns in the United States," *American Journal of Sociology* 54, 1949, p. 425.
17. Loo, op. cit. For further details, see Roger Daniels, *Asian American*, Seattle: University of Washington Press, 1988.
18. Pardee Lower, *Father and Glorious Descendant*, Boston: Little, Brown, 1943, p. 9.
19. Albert W. Palmer, *Orientals in American Life*, New York: Friendship Press, 1934, p. 2. At the same time, many of these descriptions were probably unduly negative. For a more balanced view of Chinatown in the nineteenth century, relying upon photographs and paintings, see Anthony W. Lee, *Picturing Chinatown*, Berkeley: University of California Press, 2001.
20. Sanford M. Lyman, *Chinese Americans*, New York: Random House, 1974.
21. Daniels, op. cit., p. 22.

22. See the discussion of how media has presented false images of Chinatowns in Jan Lin, *Reconstructing Chinatown,* Minneapolis: University of Minnesota Press, 1998.
23. Goldman, op. cit.
24. Richard H. Dillon, *The Hatchet Men,* New York: Coward-McCann, Inc., 1962, p. 357.
25. See Peter Huston, *Tongs, Gangs and Triads,* New York: Paladin, 1995; and Booth Martin, *The Dragon Syndicates,* New York: Carroll and Graf, 2000.
26. Ivan Light, "The Ethnic Vice Industry," *American Sociological Review* 42, 1977.
27. Gaye Tuchman and Henry G. Levine, "New York Jews and Chinese Food," *Journal of Contemporary Ethnography* 22, 1993. This pattern was strongly associated with major cities such as New York, Chicago, and San Francisco.
28. John Wildermuth and Rachel Gordon, "Chinatown Awakens to Politics," *San Francisco Chronicle,* October 23, 2003, p. A1.
29. Yen-Fen Tseng, "Beyond Chinatown: Chinese Ethnic Enterprises in Los Angeles," paper presented at the meetings of the American Sociological Association, August 1993. See also Lin, op. cit.
30. Mark Abrahamson, *Global Cities,* New York: Oxford, 2004.
31. Tseng, op. cit. See also Edward W. Soja, "International Restructuring and the Internationalization of the Los Angeles Region," in Michael P. Smith and Joe R. Feagin (Eds.), *The Capitalist City,* New York: Blackwell, 1987.
32. Namias, op. cit.
33. It is one of two very large Taiwanese concentrations in California. The other is in Richmond, in the Bay area.
34. See the preface to Timothy P. Fong, *The First Suburban Chinatown,* Philadelphia, PA: Temple University Press, 1994.
35. Patricia L. Brown, "In California Malls, New Chinatowns," *New York Times,* March 25, 2003, p. A7.
36. Fong, op. cit., p. 62.
37. John Horton, "The Politics of Diversity in Monterey Park, California," in Louise Lamphere (Ed.), *Structuring Diversity,* Chicago: University of Chicago Press, 1992, p. 223.
38. Quoted in Fong, op. cit. p. 65.
39. Quoted in Rita J. Simon and Susan H. Alexander, *The Ambivalent Welcome,* Westport, CT: Praeger, 1993, p. 93.
40. Stephanie S. Pincetl, "The Politics of Growth Control," *Urban Geography* 13, 1992. See also John R. Logan and Harvey Molotch, *Urban Fortunes,* Berkeley: University of California Press, 1987.

41. John Horton, *The Politics of Diversity*, Philadelphia, PA: Temple University Press, 1996.
42. Leland T. Saito, *Race and Politics*, Urbana, IL: University of Illinois Press, 1998.
43. Horton, in Lamphere, op. cit., p. 217.
44. Goldman, op. cit.
45. Micaela di Leonardo, "The Female World of Cards and Holidays," *Signs* 12, 1987. For further discussion, see the essays in Bandana Purkayastha and Mangala Subramaniam, *The Power of Women's Informal Networks*, New York: Lexington, 2004.
46. See the discussion in Silvia Pedraza, "Women and Migration," *Annual Review of Sociology* 17, 1991.
47. Namias, op. cit.
48. Esther Ngan-ling Chow, "The Social Construction of Asian American Feminism," paper presented at the meetings of the American Sociological Association, August 1993.
49. Bandana Purkayastha, "Contesting Multiple Margins," in Nancy Naples and Manisha Desai (Eds.), *Women's Activism and Globalization*, New York: Routledge, 2002.
50. *New York Times*, December 6, 1993, p. B3.
51. Esther Ngan-ling Chow, "The Development of Feminist Consciousness among Asian American Women," *Gender and Society* 1, 1987.

Miami's Little Havana

The center of Little Havana lies along 8th Street—Calle Ocho—in Southwest Miami. It is one of several areas in Miami and its environs in which substantial numbers of Cuban Americans reside. (According to the 2000 Census there were about 600,000 Cuban-Americans throughout Miami–Dade County.)[1] In recent years the area has also attracted immigrants from Nicaragua, Venezuela, Colombia, and other South American nations. However, the closer one moves to the 8th Street center, the more overwhelmingly Cuban is the population, and it continues to be the predominant Cuban-American commercial and financial center in Miami–Dade County and the nation.

Along 8th and adjacent streets for a stretch of several miles are homes and apartments occupied primarily by Cuban families. Many of the homes have characteristically Cuban features such as decorative Spanish tiles, Catholic shrines in the backyards, and fences enclosing the front yards. Commercial development is also focused around 8th and includes Cuban-owned cigar factories, music stores, restaurants, and financial institutions catering largely but not exclusively to coethnics. Most of the stores were built before the Cubans arrived and they are not architecturally distinguished in any way. The newer stores and shopping plazas do have Spanish elements in their facades, but it is their merchandise that is most distinctively Cuban. Some shops offer special apparel such as guayaberas—lightweight, short shirts traditionally worn by Cuban men. There are a number of *botánicas* selling religious goods, including potions for invoking saints and spirits and aerosol cans whose contents are guaranteed to improve one's love life. Many small grocery stores sell Cuban food products, and almost all the local churches offer masses in Spanish and in English.

A dozen daily and weekly Spanish-language newspapers are available at Little Havana's newsstands or from coin-operated boxes. Some of the newspapers are primarily oriented to news about Cuba, with headlines such as, "Clandestine Groups Are Plotting to Overthrow Castro." Other papers focus upon the Cuban population in the United States, with reviews of restaurants in Little Havana and stories about Cuban-American baseball players in the major leagues. A few of the papers are panethnic, directed to all Spanish-speaking residents. The area is also served by WQBA, one of several Spanish-language radio stations in Miami but the one that has historically claimed to be "La Cubanisma"—the most Cuban.

Little Havana also contains a number of cafés with outdoor tables, where a mostly elderly male clientele gathers during the day and evening to play chess or cards in the shade of black olive trees. A focal point in Little Havana is Maximo Gomez Park, where dominos is the foremost game among older Cuban immigrants who often spend much of the day playing the game, smoking cigars, and talking about the old days in Cuba. Just down the street from the park is the Bay of Pigs Monument, a memorial to the Cubans who died trying to invade the island (to overthrow Fidel Castro) in 1961.

The area's nightclubs and restaurants also conspicuously maintain Cuban culture. The most famous among them is probably the Restaurant Versailles, "the mirrored palace," which was designed to closely resemble several once-popular nightspots in Havana. Like its Cuban models, the Versailles offers many traditional dishes, such as chicken with yellow rice and plantains. Its mostly Cuban clientele is a mixture of partygoers, loan sharks, politicians, members of old Cuban society, and tourists. This restaurant

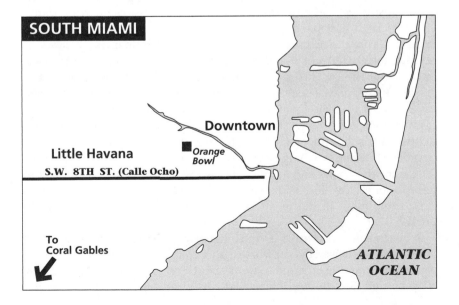

was once the scene of some legendary fights—both verbal and physical—between patrons who disagreed about U.S. policies toward Castro and Cuba.[2] Today, however, the patrons may be more likely to argue about a local sports team.

One of the newest restaurants on Calle Ocho is Tete. The name is short for Teresita, once an extremely common Cuban name. Almost everyone in Little Havana had an aunt or a grandmother with that name. The restaurant offers traditional Cuban breads and Cuban beef jerky and black and red beans. The owner explained that the name and the menu were designed to evoke a warm, cozy environment. "When people come inside," she said, "I want them to feel like they're coming home."[3] The busiest night of the week at Tete's and throughout Little Havana is the last Friday of each month, when Calle Ocho is turned into a festival. Large crowds stroll up and down the street, live bands and boom boxes blast salsa tunes, and people dance in any space available. Artists at the curbside sell paintings, photographs, and wood carvings—all depicting scenes of Havana. The pharmacy across the street from the Versailles used to display serving dishes in its front window, adorned with pictures of Cuba and inscriptions in Spanish and English such as, "How I yearn for you, my beloved Cuba."

Symbolic Attachments

Evidence of the Cuban Americans' continuing attachment to their former homeland is everywhere in Little Havana. Murals of the Cuban city, complete with street signs, decorate the walls of business establishments. Many of the businesses begun in Little Havana were symbolically linked in the minds of the entrepreneurs to former businesses in Cuba. The tie is subtly but dramatically illustrated by the tendency of Little Havana businesses to note the date of their former establishment in Cuba as their official beginning. For example, the sign over the Caballero Funeral Home in Miami states, "since 1857." Miami did not yet exist in 1857, though, and the funeral home did not appear at this location until about one hundred years after the advertised date.[4] Some stores continue to display Havana phone books from the 1950s.

Walking down Southwest 8th Street can give a former Cuban a feeling of being transported back in time to the Havana of yesterday. Little Havana in Miami is in many respects a copy of Havana in Cuba. The nostalgia this creates, however, particularly for older residents, can be mixed with bitter irony. Havana of the 1950s was in many ways like a copy of Miami Beach with its overdone hotels and garish elegance. When Little Havana proceeded to imitate Havana, the former achieved "the unreal appearance of a copy of a copy."[5]

The paradox, according to writer David Rieff, is that it was easier to escape psychologically from Cuba in Cuba than in Miami! In Cuba, educated people were always eager to find out more about the rest of the world; for example, details about the latest European movies or American pop stars. In Miami, by contrast, it sometimes seems that Cubans only want to talk about Cuban films, Cuban music, and Cuban culture, all in a romanticized way. Unduly glamorized memories of all aspects of life in Cuba are most strongly held by the older generation who were raised in Havana. One Cuban-American college student illustrated this tendency to romanticize by explaining how his Cuban mother always complained about the heat in Miami. It is a fact that the climate is very similar in Miami and Havana, but his mother insisted that it never got as hot in Cuba.[6]

The corollary to love of Cuba, in Little Havana, is hatred for Castro. Events that connect to this love/hate combination are especially likely to be incendiary and, in the view of some critics, illustrate the community's intolerance of differences of opinion on these matters. Perhaps the most dramatic event of this type was the forced return to Cuba of six-year-old Elián Gonzalez. Before dawn on April 22, 2000, agents of the Immigration and Naturalization Service (INS) raided the home in Little Havana of Elián's uncle and seized the boy. Six months earlier he had been found with two other Cubans floating in inner tubes about three miles from the Florida coast. Eleven others, including the boy's mother, began the trip but apparently drowned.

An international tug of war over the boy began. Speaking on behalf of Elián's father (who was divorced from Elián's mother and had remained in Cuba), Castro demanded the boy's return. The boy's sole surviving parent wanted him back. However, people in the Cuban-American community insisted that he be permitted to stay in the United States. In their view, his mother gave her life to obtain his freedom. How could the United States then send him back to a hated dictatorship? After INS seized the boy, almost every office and business in Little Havana closed in protest to convey "the hurt and pain of exiled Cubans."[7] Huge crowds formed along 8th Street carrying anti-U.S. placards and waving Cuban flags. They reviled the *Miami Herald* for what they regarded as its tepid stance on Elián's return. Even physicians who opened their offices that day were cursed and threatened for breaking the solidarity. Franchises that opened in the area (e.g., Denny's and Kmart) closed after receiving bomb threats. In the aftermath of Elián's return to his father, key people in the Cuban-American community, who were feeling betrayed, wanted more Cubans in local positions of power. Miami's white Anglo city manager and chief of police were both forced to resign, and both were replaced by Cuban Americans.

A Georgia College professor, Ann Badrach, presents an entirely different interpretation of the entire Elián Gonzalez affair. After researching Elián's voyage, she concluded that his mother's reasons for leaving Cuba had less to do with freedom and more to do with her desire to join her boyfriend in the United States. The community's insistence that the only acceptable course of action was for Elián to remain in Little Havana, according to Badrach, illustrates the community's unwillingness to tolerate differences of opinion. Her ironic conclusion is that the enclave is less different from Cuba than it might appear: in both there is only one acceptable political position, and those who deviate from it face threats and intimidation.[8]

The dramatic nature of the Elián Gonzalez tug of war could also make it seem that there is more unanimity in Little Havana than there is, at least most of the time. Even views toward Cuba are marked by generational differences. As previously noted, the oldest immigrants are the most attached to Cuban ways of life, Cuban food, Cuban clothing, and so on. This oldest generation tends to favor a U.S. policy that continues to punish the Castro regime until he and the rest of the communist leadership are forced out of power. Many of the younger Cuban Americans, on the other hand, either do not share this intense hatred of Fidel Castro or want to find a constructive way to be positively involved in Cuba's future despite their feelings toward Castro. These differences were vividly illustrated in the spring of 1994, when Cuba offered to ease restrictions on return visits and invited a group of about two hundred Cuban Americans to fly to Havana for "official" talks. The Cuban government's objectives were to attract investments from the exile community and to persuade them to use their domestic political influence to end the U.S. embargo on exports to Cuba. However, little progress was made in the talks, primarily because so many older Cuban Americans continued to be unalterably opposed to any acts of reconciliation as long as Castro remained.

One of the Cuban-American participants in the conference was Magda Montiel Davis. She was a very prominent attorney in Little Havana with a large staff. As the talks in Havana ended, she said good-bye to Castro and thanked him, then reached over and lightly kissed his cheek. The kiss was caught on film and was strongly denounced on Spanish-language television and radio stations in Miami. According to family friends, that kiss broke her father's heart. (Like most of his generation, he was vehemently anti-Castro.) There was such an outpouring of angry threats that she was given police protection and forced to resign from several Cuban-American organizations. Five of her employees publicly quit in protest of her actions. To reward them, they were immediately offered jobs in the private sector by wealthy businesspeople in Little Havana and jobs in government by the county commissioner, who was also a Cuban exile.[9]

Any positive link to Castro continues to evoke unalterable opposition from the older generation in Little Havana. When the Latin Grammy Awards were broadcast from Miami in 2003, for example, those who had grown up in Cuba were outraged because among the performers were some Cuban artists whose songs had praised Castro. They demonstrated outside the Miami arena hosting the award show, contending that for these singers to perform in Miami was, to them, "a slap in the face."[10] Other Cuban Americans who tended to be younger were opposed to any ban, wanting all performers to enjoy freedom of expression.

The generational difference arises because the younger Cuban Americans are American-born and see Miami as their home. While being of Cuban background is significant to them, many care more about the Miami Dolphins football team than about events in Cuba and would rather eat at the local McDonald's than at the Restaurant Versailles. (Of course, the McDonald's in Little Havana sells Cuban sandwiches.) This does not mean that the younger generation has assimilated totally, though. A survey of eighth- and ninth-graders in a predominantly Cuban school in Miami is instructive. All of their parents immigrated from Cuba. Almost all of these Cuban-American youngsters said that their knowledge of English was good, that they preferred English to Spanish, and that the United States was the best country in which to live. At the same time, most retained a strong identification with their parents' origins, referring to themselves as Cubans or Cuban Americans rather than simply as Americans, and 89 percent said their knowledge of Spanish was also good.[11] Thus younger Cuban Americans in Little Havana tend to have a more bicultural orientation than their parents or grandparents.

The Three Waves

In order to understand the development of this distinctive community and the generational and ideological cleavages within it, Little Havana is best examined in relation to three waves of immigration from Cuba.

First Wave

The first large movement of Cubans into Miami began in 1959. That was the year in which Fidel Castro's revolutionary army overthrew the Cuban dictator Batista. The Batista regime had promoted strong ties with the United States to facilitate the export of Cuban-grown sugar and the development of resort hotels and gambling casinos (staffed with local prostitutes) in Havana. To some Cubans, it seemed that Batista had turned Cuba into a colony and vice resort of the United States. Critics also regarded his regime as illegitimate because he became president as a result of a military coup. Castro's communist revolution promised to move the country away from its ties to the American business community and redistribute wealth within Cuba. As one might expect, this message played better to the peasants than to the elite.

Most of the Cubans who left between 1959 and 1961 (approximately 135,000 in all) considered themselves political exiles. They tended to be professionals, landowners, and industrialists who had seen their lands and businesses confiscated by the revolution but were still able to take assets with them to the United States. They hoped Castro's regime would be short-lived and they expected to be able to return soon to a post-Castro Cuba. Many of those who left Cuba at that time were already familiar with Miami from former visits. Located only ninety miles from Cuba, Miami's shopping centers and hotels had attracted both wealthy and middle-class tourists from Cuba throughout the 1950s. Miami offered an interesting combination of the familiar and the different to the exiled Cubans. The temperature, the palm trees, and even the architecture were largely the same in Miami and Havana. For the Cuban tourists, it was exciting to see the familiar laid on a flat Florida landscape, surrounded by a different language.[12]

The failed Bay of Pigs invasion of Cuba in 1961 and the Cuban missile crisis of 1962 seriously strained relations between Cuba and the United States. Between 1962 and 1965 it was very difficult for Cubans to leave the island, and the average number of immigrants from Cuba to Miami declined to about 25,000 per year. Most of those who left during these years were still people of means. Some were able to get their assets out of the country, but others came with little more than the clothes on their backs. For the latter, life in Miami held deprivations to which they were not accustomed. Rodolfo de Leon, for example, was eleven years old when his family left Cuba for Miami in late 1962. He remembers his life before the revolution, when his father owned several warehouses and his family lived in a large home. He also remembers Castro's victory and the soldiers and tanks driving down his street. Then, after his father's business was confiscated, his father tried to get passports quickly so the family could leave. They waited a long time in a suite in a fancy hotel, where Rodolfo recalls feeling like a millionaire. Then came a midnight telegram authorizing them to go, and all except his father (who temporarily stayed behind) left in a hurry.

Once in Miami, the family's Cuban pesos were not worth much. In helping to resettle the Cuban immigrants, the U.S. government provided all of them with food and financial assistance, but it supported only a meager lifestyle. Rodolfo remembers a whole year of eating canned meat and beans and fighting with his brother for the one pillow in their house. His mother eventually found unskilled work in a shrimp-packing plant, and when his father later arrived, he picked tomatoes for $6 a day.[13] Rodolfo's mother had never worked while the family lived in Cuba. She tended house, cooked, and watched over her children. In Miami, however, she had no choice but to work to support her family, even though being sheltered from the world outside the home was the traditional ideal for women in middle- and upper-class Cuban society.

Finding fewer barriers to paid employment for women in the United States, many immigrant women found themselves less economically dependent on men than they had been in Cuba (or other countries of origin). Under these conditions, traditional gender ideologies and patterns of social interaction usually changed. Decision-making, and social relations generally, tend to become more egalitarian.[14] For example, Rieff describes how one young Cuban-American woman, a doctor, told her husband at a party that if she ever caught him with another woman she would shoot him. In *la Cuba de ayer* (the Cuba of old), well-born females did not talk that way; they were resigned to the probability that their husbands would be unfaithful. In Miami, at least the young Cuban-American women learned to think differently, "to demand as well as to accept."[15]

Second Wave

An agreement between the United States and Cuba in 1965 allowed a program of "freedom flights" which brought a large second wave of 340,000 more refugees from Cuba between 1965 and 1973. Miami was their original destination, but it was the U.S. government's policy to try to induce Cubans who arrived during this period to leave Miami and settle throughout the nation. However, even among those relative few who did try life somewhere else, many returned. The Miami area has always been home to most Cuban Americans and it continues to have a larger Cuban population and more Cuban businesses and institutions than any city in the world except Havana. As one Cuban American explained, "Miami is the only place in America where we Cubans can be ourselves."[16]

A great deal of insight into the adjustments Cubans had to make after arriving in Miami was provided by a series of surveys conducted by sociologists Alejandro Portes and Robert L. Bach. The investigators interviewed a representative sample of nearly six hundred immigrants when they initially arrived in Miami in 1973. They then reinterviewed the respondents in 1976 and again in 1979. They were able to retain about 70 percent of the original members of their sample throughout the study, and the attrition that did occur did not seem seriously to alter the representativeness of the continuing sample. They found that many in the Cuban community were in a state of flux during their first three years in Miami. Only about 25 percent remained at their first address, and about 25 percent moved more than once. During the second three-year interval, however, there was much more residential stability; about 50 percent stayed at the same address, and only about 10 percent moved more than once. By 1979, 40 percent owned their own homes. Occupational mobility followed a similar pattern. In 1976, only about 8 percent of the Cubans who had arrived in 1973 owned their own businesses; by 1979, this figure had increased to 21 percent, as they acquired retail shops, repair services, construction companies, and so on. Others became doctors or dentists; they tended to be young adults with wealthy parents who could afford advanced education in the United States.[17]

The growth of Cuban businesses was primarily dependent on the availability of start-up capital. Particularly during the 1970s, the international role of Miami's economy was growing, in some large measure due to the import-export and banking activities of the Cubans, which strengthened links between the economies of the United States and Latin America. A number of small Latin-American banks were established in Miami. They were willing to invest in local businesses and they hired as officials a number of local Cubans who had extensive banking experience in Cuba. These banks provided start-up capital for Cuban entrepreneurs who could not have qualified for conventional loans at other Miami banks. Other capital was provided by many of the earliest refugees from Cuba, who had brought enormous assets to the United States. Once it became apparent that they could not return to their former home, they too invested in local Cuban-owned businesses.

The steady stream of refugees also provided an abundant and relatively inexpensive supply of labor. They were hired by coethnics despite being unable to speak English and lacking American educational credentials. The readiness to hire relatively unqualified Cuban help was an expression of ethnic solidarity, though the workers' willingness to work cheaply was also an inducement to the Cuban owners. At the same time, even modest jobs in the enclave often provided an apprenticeship for those who wanted to learn how to operate an independent business. After gaining some experience, industrious employees could borrow money relatively easily, start a business, and in turn hire later-arriving Cubans. Meanwhile, the continuous flow of Cuban immigrants also provided a sizeable number of customers for the goods and services that only enclave stores could provide.[18]

The socioeconomic status, on average, of the second wave of Cuban immigrants was lower than that of the Cubans who left when Castro first took power, but when compared to that of other immigrant groups throughout history, it was still relatively high. At the same time, Cuban immigrants in the second wave were diverse with respect to class, skin color, and ethnic background. "Cuban" and "American" did not exhaust the identities competing for salience, as the following two examples of second-wave immigrants illustrate:

> Antonio Wong was born in Cuba to Chinese parents. After they came to Miami, Antonio attended college in the United States, married, and bought a flower shop in Little Havana. He remembers the people in the Chinese community in Cuba experiencing open hostility. Natives made fun of the fact that they could not speak Spanish with a Cuban accent, but they still considered themselves Cuban and were frustrated by the unwillingness of other Cubans to accept them as such. Despite now being an American citizen, Antonio feels that "inside" he is "still a Chinese wanting to be a Cuban." When his son is old enough, he hopes to take him to China. He has instructed the boy in Chinese religious and cultural traditions but has not told him about Cuba. The boy does not, in his father's view, need to know about it. "I am the one with Cuba inside. He will be another wandering Chinese who happens to like Cuban food."[19]

> Isaac Cohen was a rabbi in Cuba who was raised in Havana. After emigrating to Miami he bought an electronics business. He became an active member of a Cuban Hebrew congregation, a Cuban Sephardic congregation (Jews who originally were forced out of Spain), and a Cuban Hebrew Circle. He refers to himself in summary as a "Jewban," which he defines as someone whose identity is very Jewish but who "also . . . speaks Spanish at home and eats Cuban food and dances to Cuban music."[20] He and his wife have deliberately taught their children to be Cuban, Jewish, and American. That way they will always have "two hyphens" in their self-concepts; and as a result of having two hyphens, he says, they will know with certainty who they are.

Third Wave

Between 1973 and 1979 Cuba was virtually closed to any U.S. contact. Cubans in Miami were largely unable to communicate with relatives in Cuba, while several hundred thousand Cubans who had applied for exit visas remained in Cuba under difficult circumstances. In 1980, thousands of Cubans wanting to enter the United States sought political asylum in the Peruvian embassy, and there were street demonstrations that embarrassed Castro. He invited Cubans in Miami to come to the port at Mariel and pick up their relatives. He announced that all were free to go.

During the next few months a poorly organized "freedom flotilla" financed by the Miami Cubans eventually picked up 125,000 refugees at the port of Mariel. They were taken initially to the tip of Florida, Key West, then by bus to Miami. Five thousand were brought over during the first week alone, triggering alarm that the Miami Cuban community had opened Pandora's box and could not handle a refugee influx of this magnitude. Concern increased as descriptions of the refugees began to circulate.

The Cubans who were picked up at Mariel were a heterogeneous group. Some had relatives in the United States, some did not. The only uncontested characteristic of this third wave was that it contained a much larger lower-class contingent than had previous Cuban refugee groups. Castro vindictively claimed that the Mariel refugees were the "scum of the country," describing them as drug addicts, homosexuals, mental patients, and criminals. Later analyses of this third wave indicated that Castro exaggerated the undesirable aspects of the *Marielitos* in order to make the United States look foolish for accepting them. However, this third wave did contain both criminal and mentally ill contingents, and neither the Cubans in Miami nor the U.S. government knew exactly what to do with them.

One of the most negative views of the *Marielitos* was presented by the *Miami Herald*, the major daily newspaper in South Florida. It helped to crystallize negative feelings toward the newest refugees by reporting at various times that as many as 80 percent of the refugees came from Cuban prisons; that twenty thousand were homosexuals; and that in the first three months after their arrival, local crime increased by 34 percent. The *Herald* also expressed the fear of the local Anglo business community that tourism in Miami and South Florida in general would be adversely affected by the presence of this large group of dangerous criminals.[21] Most of the media took a more benign view of the *Marielitos*. For example, *Life* magazine in July 1980 published an editorial stating that while the newcomers did not represent the upper strata of Cuban society, the worst fears about their backgrounds were unfounded. Much of the prison records of the refugees were attributed by the magazine to Cuba's tendency to punish its citizens for "buying scarce food on the black market or for speaking too openly against the government."[22]

The subsequent plights of the *Marielitos* in Miami were as varied as their backgrounds. Thousands were detained by U.S. government officials, who tried to return them to Cuba, but after extensive negotiations Castro eventually refused to take them back. They were subsequently held in federal detention centers without due process for a number of years. Psychiatric problems including depression and posttraumatic stress disorders were widespread among this group. What has been difficult to sort out is how much these problems were caused by their detention experience in the United States and how much they were a result of preexisting conditions. As many as ten thousand of the *Marielitos* may have been convicted of crimes committed in the United States. Again, however, it is difficult to know how much of the criminal behavior to attribute to adjustment stress, which may have been exacerbated by the tendency of the established Cubans to offer little help to the *Marielitos*.[23] At the other extreme, some of the refugees had close ties to established family in Miami and were readily integrated into the enclave.

The thousands of generally unskilled Cubans between the extremes described above sought whatever work they could find, mostly in Little Havana. The established Cuban community initially tried to shut out the *Marielitos*. Business owners in the enclave complained that the new refugees did not want to work, were shoplifters, and frequently became violent. The "native" white community, which had previously admired the Cubans' industriousness, responded negatively to the new image of the Cuban refugee. This negative image led to the passage in Dade County (which includes Miami) of an antibilingual referendum in the fall of 1980. The vote was received like a slap in the face by the Cuban Americans, who believed it was primarily directed at them. Until this time, the Cubans believed that they had been accepted by the mainstream of Miami, and this referendum was one of the events that led them to become a more self-conscious and political ethnic group.[24]

After Mariel

After the 1980 Mariel boat lift, the number of Cubans coming to the United States declined to an average of only a few hundred per year until 1988. When Soviet assistance to Cuba declined at that time, economic conditions on the island deteriorated, stimulating another increase in emigration. Between 1988 and 1993, immigration to the United States from Cuba increased to an average of about 3,500 per year. Illustrative of this group of refugees is the Gonzalez family: Pedro, who worked as an automobile mechanic, Maura, and their twelve-year-old daughter. In 1992, as the Cuban economy was crumbling, Pedro bought a boat on the black market and kept it with a friend who lived near the port at Mariel. They bided their time for two years, until it appeared that Cuban officials would do little to stop them if they tried to leave. They left quickly with little more than the clothes on their backs and ham sandwiches and Pepsi, also purchased on the black market. After two days at sea, the Coast Guard picked them up and brought them to Key West. From there they went to Little Havana to live with an aunt who had moved there a number of years earlier. They left Cuba expecting to improve themselves economically and to find more freedom in Miami. "I want what I've never had before," Maura said. "We never celebrated Christmas in Cuba."[25]

During the past decade there have been few Cuban immigrants to Little Havana (or anywhere else in the United States). Castro has linked the ability of Cubans to emigrate to the United States with the lifting of the U.S. embargo on trade with Cuba. That linkage was designed to induce the Cuban-Americans to pressure the United States on Cuba's behalf, but Miami's Cubans have been divided on the issue. While they favored an end to Cuba's restrictions on emigration, they opposed any action (such as an end to the U.S. trade embargo) that could help the Castro regime. Sneaking out of Cuba has been difficult, and even those who made it across the 90 miles of ocean between Cuba and Florida faced circumstances designed to discourage others from attempting it. The policy of the U.S. government has been to return would-be immigrants from Cuba or hold them, often for lengthy periods, in detention camps such as the Guantánamo Bay Naval Station.

Cuban-American and African-American Conflict

As we have noted, the Cuban-American community has often been in conflict with the Anglo community of Miami–Dade County. However, many of the most intense conflicts have occurred with African-American communities in Miami. The tension between them began during the 1960s and 1970s because of economic competition. In many cities, this was a period of economic progress for African Americans that was associated with the civil rights movement. However, in Miami, African Americans felt that not only were they not making progress, they were losing ground in the private sector because of the Cuban refugees. The Cubans competed with African Americans for the same service jobs in restaurants and hotels, the garment industry, and construction. A number of African-American groups complained that their workers were being pushed aside to make room for Cubans.[26] Then Cuban-owned gasoline stations, groceries, and laundries began springing up in African-American neighborhoods, sometimes replacing African-American-owned establishments. The Cuban enterprises were sometimes conspicuously more successful, as well. Analysis of business income by race indicated that in fact the average earnings of Cuban-owned enterprises were approximately twice those of the African-American-owned businesses.[27]

African Americans also felt that Cubans were benefiting at their expense in the public sector. For example, during the 1960s and 1970s, the U.S. government was providing Cuban refugees with relocation assistance, funds that, African Americans felt, might otherwise be used to assist people in African-American neighborhoods, who had been systematically discriminated against in Miami for many years. During this period, Cuban-owned contracting companies also received several times more minority funding than African-American-owned firms, both from Dade County and from the U.S. Small Business Administration.

The resentments of African Americans in Miami have on several occasions resulted in serious rioting. Of particular importance to the Cubans, who were feeling "picked on" during public discussions of Miami's antibilingual referendum, was a street demonstration in May of 1980. It occurred after an all-white jury acquitted four white police officers of having beaten a black insurance agent to death in Miami. It was at least the fifth racially divisive case in a fifteen-month period, which led most people in Miami's African-American communities to believe that the criminal justice system did not treat them fairly. This latest decision became the immediate precursor to a particularly violent riot. Businesses, some of which were Cuban-owned, were looted and burned. Nonblacks who were caught driving through the riot area were viciously beaten, and eight were killed. One victim, a Cuban-born butcher, was clubbed to death by a mob wielding sticks, who then set his body on fire. His wife and son were at that moment waiting at the Mariel harbor for a boat to take them to Miami.[28] The riot of 1980 was not primarily directed at Cubans but, combined with more symbolic rejections by the Anglo community, it contributed to the Cuban community's feeling that they were under siege.

In order fully to understand the continuing conflict between Cuban and African Americans in Miami, a third group, the Haitians, must also be taken into account. In 1980, simultaneous with the Mariel flotilla, thousands of Haitian "boat people" were trying to escape persecution or miserable living conditions and enter the United States. Coast Guard cutters attempted to block their way, and immigration officials either deported or jailed most of those who got through. Such magazines as *The Nation* described the treatment of the Haitian boat people as "disgraceful" and "punitive and vindictive."[29] Jesse Jackson, Andrew Young, and other leaders of the African-American community saw color as the issue. The Haitians were, of course, black. Was that why they were turned away while the Cubans were admitted? Following marches organized by African Americans in Miami and elsewhere, some Haitians were eventually admitted. They congregated on Miami's northwest side, in an area that came to be called Little Haiti. It was a poor community comprised of mostly young people living in stucco cottages. Little Haiti encroached on previously established African-American (not Cuban) communities, and the Haitians proceeded to compete with African Americans for the low-skill jobs not taken first by Cubans. However, despite the competition, Miami's African Americans continued to support Haitian immigration and relocation assistance, arguing that Haitians should receive the same preferential treatment as Cubans.[30] In the local Cuban community, this was seen as anti-Cuban.

In addition to the issues surrounding Haitian immigration, the positions of Miami's African-American and Cuban communities have dramatically diverged on other matters that have resulted in conflict. When South Africa's Nelson Mandela was invited to speak at a convention in Miami in 1990, for example, African-American leaders were enthusiastic. As part of his tour, high elected officials had already greeted him warmly in Washington, New York, and elsewhere. The African-American community felt that Miami should do the same. The Cubans, however, were opposed to according him VIP treatment because of the prior support he had expressed for the Castro regime. The Cuban position won, and Mandela's official welcome to the city was muted. When Mandela arrived to speak, African-American groups greeted him with such signs as "Welcome to Miami, Home of Apartheid."[31] A week after Mandela's visit, there were major street demonstrations in Miami as blacks (including Haitians and African Americans) protested the city's treatment of Mandela, which they blamed on the Cubans.

The Miami Cubans' intense interest in the implications of any government policy for Castro's regime, combined with the domestic conflicts described above, led to a determined effort in the Cuban community to become more powerful politically in Miami. They had the demographic base and the wealth. From headquarters in Little Havana, Cuban Americans energetically entered local and regional politics. In the 1980s and 1990s, Cuban Americans were elected or appointed to many key positions in

Miami and Dade county, including mayor, city manager, and superintendent of schools. In many instances, African Americans were the defeated candidates, and this has contributed to continuing strain between the two groups. In December 1990, the *Miami News*, a black-oriented newspaper, expressed on page one the view of many African Americans when it headlined the charge, "Miami Run by Cuban Mafia."[32]

In the 1990s, the number of Cuban Americans in major elected and appointed positions in Miami–Dade County continued to increase. And when, in the aftermath of Elián's return in 2000, still other Cuban Americans were placed into key positions, the dominance of Cuban interests seemed overwhelming to the African-American community. In 2000, black leaders spent nearly $10,000 for a full-page advertisement in the *Miami Herald* urging changes in (Cuban American's) power, and more attention to the interests of the local black community.[33]

Exiles and Immigrants

Theories of international migration have assumed that the motivation of the traditional migrating person or household is primarily economic. More jobs, better jobs, and better wages are anticipated in the country of destination than in the country of origin. The direction in which people move and the rate at which they move have therefore been explained by a world-system view that sees movement occurring in response to "disruptions" in the development of poorer countries. Specifically, in searching for cheap labor and materials and new consumer markets, firms in the capitalistic nations that dominate the world economy invest in the less-developed (frequently former colony) nations. As these investments transform the recipient communities, one result is a weaker attachment of natives to their local economies, which leads to a tendency for them to seek better opportunities elsewhere. They frequently move to major world cities—such as New York, Los Angeles, or Miami in the United States—where they typically take low-paying, low-status jobs with little possibility for upward mobility. As the stream of migration from one place to another continues, networks are established that facilitate further movement of coethnics into enclaves in world cities.[34]

The above description of the traditional immigrant fits some of the Cubans who moved to Miami, especially the *Marielitos*. It would also fit the nineteenth-century movement of Chinese, Italians, and Irish to America and such contemporary immigrants as Mexicans to Chicago and various Texas cities. On the other hand, the traditional immigrant profile misses some important features of other groups such as the first wave of Cubans to settle in Miami or the recent immigrants from Taiwan who moved into the Los Angeles area (see Chapter Six). For the latter groups, avoiding political or religious persecution is a major motivation for moving, and these people are often referred to as exiles rather than immigrants.

The distinction between traditional immigrants and exiles is associated, in general, with two sets of differences: first, the age and sex distribution of exiles is more likely to be balanced; that is, they have more-or-less typical demographics because all family members are likely to leave simultaneously in order to avoid persecution. In contrast, selective migration, which characterizes most traditional immigrants, results in an underrepresentation of women and children; men come to seek their fortunes, and their families follow later. Second, the occupational and income levels of exiles in their country of origin tends to be higher than that of traditional immigrants, but exiles frequently experience downward mobility, at least initially, in their country of destination.[35]

The differences between traditional immigrants and exiles often results in some corresponding differences in the enclaves each group establishes. Immigrants have most often formed temporary communities, way stations on the path to greater assimilation. The immigrant groups generally lacked both the economic and the demographic supports necessary to develop enclaves that were truly self-contained and that offered sufficient prospects to keep young people from moving out. They could not retain their youths because most of their economic opportunities lay outside the enclave; so too did political power. The enclaves of exiles, on the other hand, have been able to offer their residents better economic opportunities. Exiles have also been able to wield more political power and to exert more control over the conditions under which their members live and their relations with other groups. As a result of these differences, the enclaves of exiles usually prove to be more enduring than those of traditional immigrants.

Finally, it is important to note the tendency of exiles to regard themselves as being in a temporary situation; they are, they believe, in exile only until some event occurs, such as the death of a religious leader or the collapse of a political regime. Traditional immigrants are mixed in this respect. Some intend to accumulate money and return home, whereas others see their country of origin as unlikely ever to offer sufficient opportunities. Even among those exiles who always profess the desire to return, however, it is not certain that they actually would, even if the conditions they specify were to occur. For example, it is common for Cubans in Miami to solemnly toast each other with the phrase, "Next year in Havana," but they probably mean it mostly at a symbolic level. One self-defined exile claimed that he would get to Havana on the first available plane if Castro were out of the way. "Are you really sure?" he was asked. "Well," he smiled, "Who can tell?"[36]

There are, of course, many reasons to stay: businesses, families, friends, and so on. In addition, exiles often recognize that the place to which they yearn to return has itself changed. Even if they could return, they could not continue the life they left. To illustrate, after spending many years in Miami one woman returned to Cuba for a visit. She explained that even though she was born there, during her visit she felt like a foreigner. When she returned to Miami, she sadly realized there was nothing more for her in Havana. She had been "mourning for nothing all these years, and loving a place that no longer exists except inside us."[37]

Notes

1. Alex Stepick, Guillermo Grenier, Max Castro, and Marvin Dunn, *This Land is Our Land,* Berkeley, CA: University of California Press, 2003.
2. Jose Llanes, *Cuban Americans,* Cambridge, MA: Abt Books, 1982.
3. Quoted in Necee Regis, "The Soulful Attraction of Miami's Little Havana," *Boston Globe*, February 10, 2002, p. M1.
4. David Rieff, quoted in Alejandro Portes and Robert L. Bach, *Latin Journey,* Berkeley: University of California Press, 1985.
5. Llanes, op. cit., p. 129.
6. David Rieff, *The Exile,* New York: Simon & Schuster, 1993.
7. Stepick, et al., op. cit. p. 4.
8. Ann L. Badrach, *Cuba Confidential,* New York: Random House, 2003.
9. Quoted in *New York Times*, May 6, 1994, p. A10.
10. Marita Ojito, "Latin Grammy Show Puts Miami to the Test," *New York Times*, September 3, 2003, p. E1.
11. For further discussion, see Alejandro Portes and Dag MacLeod, "Educational Progress of Children of Immigrants," *Sociology of Education* 69, 1996.
12. Alejandro Portes and Alex Stepick, *City on the Edge,* Berkeley: University of California Press, 1993.
13. June Namias, *First Generation,* Urbana: University of Illinois Press, 1992.
14. For a general discussion of this issue, see Silvia Pedrazza, "Women and Migration," *Annual Review of Sociology* 17, 1991.

15. Rieff, op. cit., p. 157.
16. Ibid., p. 156.
17. Portes and Bach, op. cit.
18. Portes and Stepick, op. cit.
19. Llanes, op. cit., p. 104.
20. Ibid., p. 113.
21. Portes and Stepick, op. cit. The Cuban community's resulting displeasure with the *Herald* did not end with its coverage of the Mariel immigrants. There was a succession of news stories that gave Cuban Americans the feeling that the newspaper was not sympathetic to Cubans. In the late 1980s, the *Herald*'s parent company established an editorially autonomous Spanish-language edition of the newspaper primarily oriented to Miami's Cuban population. It is now published daily in Miami.
22. Rita J. Simon and Susan H. Alexander, *The Ambivalent Welcome,* Westport, CT: Praeger, 1993, p. 179.
23. For further discussion of stress and maladaptive behavior among the *Marielitos,* see Roberto J. Velasquez and Michaelanthony Brown-Cheatham, "Understanding the Plight of Cuba's *Marielitos,*" in Ernest R. Myers (Ed.), *Challenges of a Changing America,* San Francisco: Austin & Winfield, 1994.
24. Portes and Stepick, op. cit.
25. *New York Times,* August 19, 1994, p. A14.
26. Raymond A. Mohl, "On the Edge: Blacks and Hispanics in Metropolitan Miami," *Florida Historical Quarterly* 69, 1990.
27. Bruce Porter and Marvin Dunn, *The Miami Riot of 1980,* Lexington, MA: D. C. Heath, 1984.
28. Ibid.
29. Quoted in Simon and Alexander, op. cit.
30. For an analysis of changes in relations between established African Americans and later-arriving Haitians as seen through the prism of a high school at the edge of Little Haiti, see chap. 4 in Stepick, et al., op. cit.
31. Portes and Stepick, op. cit., p. 176.
32. Ibid., p. 251.
33. Stepick, et al, op. cit., p. 76.
34. For further discussion, see Douglas S. Massey, "Theories of International Migration," *Population and Development Review* 19, 1993.
35. See Roger Waldinger, "From Ellis Island to LAX," *International Migration Review* 30, 1996.
36. Rieff, op. cit., p. 45.
37. Ibid., p. 204.

American Writers and Artists in Paris's Left Bank District of Montparnasse

During World War I, thousands of American soldiers were stationed in Paris. When the war ended in 1918, many decided to stay, and they were soon joined by others from the United States. The French, grateful for the enormous U.S. help during the war, treated Americans well and made them feel welcome. Paris's other attraction to the Americans was the fact that it was much less expensive than most large U.S. cities. It had a diverse array of hotel rooms and small apartments that could be rented monthly for less than $20 and cafés and restaurants that served good meals for a quarter. And like everyone else, the Americans were charmed by the beauty of the city.

For those who wanted to write or paint or compose music, Paris offered special attractions: dozens of avant-garde art galleries, innovative concerts and music schools, experimental filmmaking, and more magazines devoted to literature and the arts than the rest of the world combined. In addition, there were the legendary cafés in which like-minded people could be found to discuss trends in art or literature at any time of the night. In its receptiveness to innovative ideas and new forms, Paris at the end of the war enjoyed a reputation as the "City of Light": a charmed city that permitted beauty to be created by its open atmosphere.[1]

It was not only Americans that were attracted to Paris at the end of World War I. There were thousands of Russians fleeing the Bolshevik Revolution, immigrants from all over Eastern Europe and expatriates from throughout the United Kingdom. There was a sense of community among all the artists and writers in Paris, regardless of their origins. They were aware of each other's contributions, and their art, music, and, to a lesser extent, literature transcended national boundaries. In addition to the artistic interests they held in common, most of them also shared an attraction to a bohemian lifestyle that emphasized tolerance and indulgence. Within this international community, though, there were also some (at least partly) separate ethnic subgroups, the largest of which was American.

There was a good deal of overlap among all the English-speaking artists and writers in Paris. Those who emigrated from the United Kingdom (D. H. Lawrence and James Joyce, for example) tended to live in many of the same places as the Americans and frequent many of the same bars. There were many friendships between émigrés from the United Kingdom and the United States, and a number of the U.K. expatriates also traveled regularly between Paris and New York. However, the Americans were a distinct group within the larger English-speaking group. They had their own schools, clubs, gymnasiums, and centers, and hundreds of tables at cafés where the regular clientele consisted entirely or almost entirely of Americans. They also disproportionately selected other Americans as their closest friends. In addition, their common culture and food preferences created a bond among them. At Thanksgiving, for example, some of the expatriates cajoled French restaurateurs into preparing a traditional American dinner with turkey, mincemeat, and all the trimmings.[2]

In this chapter we shall focus upon the artists and writers that formed an American enclave in the Montparnasse Quarter in Paris's Left Bank. They were mostly young and aspiring, though a few were not young, and a few were already very well known. They included dancers, poets, playwrights, photographers, singers, sculptors, composers, novelists, and others. *Artists and writers* in this chapter will be a shorthand way of referring to all of the above.

The Americans and the French

For some of the American artists and writers, coming to France was part of a rejection of American society. Compared to Paris, they found the United States socially "stifling": intolerant of all but highly conventional sexual preferences, overly religious, bigoted on matters of race, and totally opposed to alcohol consumption. The differences entailed cultural preferences, of course, but there were also legal differences. For example, in the United States, Prohibition banned the sale of alcohol between 1920 and 1933, but it flowed freely in Paris's cafés; homosexual acts and relationships were actively prosecuted under a variety of different statutes in the United States, but not in Paris. For example, dozens of American artists and writers lived openly as lesbians in Paris' Left Bank, Gertrude Stein and Alice B. Toklas being perhaps the best known of them.[3]

Even if they still wanted turkey and mincemeat at Thanksgiving, the Americans wanted to be free from all remnants of puritanical America. According to historian Hugh Ford, the "anti-America" Americans did not know exactly how to proceed. They believed they had to revolt against something, and that something became the ideas and prejudices of "the people back home."[4] To prove they were emancipated, they had to see how much they could drink, how many promiscuous sexual relations they could engage in, and how much they could flout social conventions. What happened in the uptight and repressive United States, they contended, was of little concern to them.

On the other hand, some of the Americans who were highly critical of American society and who were committed to remaining in Paris, nevertheless continued to consider America their home. For example, Gertrude Stein's writings were highly critical of the ingrained patriarchy of the United States—in literature, in sexual standards, even in grammar—and she had no intention of returning to the United States, even though she remained deeply involved in U.S. affairs. In fact, she claimed that living in Paris was indispensable, given her interests in America, because it provided her with contrast and perspective. Describing her attitudes toward America and those of her friends in self-imposed exile, she wrote, "We felt that we loved it—at a distance."[5]

There were a few Americans who tried to immerse themselves in Parisian life. The writer John Dos Passos and his friends, for example, liked to hang around, "talking bad French" with cabdrivers, loafers, workmen, restaurant managers, and so on, and they often took strong public positions on issues facing Parisians.[6] However, relatively few of the Americans spoke or read much French and, according to Ford, most had little interest in what was going on in Paris outside their own social circle. Their major conversations did not involve the serious issues of the day but gossip and personalities. As soon as any one of them left a table in a Montparnasse café, those who remained immediately tore apart his or her looks, opinions, sexual affairs, drinking habits, and so on. "Every one was living in a glasshouse and everyone threw stones."[7]

Their pettiness, their lack of interest in Paris, and their outlandish behavior led many Parisians eventually to grow to dislike the American writers and artists as memories of the war receded. In particular, the heavy drinking of the Americans frequently led to grossly unconventional actions that offended the Parisians who came into contact with them. The American men were frequently arrested for urinating in public, for example. Another illustrative example is provided by F. Scott Fitzgerald, who

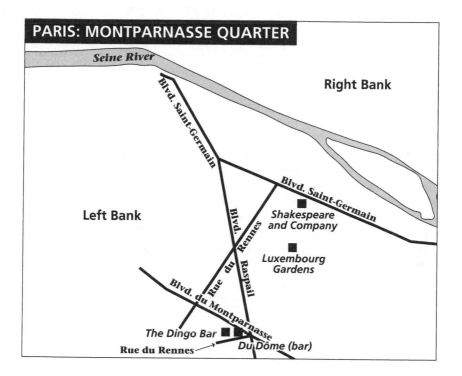

PARIS: MONTPARNASSE QUARTER

Seine River

Right Bank

Blvd. Saint-Germain

Left Bank

Blvd. Saint-Germain

Blvd. Rennes

Shakespeare and Company

Rue du Raspail

Luxembourg Gardens

Blvd. du Montparnasse

The Dingo Bar

Rue du Rennes →

Du Dôme (bar)

left a café late one night a bit drunk, and came up to a poor French woman offering a tray of trinkets for sale. Thinking it funny, he kicked the tray out of her hands and sent the trinkets flying across the sidewalk. When others in the street expressed disapproval, Fitzgerald claimed to have given her 100 francs, but no one believed it.[8]

The Left and Right Banks

The Seine River divides Paris into a Left—south of the Seine—and Right—north—Bank. The Right Bank was historically the city's banking and commercial center. It also contained many luxurious hotels and upscale restaurants that attracted wealthy American tourists but were generally too expensive (as well as too "stuffy") for the American artists and writers who were in Paris for extended periods of time. The Right Bank was also the headquarters for numerous American newspapers that published English-language editions in Paris.[9] These newspapers provided temporary employment for many struggling young Left Bank residents who later became famous writers.

The newspaper most widely read by the Americans was probably the Paris edition of the *Chicago Tribune,* sometimes referred to as the *Paris Tribune.* A number of other newspapers, including the *New York Times,* also published Paris editions. These newspapers provided extensive coverage of the openings of art shows, new novels, and the like. They also featured gossip columns, telling who was seen drinking with whom, which marriage was about to end, and the latest antics of the Americans. This information was of great interest both to Americans in the Paris enclave and to people back in the United States.

"Conventional" would be the term that applied to most of the Right Bank—with the notable exception of Montmartre, a distinctive area both socially and geographically. Its narrow, winding streets were higher than surrounding areas, providing a panoramic view of most of the city. Montmartre was the site of Paris's earliest artist colony as well as a very popular nightlife district with restaurants, bars, nightclubs, and houses of prostitution. During the late nineteenth century, the differences between most of the Right Bank and Montmartre prompted residents of the latter to only half-jokingly propose that Montmartre become an "autonomous territory" with its own capital.[10]

The Left Bank (or Latin Quarter) was dominated by college students, notably at France's premier institution, the Sorbonne, and by people connected to art and literature: "wanna-be" young artists and writers, entrepreneurs hoping to profit by discovering young talent, and wealthy people from all over the world who fancied themselves as patrons of the arts. There were also a large number of "hangers-on" and "pretenders" who copied the lifestyle of the artists and writers but lacked dedication to any craft and did not fit any of the above categories. The one thing that most of them shared in common was an attraction to the Left Bank's acceptance of people "as they were" and a general tolerance of differences. They did not risk others' disapproval for not attending church. They could dress and act as they pleased without being subject to negative judgements. And, as previously noted, people's race, sexual preferences, and drinking habits did not matter very much either.

The term most often used to describe the predominant lifestyle in many parts of the Left Bank (and in Montmartre) was *bohemian.* In Western societies over several hundred years, bohemianism became associated with young artists, broadly defined so as to include writers, sculptors, actors, singers, painters, musicians, and composers. Their creative role in society was regarded as exempting them from conventional regulations. In order to free their creative impulses, they needed "more space" than others in the community. The exemplar of the bohemian in Paris was a poor, struggling, young writer or artist with no immediate prospects, wearing garish clothes and acting in eccentric ways. This prototype was most indebted to a series of stories by Henri Murger first published in 1845 in a Paris magazine.[11] His writings popularly romanticized bohemian life, and the influence of his conception was magnified when his stories became the basis for Puccini's opera *La Bohème*.[12] When the young Americans came to the Left Bank, they embraced Murger's romantic image of the bohemian life, even its poverty. Thus young Henry Miller, who had just begun to work on *Tropic of Capricorn*, stood in front of a Left Bank café and shouted, "I have no money, no resources . . . I am the happiest man alive!"[13]

Montparnasse

A couple of miles south of the Seine, near the intersection of two major boulevards, Du Montparnasse and Raspail, is a Left Bank area called Montparnasse, or the Montparnasse Quarter. Like Montmartre, much of it was built upon a hill, and some writers poetically described the two areas as "facing" each other, though they were separated by miles and the Seine. During the early decades of the twentieth century, Montmartre was increasingly built up with apartments, nightclubs, and restaurants. Studio space was more available in Montparnasse, and that began the flight of artists, then writers and others. When the Paris subway connected Montmartre and Montparnasse in 1912, many of Montmartre's artists were said to have purchased one-way fares. The exodus from Montmartre was occurring at about the time the number of Americans coming to Paris was increasing, and most of the young American writers and artists also settled in Montparnasse. At the time, a French poet and art critic described the transition by writing that Montmartre was "full of fake artists. . . . In Montparnasse, on the other hand, you can find the real artists, dressed in American-style clothes."[14]

Montparnasse contained the hotels and apartments that housed the young Alexander Calder, Josephine Baker, Man Ray, William Faulkner, Aaron Copland, and other of the twentieth century's most notable American writers, artists, and composers. Some spent only a few months living in Paris; others remained for most of their lives. In Montparnasse there was also a concentration of bars, cafés, and restaurants with large or predominantly American clienteles; bookstores, book publishers, and galleries that typically featured the works of the Americans; and a poorly attended American Church whose minister claimed the American expatriates packed their religion in a suitcase, then left the suitcase behind in New York.[15]

An important attraction of Montparnasse to the Americans was its bohemianism, which they in fact helped to maintain. In 1922, many residents of Montmartre declared that "bohemia was at an end. Modern life had become too serious, too demanding."[16] They were responding to the ravages of World War I, the turmoil of the Bolshevik Revolution, the unsettling new ideas of Freud. The American artists and writers in Montparnasse were the group that most insisted that bohemia was not dead. They made it the center of bohemia, "swarming with people who lived sexually free and economically shaky lives in the name of art or literature."[17]

At all hours of the day and night there were public incidents on Montparnasse streets: brawls between artists who were jealous of the gallery locations in which the artwork of others was hung, drunks reciting poetry they had written, or shouting matches between composers and the critics who reviewed their work. An illustrative story was told by a reporter who covered Montparnasse for the Paris edition of the *Chicago Tribune*. He described what happened when a prominent ex–New Yorker named Louise Bryant, a poet, gave a trunk she no longer needed to two male friends. The two, who were poor artists, were carrying it down the Boulevard du Montparnasse, but it was heavy, and they were a little drunk. So they dropped the trunk in the middle of the street, sat down on it, and drank what was left of the bottles of wine they had been carrying in their pockets. Motorists began to yell at the drunks, who were blocking the street. The two grew annoyed and smashed their empty bottles in the street. Then they ran down the street waving their arms and yelling at motorists, "Detour to save your tires!" Dozens of people lined the sidewalks watching the spectacle until the police finally arrived. However, such incidents were commonplace in this area, and the police merely helped the two drunk artists lift their trunk and gently pushed them down the sidewalk toward their apartment.[18]

Most of the people who have written about the American enclave centered in Montparnasse have not offered a guess concerning its size; the fluid nature of the enclave was a major impediment. Many people who were integral to the enclave's life traveled almost continuously between Paris and New York, or Paris and London, or Paris and somewhere else. Their perpetual movement made them difficult to count and made moot the question of whether Paris was their primary residence. In addition, many Americans returned to the Left Bank every June, when schools in the United States let out. They temporarily swelled Montparnasse's population, and their inclusion would have exaggerated the size of the permanent enclave, but they would not have been easily distinguished from the more permanent residents if anyone had tried to enumerate the enclave during the summer.

An additional problem in estimating the enclave's size was due to ambiguity concerning the boundaries of the Montparnasse community. For example, some artists and writers lived in the inner Left Bank, considerably north of Montparnasse. Because they were regularly found in the bookstores, bars, cafés, and other institutions of the enclave, most analysts are inclined to include them as part of the community. However, the few population estimates there were for the enclave in the 1920s did not specify what boundaries their proposers were utilizing. Were groups such as those in the inner Left Bank included? Finally, the enclave apparently grew substantially in size during the early and middle 1920s before it slowly declined in the late 1920s and 1930s. However, when chroniclers of the American colony in Montparnasse commented on its size, they usually failed to link their estimate to a specific date. With all of the above caveats in mind, we can roughly estimate the peak size of the American enclave, broadly defined geographically, as probably containing between about twelve thousand and fifteen thousand more or less permanent residents in the mid-1920s.[19]

Enclave Institutions

The Americans' Montparnasse enclave was served by a wide range of organizations. To list just a few, they included the American Conservatory of Music (Aaron Copland, who became the premier composer in the United States during the middle of the twentieth century was the school's first American student); an American women's club (where Gertrude Stein frequently gave analyses of American politics); an American students' club (which offered space for dances, card games, and table tennis, mostly for art students), the American Baptist Center (whose gymnasium was widely used by the American expatriates), and so on.

Although the above (and kindred) organizations impacted the lives of the American expatriates, their contributions to maintaining the American enclave were probably secondary. The two types of institutions that probably warrant most attention in that respect were, first, bookstores that catered to people interested in books and were also meeting places where information was disseminated—these bookstores, some of which were linked to publishing outlets, were significant to novelists and to many painters, musicians, and others who were also writers as a secondary activity—and second, drinking establishments—cafés and bars—that catered to the Americans and were filled with them on most nights. We will discuss leading examples of each of these institutions.

The Bookstores

There were a number of bookstores in Montparnasse and most of them were more than just places to buy a book or magazine. They tended to be important meeting places for writers and artists. Some were places where novelists or poets previewed their work in public readings and some also became publishers for young writers who could not get contracts with major firms. In a few cases, the bookstores provided addresses for struggling authors who did not know where they might be living next week, and some of the proprietors could even be approached for a loan. For the Americans in Montparnasse, the most important bookstore was Shakespeare and Co., and its owner, Sylvia Beach, played all the roles noted above, plus serving as a confidant and message bearer for the Americans.

Shakespeare and Co.

Walking a short distance north from the center of Montparnasse, one came to the Luxembourg art museum and gardens. Stretching several blocks in every direction, the Luxembourg Gardens had beds of beautiful flowers, a pond, a variety of trees tagged with their Latin names, and a miniature Statue of Liberty.[20] Just to the north of the gardens lies rue de l'Odéon. In the 1920s, it was a brick-lined street that extended only one long block, and it was full of little shops, including an antique dealer, shoemaker, music shop, and several bookstores. Shakespeare and Co. was at 12 rue de l'Odéon, at that time probably the most famous expatriate address in Paris.[21]

The metal sliding door to the bookstore was nearly ten feet high, and just above it hung a picture of Shakespeare. When Shakespeare and Co. first opened, most of its books' authors and its clientele were British, but that soon changed. Inside, the shop was filled with bookshelves, some of which were as low as about four feet high, some of which went as high as the ceiling. Most of the books were in English, and the shelves always contained a lot of new experimental works. On the walls above the shorter shelves were pictures of famous authors, most of which had been taken by the noted American photographer Man Ray. There were also several tables and chairs, and enough space on the floor to sit cross-legged and read.[22]

The proprietor, Sylvia Beach, was a slight woman with wavy brown hair and a ready smile. Raised in Princeton, New Jersey, she first came to France at the age of fourteen when her father was appointed director of an American artists' center in Paris. As the owner of Shakespeare and Co. she became, by all accounts, one of the most significant people in the American enclave. One of the first stops for an American arriving in Paris, rich and famous or poor and unknown, was her bookstore. Ernest Hemingway, who became the shop's best customer, recalled his immediate fondness for it as a young expatriate. He was poor and was thrilled to discover that he could just borrow a book because he could not afford to buy any; and in the winter when it was chilly outside, the shop was warm. Twenty years later, as Paris was being liberated from the Nazis, Hemingway—bareheaded and in shirtsleeves—commandeered sixteen American soldiers and took them to Shakespeare and Co. They shot the German snipers off the rooftops, and the sound of the gunfire sent Sylvia Beach into hiding in her apartment upstairs. A few minutes later she heard a man's voice yelling, "Sylvia! Hemingway is here!"[23]

Shakespeare and Co. barely survived financially. Most of the customers came to browse and read, not to buy. Beach took an intense interest in the young, aspiring authors, however, and many credited her with dramatically helping their careers. For example, shortly after the first chapters of James Joyce's classic, *Ulysses,* appeared in a magazine, it was declared obscene and banned in the United States and the United Kingdom. Beach was very impressed with his talent, though, and personally made financial arrangements with a printer she knew to produce the entire book. She also lent Joyce what little money she could spare so he could support his family until the book was published.[24]

On the same street as Shakespeare and Co. there was a French bookstore whose name translates as "The house of friends of books." Its owner was a Parisian woman, Adrienne Monnier. Her shop, like Sylvia Beach's, was a combination bookstore, lending library, and meeting place—but for French writers and artists. Monnier opened her shop first, and it became the inspiration for Sylvia Beach. When Shakespeare and Co. opened across the street, the two women were supportive colleagues and then close friends, and eventually they shared an apartment down the street from their bookstores. The close ties between the two women became a bridge between the American and French communities, and writers in each learned from the other, to everyone's benefit. Together, the women turned

rue de l'Odéon into an (unofficial) welcoming center for newcomers and visitors to the artistic world of the Left Bank. When Paul Robeson, the African-American singer and actor, came to Paris on a tour in 1925, for example, he was "introduced" to the Left Bank at a tea given together by the two bookstore proprietors.[25]

The Cafés and Bars

On the Boulevard du Montparnasse, near the intersection with Raspail Boulevard in the center of the enclave, were four cafés. Because of their concentration and their central location, they were all among the best known in Montparnasse, though there were dozens of others throughout the area. The patrons of some of the cafés were largely or predominantly American. The most famous of these during the 1920s and 1930s was one of the centrally located cafés, Café du Dome.

The Dome

Before the American writers and artists made it a popular gathering place, the Dome was a shabby, dark tavern with a billiard table in the rear and a predominantly male, working-class, Parisian clientele. Before the end of World War I it was described as "a rundown joint, small and ugly."[26] As its popularity grew, the owners substantially expanded the interior of the café and added a terrace. This outside area became famous for permitting people to nurse a drink for hours without being hassled. Paint, lighting, and rows of tables were added to modernize the expanded back room, and the billiard table was removed in order to accommodate more customers. Many years later, the owners of the Dome turned it into a trendy restaurant with decorative orange lamps and photographs hanging on the walls showing diners the likenesses of the famous writers and artists who frequented the café in the 1920s and 1930s.

During the years in which it served as a meeting place for the American expatriates, many of the tables contained groups of people who went to the Dome together almost every night. So predictable was their attendance that one could get a message to another of the Dome's regulars by conveying it to a third party who would almost certainly be at his or her table later that evening. People sent messages, gifts, keys, and so on to each other in this way. And if they had good news or bad news to share, they knew where to go to find their friends. Others, apparently without friends, sat alone at a table on most nights.

The core of one typical group that frequently met at the Dome consisted primarily of several painters, sometimes their wives, and sometimes one or more of their models. Specifically, the core of this group included:

Jules Pascin, a noted painter born in Bulgaria who emigrated to Paris, then New York, became a U.S. citizen, then returned to Paris. He was at the Dome almost every night, often with one or more of the painters listed below. He usually wore a black hat with a narrow brim at an angle on his head and spent much of the night openly admiring the youngest females in the room.[27]

Lucy Vidil, Pascin's model and lover before and after she married the painter Per Krogh. Her husband occasionally joined this table.

George Biddle, a painter from Philadelphia who kept a studio in Paris.

Louise Bryant, the New York poet who gave the previously described trunk to the two drunk artists. She was the widow of writer John Reed before marrying William Bullitt.

William Bullitt, a writer from Philadelphia who later became the U.S. Ambassador to France.

Illustrating the nature of an ordinary evening at the Dome, George Biddle recollected one night when he, Pascin, and several other painters were seated in the tavern. Suddenly, an enraged art critic shrieked at one of the artists and threw a wad of horse manure at him. No one thought much about such an event in the Dome, though they all did get out of the way.[28]

Some years later, Pascin was ill and no longer regularly coming to the Dome. Like many of the artists and writers, he suffered from liver disease as a result of prolonged alcohol consumption. Lucy Vidil came to one of the tables Pascin had frequented before his illness, and told his artist friends that she was concerned about him. He had told her he did not want to see her anymore, but she still cared about him and was worried that no one had seen him lately. They encouraged her to go see him at once, and she walked over to his apartment. His shutters were closed, so she got a neighbor and they went into his apartment and found him dead. Pascin had sliced his wrists with a razor and used the blood to write, "Adieu Lucy," on his studio wall. In his will he directed that his artwork and money were to be divided equally between Lucy and his wife.[29] (A discussion of suicides in Montparnasse is at the end of this chapter.)

To complete our description of the Dome, let us take a virtual walk among the tables on a typical evening in 1924. From accounts in the *Paris Tribune*, what we could expect to see and hear is as follows. There is a brawl on the terrace, but the drunks are unable to do much harm to each other, and pretty soon they tire. Some regular chess players, ignoring the ruckus around them, are hunched over a chessboard. An Italian woman who almost nightly carries a large cloth doll into the Dome is stopped by a young American who embarrasses her by loudly demanding to know why she is always carrying it around. A group of American painters at another table are arguing about geometric shapes and the true meaning of love. In a corner of the room, a man with both hands to his mouth is pretending to play a musical instrument. A tall, blond American intentionally knocks over four chairs as he walks out, and as they clatter to the ground, they startle a waiter with a black moustache and he drops a bottle of wine.[30]

Henry Miller, the writer previously quoted as declaring that his poverty made him the happiest man in the world, often sat at a table at the Dome, hoping to get someone to buy him a drink. In the meanwhile, waiters would bring him stationary on which he scribbled notes for his book and "begging letters," asking newfound friends if they would put him up for a night. When he had no luck, he would sleep on the sawdust-covered floor in the Dome's WC (bathroom). In the morning he would sit at a table with a cup of coffee, sawdust still covering the back of his jacket.[31]

The Dingo Bar

While the Dome was apparently the most popular hangout for American expatriates, not all of them liked it. Some spoke very disparagingly about it and its clientele. There were plenty of other places to choose from, however, and each had its own loyal following. For example, a couple of blocks away from the Dome, a short walk up a small street with a bookstore, some artists' studios, and apartment-hotels, was the Dingo Bar. It was very small, especially when compared to the Dome. The Dingo contained only six tiny tables and a few stools that were placed in front of a short bar. Its bartender for several years was an Englishman named Jimmy Charters who was well known in Montparnasse after having tended bar in a number of establishments with large American clienteles. Because he spoke English and was always willing to lend a sympathetic ear, he had a large following within the enclave.[32]

Ernest Hemingway (and his first wife) were among the Dingo's regular customers. F. Scott Fitzgerald and his wife, Zelda, were also regulars. Other American writers predominated among the rest of the bar's habitués. It was at the Dingo that Ernest and Scott first met. They became friends, to judge by the time they spent together, but Ernest had his doubts about the Fitzgeralds because he felt they did not hold their liquor as well as he did. After a few drinks at the Dingo the Fitzgeralds would often become practical jokers and try to kidnap a waiter, for example, or plunge fully dressed into a fountain. Ernest also found Zelda irritating. Described as the most attractive woman in Montparnasse, she flirted with every man she met, and some took it seriously. Most men soon realized it was just her style and did not mean anything, but Ernest was frustrated by her. He could not believe there was a woman in Montparnasse that would not go to bed with him. His irritation may have prompted him to challenge Scott one night over which of them was better endowed as a male. The two of them, according to Hemingway's later account, strode off to the bathroom to compare.[33]

Zelda's flirting with other men was a serious matter to Scott, and it led to a number of scenes in the Dingo. One night when the Fitzgeralds were sitting with some other American writers, Scott was fuming over her playful sexual banter with another man at the bar. Finally he turned to her and called her a bitch, which led one of the other American men at the table to get up and punch him. Scott, a bit drunk, fell to the floor. Jimmy the bartender ran over, picked Scott off the floor, sat him at a nearby vacant table, and brought him another drink. That was the end of the incident, and a few nights later Scott and the man who punched him again ran into each other at the Dingo and put the incident behind them.[34]

Anomie and Suicide

There are no reliable statistics on suicides among the artists and writers who were connected to the Montparnasse enclave during the 1920s. However, there seem to have been a substantial number of them; more than would have been expected in a typical population of the same size.[35] We previously described Pascin's wrist-cutting, and there were numerous other documented suicides among well-known Montparnasse residents: the husband of San Francisco–born Isadora Duncan, the founder of modern dance, hung himself; Modigliani's model and lover threw herself off the top of her parents' apartment building; Boston-born poet Harry Crosby, nephew of the banker J. P. Morgan, shot himself in the head while laying in bed, and so on.

The apparently high rate of suicide among Montparnasse writers, artists, and their significant others would almost surely have been explained by the pioneering French sociologist Emile Durkheim as due to *anomie,* or the absence of restraining norms within community. The shared orientation within the enclave stressed extreme, hedonistic indulgence. Ideally, in this view, people should have as many (and as varied) sexual partners as possible; experiment with whatever drugs and alcohol are available; party whenever and however they wish. The objective was to make sure that one did not miss out on any possible pleasure. Conventional rules, they believed, applied to conventional people; as creative geniuses, they were exempt.[36] However, "anything goes" attitudes result in normlessness, and in the absence of norms there are no standards against which people can evaluate their outcomes. How can they tell whether they should feel contented? Because people cannot deduce how much is enough in a normless setting, genuine feelings of satisfaction are always just out of their reach.

Some of the artists and writers in Montparnasse worked diligently to perfect their skills, and a few of them ultimately made enduring contributions to art, music, dance, literature, and other fields. According to many observers, though, most of the young exiles actually worked only rarely. They were always promising themselves and any one else who would listen that they were going to get to work next week; but next week never came. It was always postponed because of another party, an exciting sexual liaison, opium, alcohol, or entire nights in a café spent *talking* about working. Montparnasse presented the artists and writers in the enclave with a new approach to life. In their American past they were taught to value industriousness, but Montparnasse encouraged them to indulge themselves. Whatever talent they may have once had was eventually wasted. When they did sober up long enough to try to do something, in the opinion of one observer, they painted "worthless pictures which no one will buy," or produced "reams of piffling drivel which no . . . normal person would read."[37]

The days just slipped by, and promising young people found themselves older with little to show for the years that had passed. Meanwhile, repetition diminished the excitement they received from their uninhibited lives. Experiences that were thrilling yesterday tend to seem commonplace today and boring tomorrow. To explain the seeming rash of suicides, a *Paris Tribune* reporter surmised that the unproductive, self-indulgent artists and writers in Montparnasse became dismayed and disillusioned, eventually finding themselves unable to perceive any alternative to pursue. They concluded that it must be time to leave the Montparnasse enclave, but "deciding they can go no better place, go to their graves."[38]

The universal relationship between suicide and the absence of regulatory norms—anomie—was first explained by Durkheim in the 1890s. When the people in any community do not share the norms that limit people's aspirations, he wrote, people continue to want *more*—more than however much they have had in the past: more novel sexual liaisons, more potent drugs, more unconventional parties. Heaven forbid, they may be missing out on something! Such unlimited desires, Durkheim contended, are necessarily insatiable. They offer people no respite from their cravings, no opportunity to feel contented. By contrast, in a community with shared norms that regulate and control aspirations there is a greater possibility for people to feel satisfied with what they have. When there is anomie, he wrote, "A thirst arises for unfamiliar pleasures, nameless sensations, all of which lose their savor once known."[39] The result is disappointment, despair, and ultimately suicide.

Notes

1. Vincent Cronin, *Paris: City of Light 1919–1939,* London: HarperCollins, 1994.
2. Arlen J. Hansen, *Expatriate Paris,* New York: Arcade Publishing, 1990. In the same vein, one day in a celebrated French restaurant, the writer F. Scott Fitzgerald threw down the menu and demanded in English that the waiter bring him a club sandwich—endearing himself to fellow Americans-in-exile with similar longings.
3. See chap. 12, "The Left Bank of Lesbos," in William Wiser, *The Crazy Years,* New York: G. K. Hall & Co., 1985.
4. Hugh Ford, *The Left Bank Revisited,* University Park, PA: Pennsylvania State University Press, 1972, p. 33.
5. Ibid., p. xix.
6. See Cronin, op. cit.
7. Ibid., p. 34.
8. William Wiser, *The Twilight Years,* New York: Carroll and Graf, 2000.
9. Detailed maps of Left and Right Bank areas, showing the locations of various people, events and places, are provided in Hansen, op. cit.
10. They even held an election for their own mayor. For further discussion, see Dan Franck, *Bohemian Paris.* New York: Grove Press, 2003.
11. It was later published as a book which has been recently reissued. See Henri Murger, *The Bohemians of the Latin Quarter,* Philadelphia: University of Pennsylvania, 2004.
12. For further history and analysis of bohemianism, see Ephraim H. Mizruchi, *Regulating Society,* New York: Free Press, 1983.
13. Quoted in Wiser, op. cit., p. 14.

14. Attributed to Guillaume Apollinaire, quoted by Jackie Wullschlager, "Models, Muses and Mistresses," *Financial Times,* Arts section, June 3, 2002, p. 14.

15. Ford, op. cit.

16. Jerrold Seigel, *Bohemian Paris,* Baltimore, MD: Johns Hopkins University Press, 1999, p. 367.

17. Ibid., p. 368.

18. Wambly Bald, *On the Left Bank,* Athens, OH: Ohio University Press, 1987, pp. 94–95.

19. The American Chamber of Commerce in Paris estimated that there were fifteen thousand Americans living *anywhere* in Paris in 1927. However, there could have been two to three times that many because not all expatriates registered with French officials. See William Wiser, *The Crazy Years,* New York: G. K. Hall and Co., 1985. Cronin, op. cit., placed the number in Montparnasse at twenty thousand, but that included both American and British residents. On the growth and decline of the enclave, see Wiser, *Twilight Years,* op. cit.

20. The gardens in the 1920s are described by Wiser, *Crazy Years,* op. cit.

21. See Hansen, op. cit.

22. For more details, see the description given many years later by the proprietor herself: Sylvia Beach, *Shakespeare and Company,* New York: Harcourt, Brace, 1959.

23. Quoted in Hansen, op. cit.

24. See Merrill Cody with Hugh Ford, *The Women of Montparnasse,* New York: Cornwall Books, 1984.

25. See Ford, op. cit.

26. Hansen, op. cit., p. 124.

27. Wiser, *Twilight Years,* op. cit.

28. Hansen, op. cit.

29. Wiser, *Twilight Years,* op. cit.

30. Ford, op. cit.

31. Wiser, *Twilight Years,* op. cit.

32. Hansen, op. cit.

33. Recounted in ibid.

34. Morrill Cody, a reporter for the *Tribune* and a writer, was the man who punched him. See Cody with Ford, op. cit.

35. I am including the suicides of writers, artists, and their significant others that occurred both in Montparnasse and elsewhere if the victim was strongly tied to the enclave. Given the previously discussed tendency for many of the artists and writers routinely to spend periods of time traveling outside Paris, one would expect that some suicides

that might still be attributable to distinctive aspects of the Montparnasse community, could still occur elsewhere.

36. See the discussion in Wiser, *Twilight Years,* op. cit.
37. Ford, op. cit., p. 26.
38. Ibid., p. 25.
39. Emile Durkheim, *Suicide,* New York: Free Press, 1951, originally published in 1897. It was in 1910 that Durkheim moved to the Sorbonne, just a couple of miles from Montparnasse. However, there is no reference to Montparnasse in Durkheim's writings, as best as I can tell.

Gays and Lesbians in San Francisco's Castro and Mission Districts

San Francisco is a city in which many alternative lifestyles flourish, often side by side. Of particular interest to us in this chapter are the gay, lesbian, bisexual, and transsexual enclave and subenclaves that have formed in the city. A similar mix is found in other large cities, notably including Los Angeles and New York. However, the largest and institutionally and commercially most complete alternative-lifestyle enclave comprised primarily of gays and lesbians is in the Castro and Mission districts in San Francisco. It may be considered the core of an enclave whose outer boundaries extend into adjacent areas in San Francisco. We begin, therefore, with a brief overview of the city.

A San Francisco Overview

At the northeast edge of the city a number of piers jut into San Francisco Bay. If one started there and began walking toward the center of the city, North Beach would be reached in less than one mile. This area contains a number of bars, restaurants, and theaters, and, as in many other parts of San Francisco, the recreation and entertainment are oriented to diverse tastes. For more than one-half century, until it closed in 1999, the area's best-known attraction was probably Finocchio's, a nightclub that featured female impersonators and live music in three nightly shows. Continuing south and west toward the center of the city, one brushes the outskirts of Nob Hill (discussed in Chapter Two). At the edge of Nob Hill is a concentration of playhouses and theaters hosting both traveling and local productions. Included among them is the Nob Hill Male Show Palace, which offers live male strippers on stage, along with private viewing booths, magazines, and novelties.

In just a few more blocks one reaches Market Street, the major thoroughfare in the central city. It begins near the Bay Bridge, just below North Beach, and runs diagonally south and west. On the south side of Market Street is an area aptly called "South of Market." It was once a warehouse district, but the addition of a large number of bars, nightclubs, restaurants, and discotheques turned South of Market into a center for nightlife. It attracts an extremely diverse clientele: people dressed in conventional business suits and others in outlandish outfits, young and old, gay and straight, laborers and professionals.

In San Francisco's gay community, the South of Market area is often referred to as the "Valley of the Kings" because many of the gay-oriented bars, bookstores, and nightclubs have a highly masculine ("leatherman") emphasis. Commonplace dress includes motorcycle jackets and boots and studded wristbands. The names of many current and former establishments in South of Market have conveyed this macho emphasis: the Stud Bar, the Arena Bar, and Folsom Gulch Adult Books, to name a few. Entertainment in the gay bars and nightclubs has also tended to be congruent with this theme. For example, one bar staged "slave auctions" in which a volunteer was stripped and tied up by men in black masks, and the "slave" was sold for the night to the highest bidder.[1] In recent years, at least one South of Market establishment—the Eagle Tavern—has also featured lesbian leather nights, and the Cherry Bar Lounge is a bar and dance club for women only.

Moving down Market, just to the north is the city's fabled Tenderloin district. The name apparently goes back to the nineteenth century, when police were paid more to patrol this dangerous neighborhood and could therefore afford to buy better cuts of meat. The Tenderloin once served as a transit point for sailors and was home to most of the city's prostitutes, and many still work out of its street corners and cheap hotels. In the 1950s the Tenderloin also contained most of the city's gay bars. It still contains a few, mostly catering to men who cross-dress—transvestites or "drag queens." This fact earned it the nickname "Valley of the Queens" (in contrast to the Valley of the Kings) in local gay circles.[2]

Richard Slezak, who writes about San Francisco's neighborhoods, states that his favorite Tenderloin story occurred one summer evening in 1996. A group had gathered at a hotel for a sex party in which the featured guest was a man who had been paid to dress as a woman for the night. Another man, whom no one in the group knew, saw the gathering and tried to

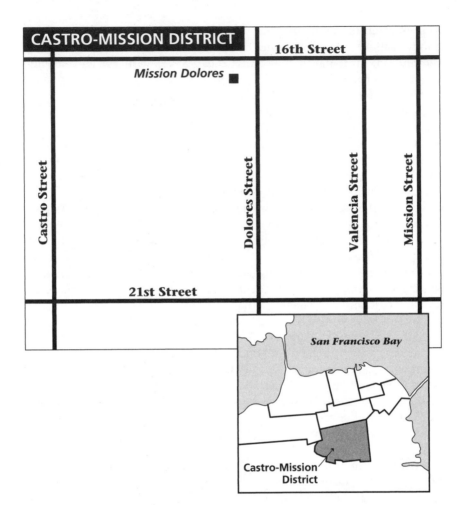

join in, but was told to leave. After threatening to stab everyone with a syringe, the would-be party-crasher ran up to the roof of the hotel, jumped over to the roof of an adjoining bar, then leaped through the skylight to the floor of a restroom. He was fine—but twenty police vehicles and two fire trucks responded, giving the street a surreal look.[3]

At its western edge, along Polk Street, the Tenderloin district blends into an area called "Polk Gulch." It, too, is a seedy area, crowded with drag queens and hustlers, yuppies and alcoholics. Along Polk Street is an assortment of bars and lounges and a store named Good Vibrations that sells erotic books, sex toys, and the like to a mostly female clientele. (We shall describe this local chain of stores when we discuss the lesbian concentration in the Mission district; that is where the chain began.)

Continuing down Market again, just to the north the next neighborhood is Haight-Ashbury. During the 1960s it was the center of the hippie community, which contained a number of gays and lesbians, and some of the Haight's bars became notable hangouts for them. A lesbian bar named Maude's, which opened in 1966 and closed in 1989, later inspired the documentary film *Last Call at Maude's*.[4] This neighborhood still contains a number of gay-oriented bars, such as Aunt Charlie's Lounge.

A little to the south of Haight-Ashbury, where Market, 17th, and Castro intersect is the beginning of the Castro district. As one gets closer to it, there is an increase in the number of six-colored rainbow flags hanging from apartment buildings, bars, and stores. (The multiple colors of the flag stand for the diversity of the alternative-lifestyle community.) Entering the Castro district from Market Street, one arrives at the LGBT (lesbian, gay, bisexual, and transsexual) Center on Market Street near Castro Street. It opened in 2002, providing conference rooms and classrooms for its more than two thousand members and offices for a number of organizations serving the area. The center's programs, "for LGBT people," include counseling, social activities, and community development.

Down Castro Street are bookstores, travel agencies, bars, theaters, professional services, and even religious institutions designed explicitly to serve the gay clientele that predominates in surrounding residential areas. Here the rainbow flags are everywhere; and some pink triangles, first used to label homosexuals in Nazi concentration camps. Unlike centers of nightlife, which may be strongly gay-oriented but remain limited in scope, the Castro is an enclave in every sense of the term. Its residents share an identity that is linked to the place, and that place offers them a full range of *distinctive* commercial and cultural services.

About one mile east of Castro Street, running parallel to it, is Valencia Street in the Mission district. It is a center of retail stores and institutions, many of which serve a lesbian clientele. There are also lesbian residential concentrations surrounding it. The area around Valencia Street has some of the qualities of an enclave but, as we shall later see, it does not hold a lesbian majority and is not as commercially and institutionally complete as the Castro district. However, given the linkages between the gay and lesbian communities, they are probably best regarded as constituting a single enclave, though Valencia Street in the Mission district is the commercial and institutional center of the most fully developed lesbian community in the United States.

Most of this chapter will be devoted to a discussion of the gay and lesbian concentrations in the Castro and Mission districts of San Francisco. To complete the picture, we must note that interspersed among both are smaller numbers of people who are bisexual (i.e., whose sexual partners are both male and female), transsexual (i.e., who have changed, or would like to change, their conventionally defined sex), and transgendered (i.e., who feel that present gender definitions are not adequate to define them). They usually assumed that the Castro or Mission districts would more hospitable to them than their former hometowns, and after gravitating to these communities, they often became parts of the gay-lesbian coalitions.

Neither the Castro nor Mission district began to take its contemporary form until after 1970, but if we want to understand how they emerged in the center of San Francisco and the meaning of these places to the groups who live in them, it will be helpful to begin with a look at some of the effects of World War II on American life. During World War II, San Francisco was a major port for military personnel going to or coming from the Pacific. When service people were periodically labeled homosexual and purged by the military from the Pacific theater, they were usually shipped back to San Francisco. Thousands remained in this city rather than return home in the disgrace of a dishonorable discharge.

When the war ended, thousands of other gay ex-GIs also chose to remain in San Francisco rather than return home to small towns in the Midwest, for example, where life as a gay person now seemed impossible. Many of these veterans who did go home after the war soon returned to the less oppressive climate that they knew from their wartime experience they would find in San Francisco.[5] The war is also credited by many with having created settings in which people were given opportunities to discover their same-sex preferences. Millions of young servicemen and women were living in same-sex quarters in the military, and millions of young civilian women were living in communities from which most of the young men were gone. For some people, the living arrangements imposed by the war merely reinforced their own previously established patterns. For others, however, same-sex living was conducive to experiences that led them to realize that they were sexually interested in people of the same sex.[6] With this discovery, many gays sought out others who were like them, and San Francisco was a magnet to them.

Tearooms and Bars

Before and immediately after the war, gay men were largely limited to seeking each other out in two types of places: tearooms and bars. We will discuss each in turn. Tearooms—that is, *t-rooms*, short for toilet rooms—referred to public facilities used for casual sex between men, and not to refined cafés that served afternoon tea. During the early twentieth century, men discretely looking for male partners often found them in the public bathrooms of city parks or bus or subway stations. Later, with the expansion of interstates, highway rest stops also served as tearooms. For men who were bisexual and desperate to keep their same-sex contacts hidden from family, coworkers, and others, these public facilities became "private sexual spaces."[7] However, for as long as men used tearooms, the police monitored them: spying through holes in the ceiling, planting undercover policemen in the facilities to entrap them, and so on.

The tearooms were used solely for sexual gratification, with minimal social contact between men who were trying to conceal this sexual activity from everyone. Rather than choosing each other, men would typically pair off with whoever was hanging around at the time. The two men would go into a stall together, and if available, a third man (sometimes waiting his turn, sometimes a voyeur) would serve as a lookout. The two participants would complete the sex act as quickly as they could, then rapidly disperse. Specialized bars, by contrast to tearooms, served both men and women and had more varied uses: as places where gay men or lesbians could select each other for sexual purposes and also as places where they could "come out," at least temporarily, as long as they felt they were in a supportive place.

After the war, concentrations of gays and lesbians supported a proliferation of bars primarily catering to specialized clienteles. Before the war in port cities such as San Francisco and New York, gay and lesbian bars had been established but they were not specialized. In New York's Harlem during Prohibition (the 1920s), for example, middle-class gay and lesbian whites and African Americans all mixed in small clubs that featured transvestite floor shows and bootleg liquor.[8] However, with the more concentrated markets that developed after World War II, it became economically feasible for bars to specialize. In fact, competition among bars spurred each to find its own niche by attracting a gay or lesbian clientele with distinctive interests and lifestyles.

An interesting illustration of this specialization process is provided by the lesbian bars of Montreal. The first lesbian-only bar in the city opened in the 1960s. Called Baby Face Disco, it was owned by a tough-acting, short-haired ("butch") lesbian known only as Baby Face, who was also the manager and bouncer. It had a jukebox, a dance floor, and only a few tables, which encouraged people to move around and meet others. Even so, groups of women tended to be segregated within the bar. The (many) women whose behavior deliberately followed the butch and the more passive "femme" roles tended to separate themselves from those women who were not committed to playing these roles.[9] However, the feminist movement of the late 1960s led many lesbians to reject the butch and femme roles, regarding them as imposing patriarchal standards. Other divisions among women became more salient, based on class, age, and ethnicity. In the 1970s, as the city's openly lesbian population increased, entrepreneurs opened new and more specialized establishments. The newer bars reflected a clear class hierarchy, from stylish private clubs with professional memberships to beer and pool halls with working-class patrons. In the 1980s, butch and femme roles reemerged, but as parts of a different social configuration.[10]

Bars have been very significant in gay and lesbian life because they provided the primary settings in which people could find companions and/or sex partners of the same sex. In workplaces or neighborhood stores, people had to work hard to hide this aspect of their lives, which made it very difficult (and risky) for them to find each other. If you were a lesbian and thought another woman was also, you would have to go through "lengthy verbal games, dropping subtle hints . . . waiting for her to pick up your clues before you dared to reveal yourself."[11] The problem was the same, of course, for gay males and they too developed code words to enable them to recognize each other.[12] None of these word games were necessary in a lesbian or gay bar, and prior to the development of gay enclaves, such bars were the only places where people of the same sex could talk, touch, and dance, "cruise" in search of sexual partners, and interact openly. Thus these bars were the one kind of environment that could provide homosexuals with a territorial referent, or sense that a place belonged to them.

Given the centrality of bars to gay and lesbian life, visiting these bars was often an important "coming-out" experience. Going to such a bar meant crossing a symbolic line, translating a private identity into public interaction. One man was thirty-two years old before he took this step, but he remembered it vividly five years later. His first terror, which struck him as he drove to the bar, involved his car. "Oh, my God," he thought, "I hope nobody sees my car because they'll know right where I'm going." He found a place to park across the street from the bar but then just sat there with the car doors locked. To go in, or not to go in, he deliberated. "I just knew there would be somebody in the bar I knew." Finally, after about thirty minutes he ran across the street but, glancing back, he noticed that he had left his car lights on and returned to the car. The anxiety came back, and he sat inside the car again for a while. Eventually, he once again gathered his nerve, walked across the street, and went into the bar.[13] Prior to coming out, many lesbians, bisexuals, transsexuals, and transgendered people describe similar anxieties over having their secret discovered by others, even the people who are closest to them.[14]

Fear of coming out, especially during the decades right after World War II, resulted from people's knowledge of the sanctions they could typically expect, which could include rejection by friends and family, eviction from housing, and termination of employment. There were also the "gay-bashing" forays organized by heterosexual gangs and the routine harassment by police, who periodically raided their bars and arrested patrons.[15] Although gay men and lesbians were tormented in San Francisco during this period, the harassment was probably less severe than in most places. For example, California was one of few states not to prohibit "congregations of homosexuals" in public places. In New York State, by contrast, same-sex touching, dancing, or the like was classified as "degenerate" and punishable by fines or arrest.[16]

The Stonewall Riots

Because of the importance of bars in gays' lives, police intrusion into these bars cut to the heart of their shared social life. However, police raids and bar closings, often based on frivolous grounds, were common. In almost every instance, patrons suffered their indignities quietly. Then came the Stonewall Inn riots, which turned out to be of national symbolic significance to the gay and lesbian movement. The Stonewall Inn was a small bar on Christopher Street in Greenwich Village, New York's closest approximation of Castro Street and the Castro district. The bar served a predominantly male gay clientele, many of whom wore shoes with four-inch heels, gowns, strings of pearls, wigs, and long, painted fingernails. The bar was apparently owned by the Mafia, which found it lucrative not only for selling drinks but for blackmailing patrons.[17]

On June 27, 1969, a small group of police tried to close the Inn. Forced closings were not an unusual occurrence, and patrons had not objected too strongly in the past. The police knew, as one drag queen later put it, that "little fairies never fight back."[18] This time, however, when the police threw the bartender and several "queens" into a paddy wagon, the mood of the crowd suddenly changed. People began to yell and boo. When the police next dragged out a struggling lesbian, bystanders began to throw bottles at the police. Facing the police, the gay men formed a chorus line, kicking and singing "We are the Stonewall girls." They then threatened to rape the policemen, who barricaded themselves inside the Inn. Several demonstrators uprooted a parking meter and used it as a battering ram on the door. The police turned a fire hose on the crowd, which then temporarily dispersed. While the demonstrators were regrouping, several carloads of police reinforcements arrived, and the demonstrators disappeared. However, the next night, when a large police contingent returned to the area around Stonewall, they confronted an army of middle-aged gay men, transvestites, teenage male prostitutes, a few lesbians, and some passersby. There was more bottle-throwing, more marching and singing, and more arrests.

The resolve and defiance of the demonstrators at the Stonewall Inn became a rallying point for gay and lesbian organizations in many U.S. cities. In New York, an umbrella organization declared the anniversary of the street demonstrations to be Christopher Street Liberation Day, which is still celebrated, though it is now part of a Lesbian, Gay, Bisexual, Transgender Pride march through Midtown Manhattan. The men who were (or claim to have been) at the 1969 Stonewall riots formed the Stonewall Veterans Association, one of the groups that continue to march in the parade under their own banners. In the Castro district of San Francisco, the anniversary of the riots is marked by the annual Gay Freedom Day Parade, which attracts hundreds of thousands of people.

The years following the Stonewall riots were characterized by an increase in the number of gays who came out seeking openly gay and lesbian lives and by an increase in the size and strength of organizations pursuing gay (and other alternative-lifestyle) interests in politics, religion, and other institutions. With growing numbers of openly gay people interacting with each other, gay and lesbian cultures emerged, and it became possible to differentiate among homosexuals by their various lifestyles.

Sexuality and Lifestyle

The term *homosexual* is usually applied to people who engage in sexual acts with persons of the same sex. However, within this category, people's intimate relations vary along a number of dimensions: they may or may not exclusively engage in one type of sexual behavior; their liaisons may be secret or known, frequent or sporadic, central to a person's identity or peripheral. To apply the same label (i.e., homosexual) across this entire range of people and relations captures only one quality they share, but it does not address the place of such sexual activity in their lives. Put in other terms, homosexual or bisexual can be viewed as an adjective because it describes some of the (sexual) things a person does; the terms gay and lesbian are often used as nouns because they describe who a person is.[19]

Some writers also believe that the emphasis on sexual conduct in labeling is misplaced. In the view of some lesbians, for example, it is the way they think, feel, and relate to each other that differentiates them from straights; they consider themselves most *like* straights in terms of their sexual behavior.[20] To illustrate further, some men have wives or long-term girlfriends and also have occasional, brief sexual encounters with other men; but they do not consider themselves gay or bisexual—their traditional arrangements with women define who they consider themselves to be.[21]

Gay men and lesbians (and bisexual and transgendered people) for many years lived under an oppressive fear of disclosure that ensured that their social circles remained small, barely visible, and confined largely to furtive sexual contacts. If one goes back to the 1920s, however, at least in sections of New York City, some gay social circles were only half-hidden. Gay men had codes for identifying each other (such as red ties), used certain parks and cafeterias as meeting places, and held large "drag balls" that attracted thousands of participants and voyeurs. It was not until the 1930s, historian George Chauncey argues, that sexual choices and identities came to be viewed in society as rigidly fixed, with little tolerance shown to those who deviated.[22]

In recent years, many states and cities have passed laws extending civil rights protections so that homosexual activity per se cannot be the basis for firing someone from a job, evicting a person from an apartment, or the like. Marriage or marital benefits have also been extended to gay couples. These safeguards and benefits seem more the result of organized political efforts by gays and lesbians than changing attitudes in the general public.[23] However, the minimal rights and protections extended to gays (and sometimes to bisexual and transgendered people) along with post-Stonewall feelings of assertiveness have led to larger and more visible associations. Being a part of one of these groups is frequently very important to people who pay the price for coming out—often rejection by family and former friends. These new relationships replace those that are lost and afford an opportunity for people to play more inclusive gay and lesbian roles.[24]

Not everyone makes this transition, of course. Some continue to hide their sexual orientations and behavior, projecting an exclusively heterosexual social identity. Others do not deny their same-sex preference but regard the sexual dimension as being confined to one part of their lives and are attracted neither to local gay communities nor to gay culture. For example, one man's description of himself as a homosexual stressed his erotic fascination with masculinity. He has thought at length about the kinds of clothing and style that rouse his attraction to another man and has not tried to hide his many and diverse homosexual experiences. However, he does not identify with gay culture and does not feel his attitudes are like those of other men whom he thinks of as gay. His description of them is that they, unlike himself, are "men who live in a gay neighborhood, have gay friends, go to gay bars, and have a kind of specialized ghetto mentality."[25]

In a book about enclaves, we shall of course be primarily focusing on people with gay or lesbian identities, because they are the core of gay and lesbian enclaves. It must also be recognized that even people with highly salient gay or lesbian identities differ from each other in such aspects as race, social class, and religion. They are not of a single social type, but space will not permit us fully to describe the variations.

Gays in the Castro

The Castro district today includes a middle- and upper-middle-class residential neighborhood of apartments in renovated Victorian houses, many of which are pastel-colored. It contains a typical commercial center with a full complement of clothing stores, hairstylists, banks, restaurants, and laundries, and it houses the religious and political institutions that can be found in any community. The only thing out of the ordinary about the area is the fact that most of the residents and store owners are gay—and they are not trying to disguise or camouflage it.

Until the late 1960s, the Castro was a somewhat run-down, Irish, working-class neighborhood. An anomaly was the presence of two gay bars that had opened in the Castro to serve hippies from the nearby Haight-Ashbury district. Many in the traditional working-class Castro community were leaving during the 1960s because the factories in which they had been employed had left the area; most of the local manufacturing jobs moved across the bay to Oakland or left the country entirely. Housing prices fell, attracting young homosexuals who "spilled over" from the Haight. During the 1960s Haight-Ashbury was a center for antiwar counterculture hippies. The heterosexual hippies were relatively tolerant of the gays among them, and the gays were relatively comfortable with the hippies' advocacy of peace, love, and nonconformity. Young gay hippies were initially attracted to the Castro by cheap rents, but as the district's reputation as "a liberated zone" increased, they and nonhippie gays were attracted by its social climate. During the mid-1970s, Castro property values began to rise as an estimated thirty thousand homosexuals from elsewhere in San Francisco and from around the country moved into the district.[26]

The resurgence of a declining neighborhood resulting from an infusion of gays and lesbians is a familiar pattern across the country. It has been repeated in a number of neighborhoods in other cities, such as Seattle's Capital Hill, Houston's Montrose section, Cincinnati's Liberty Hill, and Washington's Dupont Circle, to name just a few. In each case, a community in transition became the destination for gay and lesbian migrants, whose influx increased property values and who became increasingly open in their lifestyles as their numbers increased.

It was a diverse group of men who moved to the Castro during the 1970s. Included in it were gay physicians and psychologists who specialized in treating gay patients; gay lawyers specializing in the types of discrimination and child custody cases experienced by gay men; a gay-owned savings and loan association that did not discriminate against gay applicants; and travel agencies and insurance brokers catering to the distinctive needs of a gay clientele. What they all had in common was a belief that the Castro was their refuge; a place to start life over without having to hide or deny their sexual preference. They also established religious congregations suited to their way of life. For example, the pastors of the Metropolitan Community Church performed gay marriages decades before the legality of such marriages was even debated. The Castro Theater, an old movie palace, nearly closed until it was given a new life by the gay community. In place of mass-market films, it began to show camp classics (e.g., *Rocky Horror Picture Show*) and documentaries of interest to the community; an organist performs before most shows and the audience usually sings or claps along. In short, they built a self-contained gay community.

As the enclave grew during the 1970s, it offered men the freedom to explore new kinds of sexual relationships: some open and communal, some exclusive; some patterned after heterosexual relations and some not. "In the Castro," one resident said, "How you live together is a matter of negotiation."[27] Monogamous pairs could spend their lives together; or, for men who simply wanted as much homosexual sex without commitment as they could find, the Castro offered bathhouses, where any evening a man could pair off anonymously with as many other men as his stamina would allow. There were also numerous bars and even busy streets that were perfect for cruising. To grab another man's body was about as easy as getting a hamburger, which was why Castro residents called it "fast-food sex."[28]

As the gay community grew and linked its identity to the Castro district, it finally had a place to erect "shrines" that captured the collective experiences of gays everywhere. In 2003 near the intersection of Market and Castro Streets, the community dedicated "Pink Triangle Park" in memory of the thousands of gay men and women who were killed over one-half century earlier in the Holocaust. In this regard, the Castro district's place in the life of gays everywhere became comparable to that of more conventional enclaves based upon race or ethnicity, such as Little Havana's meaning to Cuban Americans.

Both as a lifestyle enclave and repository of collective experiences, the Castro district became a national and international tourist attraction. A largely though not exclusively gay clientele from throughout the world was attracted by descriptions of the district in gay publications emanating from the Castro and by the marketing of the San Francisco tourist bureau, which included the exotic Castro as a "must-see" neighborhood for tourists. The increasing number of visitors spurred other developments in the district, such as specialized lodging and sight-seeing. For example, the Parker Guest House in the district describes itself as catering "primarily to the gay and lesbian travel industry,"[29] and a local tour guide operates "Cruisin' the Castro."

The largest influx of visitors to the Castro from the San Francisco metropolitan area is probably on Halloween. The Castro district began publicly celebrating the holiday in the 1970s, when it was essentially a street party, and gay residents informally competed to see who could assemble the most outlandish costume. The revelry and the drinking, along with the spectacle, began to attract suburbanites in the 1990s. Because the Halloween crowds were becoming difficult for police to handle, the city designated the Civic Center Plaza as the "official" site for the city's party. However, it is only a short walk down Market Street from the Civic Center to the Castro district, and the city's comparatively tame event could not compete. By 2002 as many as one-half million persons were estimated to have crowded into the Castro district on Halloween.[30]

Tourists from near and far also supported an extensive array of restaurants and bars, many designed to fill a particular niche. To illustrate, Twin Peaks Tavern, at the corner of Market and Castro, is an upscale bar that attracts well-to-do, elderly men. The large front windows of Twin Peaks made it one of the first gay bars that did not try to hide patrons from the street. Another very popular bars with tourists is Harvey's. On Castro Street near the center of the commercial district, it has a peach-colored exterior and gay memorabilia on its inside walls. Harvey's is named in memory of Harvey Milk, often referred to as the "Mayor" of Castro Street.

"Mayor" Harvey Milk

One of the men who moved to the Castro to find himself in the early 1970s was Harvey Milk. An ex–New Yorker, in 1973 at forty-two years of age he opened a small camera store on Castro Street and moved into an apartment above it. His store was one of the first of the wave of gay-operated stores to move into the then-deteriorated working-class area. He thought the Castro promised an interesting future because of its central location in the city, its charming nineteenth-century Victorians, and its cheap rents.

Over time, Milk's store devoted less space to camera supplies and more to notices, petitions, and brochures. Many of the issues were gay-related and arose as the gay newcomers clashed with the working-class holdovers. For example, the old-line store owners excluded the new gay businessmen from their meetings. In response, Milk helped to organize the gay store owners into a new group, the Castro Village Merchants Association. He was openly gay and advocated gay interests, but his concerns were not limited. He aggressively advocated more funding for public schools, libraries, and public transportation, among other things.[31]

Milk, in sneakers and Levi's with a thick black mustache and long hair in a ponytail, saw himself both as a street person and as the unofficial mayor of Castro Street. At the age of forty-three, for the first time in his life Milk ran for public office. He lost the race for city council because voting was citywide, but he was the top vote-getter in gay areas such as the Castro. He lost several more times before finally being elected as the Castro's city supervisor in 1977. In the course of his campaigns, Milk became a central figure in the neighborhood. He organized business associations and the annual Castro Street Fair; he rallied gay groups to economic and political issues with slogans such as "Gay Buy Gay" and "Gay Vote Gay"; and he forged alliances between the young gays, who were his core constituents, and a variety of other business, civic, and union organizations. As a result of his organizing ability he became an effective legislator, seeing through to passage a bill that he introduced forbidding discrimination against gays in housing and employment in San Francisco.

His legislative career was brief, though. In 1978, Harvey Milk was one of two city supervisors who were shot and killed by a former supervisor. That night an estimated forty thousand people, carrying candles, crying, and singing, marched from the Castro to City Hall.[32] It was the end not only of Harvey Milk, the man, but also of his politics, because the Castro had dramatically changed during the 1970s. By 1978 the transition was largely complete. The Irish working-class families were virtually all gone;

so, too, were the hippies. The interior and exterior of most of the housing had been renovated. Real estate values were doubling every six months, as gay tourists were coming from everywhere in the world to eat in Castro's gay restaurants and shop at its upscale gay men's clothing stores.

However, Harvey Milk's contributions to the Castro district have not been forgotten. He continues to be a topic of discussion in Castro establishments such as Harvey's and at the LGBT Community Center. Twenty-five years after his death, for example, in 2003, the center had a "Remembering Harvey" evening at which guests showed slides from the 1970s and talked about how his life and death had personally impacted them.

HIV-AIDS

It was shortly after Milk's death that rates of HIV-AIDS began to increase dramatically and became a focal issue in the gay community. The number of new HIV infections in San Francisco reached as high as about eight thousand per year, and remained at that high level throughout the 1980s. The number of HIV-infected people who developed AIDS lagged a few years behind, reaching a peak of 3,300 new cases in 1992. The Castro district had the highest HIV and AIDS rates in San Francisco, which in turn had the highest rate of any American city; and almost all of those infected in San Francisco were gay or bisexual men.[33]

As the epidemic spread, leaders of gay organizations looked inside and outside the community for help. The U.S. government was urged to increase funding for HIV research and to speed the process by which new drugs to treat AIDS could be approved, but the government was very slow to respond. Looking to change behavior inside the community, several gay organizations, along with San Francisco public health officials, tried to convince gays to discontinue high-risk sexual practices. The bathhouses of the Castro were an obvious target, but one that divided the community. Engaging in anal intercourse with multiple partners and no condom—typical conduct in the bathhouses—seemed to many public health officials the single best way to spread HIV, and they wanted the bathhouses closed. Some local organizations, such as the Harvey Milk Club, agreed and put out pamphlets warning men about high-risk practices. Other organizations, however, such as the Stonewall Gay Democratic Club, were suspicious of outsiders and were not prepared to give up any of their freedoms. The bath owners fought to remain open, of course, and they were prepared to invest a lot in the battle because the bathhouses in the Castro were a big business, attracting both local gays and tourists.[34]

An important person in the conflict over the baths was Randy Shilts, Harvey Milk's biographer. Shilts, who spent the last dozen years of his life as a reporter for the *San Francisco Chronicle,* was an openly gay activist who began writing about the AIDS peril in the early 1980s. In his stories he was critical of the government, the medical establishment, and some gay organizations for their seeming indifference to the epidemic; and he urged that the baths be closed.[35] As the issue went through the courts in the mid-1980s, the baths were periodically closed and reopened, but the most significant by-product of the struggle was the educational campaign it inspired. Local organizations developed a number of model prevention programs that eventually proved highly effective. By 1993, the number of new AIDS cases in San Francisco dropped by 50 percent, even though the epidemic had not yet peaked in the rest of the nation; and the San Francisco Department of Public Health forecast a continuing decline in the number of new cases.

During the 1990s, however, surveys indicated that high-risk sexual behavior was again increasing, portending future increases in AIDS rates. There were a variety of possible explanations. Perhaps a few years of success had led to unwarranted complacency? Some therapists in the Castro district attributed men's disregard of the risks to depression brought on by so much death and suffering. "Depression is now a community norm," one said in 1993.[36] Another therapist reported that his Castro clients had lost so many loved ones that they fantasized about dying themselves in order to be reunited with them. For some men, AIDS became so interwoven with life in the Castro that they regarded getting the disease as a sign that they belonged. In any case, after declining and then holding steady at about five hundred new infections per year in the mid-1990s, the number of new HIV cases in San Francisco began to increase again in 1997 and was estimated to have reached nearly nine hundred new cases in 2002.[37]

Perhaps the most steadfast ally of the Castro gays in their struggles with AIDS has been the lesbian community of the nearby Mission district. They hosted fund raisers and staffed educational clinics, even though rates of infection among lesbians have been very low.

Lesbians in the Mission District

About one mile to the east of the Castro district is the Mission district. There are no formal boundaries to either, but the area that is generally regarded as enclosed within Mission is substantially larger than Castro.

Across the entire district, Mission is characterized by the large number of murals painted everywhere—on the outside of schools, cafés, garages, and so on. They depict historical figures and events from different cultures and diverse groups' struggles for civil rights. The variations in the content of the murals reflect the variations within the district. It is highly diverse in every respect: economically, culturally, ethnically.

The major thoroughfare near the western edge of the Mission district is Dolores Street, only a few blocks from the center of the Castro district. Along several blocks of Dolores Street is Dolores Park, the largest park in the area, and its diversity mirrors that of the district. Some sections of the park are regularly used by lesbians who live nearby to picnic or walk their dogs. Another part of the park has tennis courts and ball fields—but also drug dealers, and it can be dangerous at night. Finally, in one corner of the park there is a ledge overlooking the city that muscled gays refer to as "Dolores Beach." They often sunbathe there on Sundays, sharing the space with Latino families barbecuing chicken and corn.

Dolores is a hilly street lined with palm trees and old Victorian homes. Valencia Street, the commercial center of the lesbian community, is a few blocks east of Dolores, and several of the streets that run between Dolores and Valencia have been gentrified, containing a mix of old Victorian and modern apartments and condominiums. This is now a mostly upscale area that is home to large numbers of young, professional lesbians living alone, in pairs, or in groups. Other lesbians, who are highly varied racially and socioeconomically, are found throughout the district and in adjoining neighborhoods.

The southern part of the Mission district has a large number of residents with origins in Mexico and Central America. Near the southern edge of the district, 24th Street—often called "El Corazon de la Missione" (the heart of the Mission)—has a concentration of Latino establishments that serve both the local residents and people from across Mission and beyond: Latino art galleries, produce markets, bars, and restaurants. Throughout the year, Latino festivals and processions are also held on this wide, tree-lined street.

Valencia Street, as noted, is the commercial and organizational center for the lesbian community. It is to the lesbian community as Castro Street is to the gay community. Many of the stores offer products and services that anyone might purchase, and their clienteles are, in fact, varied. However, in many of the establishments, a majority of the customers are lesbians, and the products and services are geared to them. On and just off Valencia Street, shops offer "flirty" accessories for "bohemian femmes," sixties-style sweaters and jackets for the "hipster," assorted chain spike jewelry, and so on. The Roxie Theater shows underground films and documentaries of special interest to a lesbian audience. There are lots of bars and restaurants that are local hangouts, such as Blondie's Bar and No Grill and the Elbo Room, a women's dance bar. There is Osento, the women's bathhouse, and a store named Good Vibrations. The latter sells books and magazines of interest to women in general and lesbians in particular, and, as the name implies, an assortment of vibrators and sexual aids. It also includes an antique vibrator museum, with relics going back to the nineteenth century that physicians prescribed for nonorgasmic women.[38]

Valencia and adjacent streets also house a number of bookstores catering to "radical" politics or lifestyles. The historically most significant was The Old Wives' Tales Bookstore. During the early 1970s, when the gay and lesbian enclaves were forming in San Francisco, Carol Seajay left Michigan and headed west because she thought that in San Francisco she would be free to live her life as a lesbian woman. From notices in the women's bathroom of the main library she learned about the Mission district, where she met Paula Wallace. They become lovers and then business partners when they decided to open a feminist/lesbian bookstore. With a loan from the local Feminist Credit Union, they opened Old Wives' Tales on Valencia, just down the street from the women's bathhouse, Osento, and the RoxieTheater. Their bookstore stocked a wide range of specialty books by and about lesbians and greeting cards written in a way that assumes both sender and recipient were women. It also had a bulletin board that became central to the community.[39] It functioned as a kind of "town crier," like Harvey Milk's camera store in the Castro district. Posted on the bulletin board were notices of apartments to rent, services being offered, and organizational meetings—all of which were intended for a lesbian audience. Thinking back on the early days, Carol Seajay smiled at recalling the reluctance of women who had not come out to enter Old Wives' Tales but how it helped to change their lives once they did. She watched some women walk around the block a few times, working up their courage. But "once they made it through the doorway, they . . . changed their lives . . . found new self-images, came out, found sisterhood and community."[40] (After several management changes and competition from a new bookstore, Old Wives' Tales finally closed in 1995.)

The Mission district and the neighborhoods adjoining it offer openly lesbian women the opportunity to associate primarily with others who are the same as them and largely eliminates those who are intolerant of lesbians. This defining feature of the district was captured by a visitor who accompanied two residents of the Mission, Sandy and Jean, on a Saturday night outing. These two women lived together in a condominium just off Valencia Street, and one evening they took their guest to a neighborhood lesbian bar. She saw that downstairs was a narrow bar packed with hundreds of women, mostly single and looking to connect, and a few couples out to celebrate. Upstairs was a dance floor where women, mostly wearing sneakers and jeans, were dancing with each other. The three of them watched for a time, then left. Walking back down Valencia Street, Sandy grabbed Jean's hand and held it aloft. "This is what it's all about!" Sandy cried. "We can walk . . . like this."[41]

Olivia is a commercial company that has served and benefited from lesbians' desires to be more open about their relationships without fear of reprisal from disapproving outsiders. Located in Emeryville, just over the Bay Bridge from San Francisco, Olivia is the largest travel organization specializing in lesbian travel. For special bookings, Olivia puts together an entire cruise ship or resort for lesbians-only vacations. Its chartered ships offer honeymoons Olivia-style, with lesbian film festivals. Travel with Olivia is unique, the company stresses, because "you will truly feel free every minute."[42] In recent years, like most other companies with a once-distinctive gay or lesbian clientele, Olivia has broadened its service market, booking cruises and resorts exclusively for gay male travelers.

The largest of the nonprofit organizations serving the lesbian community also tend to be near but outside the Mission district in the previously described LGBT Center on Market and Castro. Particularly noteworthy is the Bay Area Career Women (BACW). It began in 1980 and, like a number of other organizations, moved into the center when it opened in 2002. BACW is dedicated to promoting business networking among lesbians and recognizing their accomplishments. With a couple of thousand members, it is the largest organization of its kind. BACW hosts a "Thank God It's Friday" get-together on the second Friday of each month, often at a gay bar in the Castro. The largest event it sponsors is an annual dinner-and-dance benefit to acknowledge the most important contributions by lesbians to the lesbian community. In recent years, BACW has also become somewhat more inclusive, describing itself as for lesbians but recognizing the contributions of lesbians to gay, bisexual, and transgendered people as well.

Illustrative of the organizational-institutional links between the Castro and Mission districts is Congregation Sha'ar Zahav. It is a small Reform synagogue established in 1977 and located on Dolores Street, at the eastern edge of the Castro district and therefore close to Mission as well. The congregation aims to serve Jewish people of all sexual identities. When writer Neil Miller visited it on a Friday night, it was filled mostly with men wearing skullcaps, or yarmulkes. Shortly after the service began, the rabbi asked two women to come to the pulpit. He removed his prayer shawl and, with the help of a few others, held it over them. He was going to marry the two women the following week, and this was the traditional prenuptial blessing. The congregants chanted a phrase believed to provide good luck to newly married people and threw candy at the couple, who kissed and returned to their seats. Then the regular Friday night service continued. (When a rabbi is going to marry a Jewish man and woman, an identical service occurs in most congregations.)

In conclusion, to some degree the lesbian concentration in the Mission district fits the definitional requirements of an enclave. There is a concentrated number of people in a residential area who share a distinctive quality. They feel attached to this area, and it houses specialized stores and institutions that serve the group. However, in other important respects it is not a complete enclave. One ordinarily assumes that people who share a distinctive quality will predominate in any area that is considered their enclave, but only a minority of the residents in the Mission (and adjoining areas) are lesbians, even though they do predominate in a few subareas. In addition, many of the organizations and institutions that are most integral to their distinctive community are located outside the Mission, in the Castro district in particular. Finally, lesbians' identification with the Mission district is also blunted by the entire city's openness to alternative lifestyles. Thus to some degree they (as well as many gays) may identify as much with the city of San Francisco as with their specific place of residence.[43]

One might also think of a single lesbian-gay (and bisexual and transgendered) enclave centered in the Castro-Mission districts, with two separate residential concentrations and links throughout the inner city of San Francisco. This one enclave conception is supported by the fact that various lifestyle groups are finding themselves increasingly comfortable under the same label—for example, LGBT people or those who identify as queers. In addition, they tend to march in the same parades, shop in each other's stores, and support the same candidates for public office.

Notes

1. Frances FitzGerald, *Cities on a Hill,* New York: Simon & Schuster, 1986, p. 33.
2. Ibid., p. 32.
3. Richard A. Slezak. Formerly wrote about San Francisco neighborhoods in an Internet forum that closed in 2003.

4. The proprietor of Maude's, Rikki Streicher, was also the creator of the Federation of Gay Games. See her obituary, *New York Times*, August 24, 1994.

5. John D'Emilio, *Sexual Politics, Sexual Communities*, Chicago: University of Chicago Press, 1983.

6. Allan Berube, "Marching to a Different Drummer," in Martin Duberman, et al. (Eds.), *Hidden from History*, New York: Meridian, 1989.

7. For further discussion, see the papers in William L. Leap (Ed.), *Public Sex/Gay Space*, New York: Columbia University Press, 1999.

8. Lillian Faderman, *Odd Girls and Twilight Lovers*, New York: Columbia University Press, 1991.

9. Line Chamberland, "Remembering Lesbian Bars: Montreal, 1955–1975," *Journal of Homosexuality* 25, 1993. For a discussion of similar types of specialization in other lesbian bars during this period, see Elizabeth L. Kennedy and Madeline D. Davis, *Boots of Leather, Slippers of Gold*, New York: Routledge, Chapman and Hall, 1993.

10. Heidi M. Levitt, Elisabeth A. Gerrish, and Katherine R. Hiestand, "The Misunderstood Gender," *Sex Roles: A Journal of Research* 48, 2003.

11. Faderman, op. cit., p. 163.

12. William L. Leap, *Word's Out*, Minneapolis: University of Minnesota Press, 1996.

13. Frederick R. Lynch, "Nonghetto Gays," in Gilbert Herdt (Ed.), *Gay Culture in America*, Boston: Beacon Press, 1992, p. 174.

14. See, e.g., the autobiographical comments of a transsexual in Donna Rose, *Wrapped In Blue*, Round Rock, TX: Living Legacy Press, 2003.

15. I do not mean to imply that violence or discrimination against gays was confined to the postwar period. These hate crimes obviously continue.

16. Warren J. Blumenfeld and Diane Raymond, *Looking at Gay and Lesbian Life*, Boston: Beacon Press, 1988.

17. For a detailed description of the Inn and of the actual riots, see David Carter, *Stonewall*, New York: St. Martin's, 2004.

18. Quoted in *New York Times*, June 23, 1994, p. 1.

19. Michael Denneny, "Gay Politics," in Denneny, et al. (Eds.), *The Christopher Street Reader*, New York: Coward-McCann, 1983. See also Stephen O. Murray, "Components of Gay Community in San Francisco," in Herdt, op. cit.

20. This argument is explored in several interviews and personal essays included in Lily Burana, et al. (Eds.), *Dagger: On Butch Women*, Pittsburgh: Cleis Press, 1994.

21. See the analysis of black men who engage in bisexual relations but do not acknowledge them even to themselves. J. L. King, *On the Down Low*, New York: Broadway Books, 2004.

22. George Chauncey, *Gay New York*, New York: Basic Books, 1994.

23. Armstrong argues that by the 1970s gays in San Francisco had recognized that they could not change society, so they concentrated their organized efforts on affirming gay identities and securing gay rights. Elizabeth A. Armstrong, *Forging Gay Identities*, Chicago: University of Chicago Press, 2002.

24. Margaret Cruikshank, *The Gay and Lesbian Liberation Movement*, London: Routledge, 1992.

25. George Stambolian, "Interview with a Fetishist," in Denneny et al., op. cit., p. 160.

26. FitzGerald, op. cit.

27. Ibid., p. 55.

28. Andrew Holleran, "Fast-Food Sex," in Denneny et al., op. cit., p. 71.

29. See http://www.parkerguesthouse.com.

30. Because of public drunkenness and several stabbings, police planned to impose crowd controls on future Halloweens. Rachel Gordon, "S.F. may rein in Castro Halloween Bash," *San Francisco Chronicle*, June 9, 2003, p. B1.

31. This description of Milk is based on Randy Shilts, *The Mayor of Castro Street*, New York: St. Martin's, 1982.

32. When Milk's assassin was convicted only of manslaughter, there was serious rioting in the Castro and open fighting between gays and police. One consequence was the San Francisco Police Department's recruitment of gay officers, most of whom were assigned to the Castro. See Neil Miller, *In Search of Gay America*, New York: Atlantic Monthly Press, 1989.

33. Yearly figures for San Francisco are provided by the San Francisco Department of Public Health. Consider the following 1993 comparisons: in San Francisco there were 280 cases of AIDS per 100,000 people; in New York City there were 155; in Youngstown, Ohio, 5. All of the preceding figures are from *New York Times*, February 16, 1994, p. A10.

34. FitzGerald, op. cit.

35. His best-selling book on the slow response to AIDS, *And the Band Played On*, New York: St. Martin's Press, 1987, was nominated for a National Book Award and made into a 1993 movie. Ironically, Shilts tested positive for the HIV virus on the day he completed this book, and he died in 1994.

36. Quoted in *New York Times*, December 11, 1993, p. 10.

37. San Francisco Department of Public Health, *HIV/AIDS Epidemiology Annual Report*, San Francisco, 2002.

38. The shop's founder has compiled a guide to vibrators; see Joani Blank, *Good Vibrations*, San Francisco: Down There Press, 2000.

39. Martha B. Barrett, *Invisible Lives,* New York: Harper & Row, 1990.
40. Estelle B. Freedman, *No Turning Back,* New York: Ballantine, 2003, p 306.
41. Barrett, op. cit., p. 82.
42. Safety and freedom have been important issues to lesbians and gays because of periodic incidents of violence against them on conventional cruise ships. For more information about Olivia see: http://www.olivia. com.
43. The strongest argument for the existence of a more or less self-contained lesbian enclave with recognizable boundaries in San Francisco was presented by Deborah G. Wolf, *The Lesbian Community,* Berkeley: University of California Press, 1979. However, she focused primarily on one group of feminist lesbians, who would not constitute an enclave by our definition. Most authors conclude, as we have, that a true lesbian enclave/community does not exist in San Francisco. See, e.g., Ellen Lewin, *Lesbian Mother,* Ithaca, NY: Cornell University Press, 1993.

Hasidic Jews in Brooklyn

The Hasidic movement began in the Ukraine in the middle of the eighteenth century and grew to comprise over a million followers in Russia, Poland, and Hungary. The growth in the number of adherents was reversed by the Holocaust, in which most of the Hasidim perished. At the end of World War II, most of those who survived the Holocaust immigrated to Israel or to English-speaking nations: the United States, Canada, England, and Australia. Of those who came to the United States, most resettled in Brooklyn, New York. In fact, of the approximately 200,000 Hasidim in the United States, over 80 percent live in Brooklyn.

To outsiders, what is initially the most conspicuous feature of the Hasidim ("the pious ones") is their appearance. There are some variations among sects, but all women must for modesty's sake cover their bodies, which means heavy stockings and dresses (typically dark in color) that have long sleeves and high collars. Their heads, with hair cut short after marriage, must be covered with kerchiefs or wigs. This prescription has led to a large number of wig stores in their Brooklyn enclaves. Wigs made of human hair imported from India can cost over $1,000 but are particularly prized because the women think they look better and last longer. Their lives were thrown into turmoil, however, when a group of Israeli rabbis ruled that they could not wear wigs from India if the person whose hair was used had been in Hindu religious ceremonies. Who knew anything about the person whose hair it used to be? Most of the Hasidic women reluctantly put their wigs aside and hoped they would eventually be considered acceptable. "Otherwise," one woman complained, "you put a thousand dollars in the garbage."[1]

The Hasidic men have full beards and ear-ringlet locks of hair, and they usually wear long black coats and black hats with wide brims and high crowns. There is a similarity in dress between the Hasidim and the Amish, and both groups emphasize tradition, piety, and separation from the larger society, though most of the Amish live in rural areas. Their clothing clearly

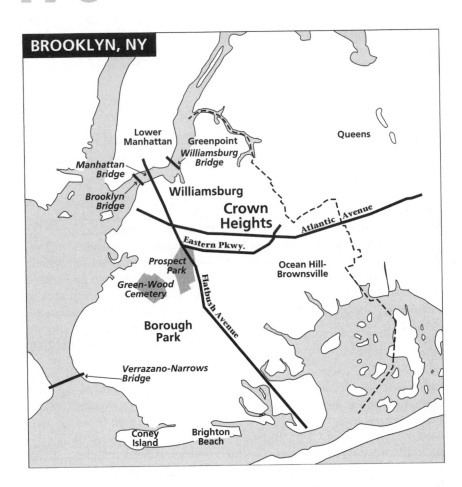

sets them apart and it is intended to do so. The Hasidim are vehemently opposed to assimilation. Most do not own television sets and in fact many do not even speak English.[2]

The Brooklyn Neighborhoods

In Brooklyn today there are three distinct Hasidic enclaves. Each contains a different mix of Hasidic sects, but there are overriding similarities among all of them. This chapter will focus primarily on the Lubavitch in Crown

Heights. (Their name comes from the Russian city of Lubavitch, where they were first organized.) We begin, however, with a brief overview of the three Brooklyn neighborhoods with Hasidic concentrations: Williamsburg, Crown Heights, and Borough, or Boro, Park.

Williamsburg is located at the northern edge of Brooklyn, just across the Williamsburg Bridge from Manhattan's Lower East Side. It is a community crowded with old brownstones, apartment buildings converted from factories, and a few high-rise housing projects. Large numbers of Orthodox but non-Hasidic Jews lived in Williamsburg as early as the 1920s. Most left during the middle of the century, when there was an influx of both Puerto Ricans and Hasidic Jews. The Hasidic community, now estimated at about 45,000, dominates the southwest section of Williamsburg. It is served by family-owned stores that sell food, clothing, and books. Located here are the religious facilities of the Satmar (originally from Satu Mar in Hungary), the largest sect, and those of several smaller sects. There is also a variety of clinics, physicians, and psychiatrists that cater to the distinctive needs of the Hasidic population.

Crown Heights is located in the center of Brooklyn about three miles south of Williamsburg. It is densely settled, with three-story brick buildings and two-story town houses, some of which are well preserved, some of which are in run-down condition. Of the approximately fifteen thousand Hasidim in Crown Heights, about ten thousand are Lubavitch. The center of their Brooklyn enclave is their world headquarters on Eastern Parkway, an imposing red-brick building with bars over its windows for protection. In terms of population, the Hasidim are dwarfed by the estimated 160,000 black residents of Crown Heights, who are both African American and West Indian. Despite their vast differences in lifestyle, food, and dress, many live on the same streets in Crown Heights, sometimes in the same apartment buildings. However, the Hasidim maintain their distance, and relations between them and their neighbors are frequently strained.

Borough Park is the third enclave, located in the southwest corner of Brooklyn about four miles from Crown Heights. It contains two-story apartment buildings, high-rise dwellings with terraces overlooking the Manhattan skyline, and some hundred-year-old mansions that have been converted to apartments. The principal commercial street in Borough Park, 13th Avenue, houses a large assortment of relatively new restaurants, candy stores, and bookstores. Few Hasidic families lived in this neighborhood until the mid-1960s, when there were sizeable migrations from Williamsburg and to a lesser extent from Crown Heights. The largest sect in Borough Park is Bobover (from Bobova, Poland), with over fifty thousand adherents.

Some of the Hasidim who moved there were attracted to Borough Park's better housing, others feared rising crime rates in their former neighborhoods, and still others merely wanted to remain close to family members who were moving. Ties between members of the same sects in different communities remained close; for example, Satmar instituted a private bus service for its members between Williamsburg and Borough Park. However, Borough Park is seen by many Hasidim as offering shopping and restaurants that are too upscale; and it is sometimes criticized for providing too modern and too secular an environment. One Williamsburg resident said he would not want to live in Borough Park because, "over there . . . you have more women driving cars . . . over there you hear kids speaking English."[3]

Hasidic Religious Views

The founders of the Hasidic movement attempted to reach out to the masses of Jews with a nonintellectual message that stressed the importance of simple devotion in leading to spiritual elevation. They were charismatic leaders, who extolled prayer, song, and comradeship. Each major Hasidic figure continues to be widely regarded by his followers as very special: a genius, a person capable of miracles and prophecies. His powers, most believe, might be able to hasten the coming of the long-awaited Messiah, who will be sent by God to provide righteousness and redemption. Perhaps their rebbe might even be ultimately revealed to be that Messiah. More conventional, mainstream rabbinical leaders tend to be highly critical of the strong mystical element in Hasidic beliefs and opposed to what they consider to be Hasidic personality cults that offer false messianic visions.[4]

A majority of non-Hasidic Jews see the dress and customs of the Hasidim as strange anomalies in modern times. Some privately view the Hasidim as "ethnic embarrassments." However, giving public voice to these sentiments can provoke rebukes. For example, the executive director of the American-Israel Public Affairs Committee, a non-Hasidic Jew, described the Hasidim as "smelly" and "low class" with a "poor immigrant image," and he said he was pleased never to have been to their Brooklyn enclaves.[5] When both secular and fundamentalist Jews besieged the board with complaints in response, he was forced to resign.

The Hasidim's lives are circumscribed by 613 *mitzvot*—commandments that they share with all Jews, but they are more zealous in their compliance. Examples include observing the Sabbath, giving to charity, and eating only kosher food. Unlike other Jews, however, they believe that failure to observe the *mitzvot* can literally cause catastrophe for the negligent individual or the entire community. Furthermore, to be a Hasid entails zealously going beyond the letter of the law, as their observation of the Sabbath illustrates. The Hebrew Sabbath extends from just before sundown on Friday to just after sundown on Saturday. Observance requires ritual lighting of candles, special prayers, and prohibitions on activities such as working, traveling in vehicles, turning anything on or off, and carrying objects. Hasidic compliance is so literal and precise that they will not take jobs whose hours might ever conflict with observance of the Sabbath. They do not consider this much of a sacrifice; quality of life for Hasidim does not depend on material possessions.

By mid-afternoon on Friday the streets of Crown Heights are filled with men in black suits and hats hurrying to prayer services at the Lubavitch synagogue. The places where they are employed in large numbers, such as the 47th Street diamond exchange in Manhattan, appear deserted. During other parts of the week, Hasidim can regularly be seen moving briskly between stores and offices in the diamond exchange carrying black sample cases. By 3 P.M. on Friday afternoons, however, the streets are nearly empty, as the Hasidim make certain their travel is complete before sundown, when the Sabbath begins. At the same time, women with baby carriages and arms full of grocery bags are hurrying home to prepare the Sabbath dinner. Young girls help their mothers in the kitchen, and young boys tape the light switches in the house to make sure none are accidentally pushed on or off.[6]

In addition to differences in degrees of observance, Hasidim have also been separated from most American Jews by the former's lack of support for Israel. The Hasidic emphasis on the coming of the Messiah has led many of them to take an antagonistic attitude toward the State of Israel, in marked contrast to non-Hasidic Jews, who tend to be extremely supportive of Israel as a Jewish but secular state. Some Hasidic groups believe that the Holy Land should be restored to Jews only by the Messiah. The Zionist movement, in their view, preempts God's role and, by violating the Messianic prophecy, may actually delay redemption. The Orthodox Union, a religious Zionist organization, has identified the Satmar sect as particularly anti-Israel and, they claim, pro-Palestinian. In retaliation, the Orthodox Union called for a boycott of all food products certified kosher by Satmar rabbis.[7] Some Hasidic groups might be prepared to accept the establishment of the State of Israel as signaling the beginning of redemption were it not for the fact that it is a secular society that has sometimes permitted bus service on the Sabbath, archaeological digs in ancient grave sites, secular schools, and so on.[8]

In addition to the emphasis on the Messiah, a central Hasidic conception, according to philosopher Mordechai Rotenberg, entails the distinction between form and matter and a belief that they are integrally related. This dichotomy applies to several referents, one of which involves types of people. The "people of form" are the scholars, the moral leaders, who bestow spirituality upon the community. They require support from the "people of matter," who provide for the material needs of the collectivity. The survival and salvation of the entire community is believed to require the interconnectedness of its body (matter) and soul (form).

The distinction between form and matter and their necessary interconnectedness also pertains to psychological states within people, namely their spiritual and material selves. The individual seeks a state of redemption, they believe, by combining community and material attachments with individual spiritual meditation. For example, to feel real spiritual joy, singing and dancing are considered helpful in "warming up" the material body and in spreading a feeling of elation among participants. Through the interconnectedness of form and matter, each individual hopes to ascend spiritually to a higher level of self-realization in which he may know God more fully. In this process the Hasid is admonished to "put himself as one who is not . . . in this world."[9] The founder of the Hasidic movement is described as having trembled during prayers when he was inspired, his face burning like a torch, eyes bulging and fixed like a person in the throes of death.

The Rebbes

Each community of Hasidic Jews, from as few as one hundred families to more than five thousand families, has historically been tied to a particular place in which their leader, a rebbe, establishes his "court." If the membership grows too large, new residential communities can form, but they usually remain tied to the same rebbe. The rebbe is the ultimate authority on both secular and religious matters. A Hasidic rabbi, by contrast, is an expert in ritual law who decides what behavior can be permitted under varying conditions. The rabbi also officiates at weddings and funerals and periodically addresses the congregation. He may be held in high regard, but a Hasidic rabbi is not presumed to possess the spiritual power or mystical insights of a rebbe.

At least once a year all the followers of a rebbe will come to seek his blessing. Those who live close by may see him regularly. For example, every

Sunday morning at his Crown Heights residence, Rebbe Schneerson individually greeted thousands of his Lubavitch followers. They filed past him, and to each one he gave a crisp dollar bill and a blessing. The dollar was to encourage them to give to charity. Followers also seek the aid of their rebbe with "petitions" that present problems they are facing, such as a sick child or loss of a job. Most petitioners are men. Although a woman may speak to the rebbe, he will not shake her hand or look directly at her. She is expected to stand to the side of her husband, and he, as head of the family, faces the rebbe directly.

The rebbe may respond to a petitioner by simply giving some general assurance and offering a blessing. However, the petition gives the name of the follower's mother so that the rebbe can trace the lineage of the petitioner's soul and pray for resolution at the root of the problem. Because the prayers of rebbes are believed to fly upward unimpeded, they can intercede on behalf of their followers in Heavenly Court. Even when the assistance of a physician or other secular specialist is recommended by the rebbe for a specific problem, the prayers of the rebbe are still always considered to be necessary and of maximum importance.[10]

Allegiance to a particular rebbe is traditionally passed on within a family, but some especially charismatic rebbes attract new members. Many of the rebbes have international followings with branches in a number of countries. In the outskirts of Tel Aviv, for example, a group of Israeli Lubavitch in 1990 built an exact replica of their world headquarters in Crown Heights. It even includes the Brooklyn address—770 Eastern Parkway—in large letters over the front door. A rebbe's court on any given day may have an international constituency, even though everyone looks the same, dressed in the garb of that particular sect. The rebbe is therefore in a position somewhat like the chief executive of a multinational corporation, having to make such global decisions as whether a new school should be built in Montreal or in Philadelphia. In addition, because most marriages occur within the sect, rebbes face additional questions not confronted by chief executives, such as: Should the newly married couple reside in the bride's or the groom's country? What would be best for the sect? What would be best for the families?[11]

The importance of a rebbe to his followers is indicated by the reactions of the Lubavitchers when Rebbe Schneerson became critically ill and then died in the spring of 1994. He suffered a stroke and heart attack in March and was brought to a New York hospital. A dozen young men and their teachers convened daily in the hospital's chapel, splitting their days between a vigil for the rebbe's health and continuing their schoolwork. (Their studies were largely devoted to the rebbe's writings.) Thousands of his followers held rallies in a nearby park and Sabbath services in the hospital's auditorium. For weeks, the fragile ninety-two-year-old rebbe grew steadily weaker, but they continued to expect him to make a miraculous recovery.

Despite their faith and prayers, he died in May. Lubavitchers from Canada, Europe, and Israel immediately chartered planes and flew to New York for his funeral. His coffin was carried out of their Crown Heights headquarters by twenty men as an estimated twelve thousand grief-stricken people watched. Women wailed and hugged each other. Men prayed and cried and pushed over police barricades in an effort to touch his coffin. Many regarded him as their personal spiritual mentor and felt "orphaned" by his death. Weeks after he was buried, thousands continued to leave notes for the rebbe on his grave. Some of the Lubavitch faithful had long been sure that Rebbe Schneerson was God's messenger, the Messiah, and he had only mildly discouraged this belief. "We are certain he will . . . be resurrected," claimed the rabbi who headed the Lubavitch Youth Organization. Now that he is "out of the body," claimed another Lubavitch rabbi, there are "no more limitations" on what he may accomplish.[12]

On Friday nights nearly ten years after his death, groups of Lubavitchers continued to congregate in the basement of 770 Eastern Parkway and pray for their departed rebbe. In the basement, with its peeling paint and dirty linoleum floors, twenty to twenty-five men danced hypnotically in a circle. They chanted for Schneerson, "may he live forever." They meant it as a statement of faith that he will soon arise.[13] The fact that ten years later he was still not resurrected did not seem to disillusion most of his followers. Some believed that he was in another realm, still watching out for them. Others claimed that when the world was ready, he would return and prove to be the Messiah. The Hasidim reacted like other devout religious groups have customarily responded when their prophecies seem not to be confirmed. Adherents typically offer interpretations rearranging events to explain away any appearance of a contradiction. As a result, their faith is left intact or actually strengthened by the "failed" prophecy.[14]

Faith sustained the older Lubavitchers, but a lot of the younger ones found it increasingly difficult to regard Schneerson as the Messiah or to remain confident of his resurrection. Baruch Thaler, raised in Crown Heights, was twenty-five years old when Schneerson died. He was a promising Lubavitch student and part of the crowd outside of 770 when the rebbe's coffin was brought out—with his physical body presumably departed. But Thaler reached his hands under the coffin and felt the dead rebbe's weight. "Physical-touch confirmation," he called it, and began to argue with his still-believing parents. Shortly after he moved out and left the Hasidic life behind. Malkie Schwartz was twelve when the rebbe died.

She remembered lining up on Sundays to get his blessing and dollar bill. For many years after his death she yearned for him, then had doubts that led to arguments with her parents. She finally felt resentment toward the deceased rebbe. How could he not realize where encouraging people to believe he was the Messiah would lead, she wondered? What was he thinking? She also left Crown Heights.[15]

Ten years after his death, the Lubavitchers had still not replaced Rebbe Schneerson. He had no children, hence no heir to succeed him. A committee of senior rabbis oversees the Lubavitch movement. Its spokesmen insist that Schneerson will continue to be their rebbe until the Messiah comes, and his followers flock to his grave in Queens. Visitors from around the world, in buses and in cars, make pilgrimages to his graveside, where they claim they can still feel his presence hovering above his grave. The Queens cemetery in which Schneerson is buried is in a predominantly black, non-Jewish neighborhood, and the influx of Hasidic visitors has sometimes felt like an invasion to the residents. Some resented the intrusions of men in black fedoras and women in long dresses, but most of the people in the neighborhood were more perplexed than angry. One elderly resident said she did not understand what they were doing at the rebbe's grave. "Maybe they are waiting for him to rise," she guessed, then concluded, "I think they're going to have a long wait."[16]

A Rebbe's Court

The principal structures of a rebbe's court consist of his home, where he accepts visitors, the synagogue and *yeshiva* (school); and the *mikvah* (ritual bath). There may also be other facilities, such as a library, summer camp, or neighborhood property; and any or all of these structures and facilities can be collectively owned by the community or held in the name of the rebbe. Schneerson, for example, owned everything and, when he died, left all to the Lubavitch council.

The Yeshiva

A central part of every Hasidic community is one or more yeshivas, or schools. The Hasidim, who do not practice birth control, often have extremely large families, forcing communities to continuously add yeshivas unless some of the membership moves to another neighborhood. The study halls of large yeshivas are also used by members for services, thereby serving as synagogues.

Hasidic males and females are always kept separate, and school is no exception. Girls have traditionally received a limited religious and secular education in the community's girls' school, consistent with the domestic role that is expected to dominate their lives as adults. More recently, some sects have enlarged the educational opportunities they offer to women. Postsecondary training is now offered to young Bobover women in Borough Park, for example. Correspondingly, there has been some expansion in the kind of work considered appropriate for Bobover women, and within the community they have found work as teachers in the sect's nursery school and kindergarten.[17]

Larger yeshivas have long encompassed diverse educational levels for boys, and the most able young men continue their studies in a Talmudic college. From the high school level on, boys begin fourteen-hour school days at 7:30 A.M., with breaks for meals and recreation. For part of a typical day, the boys attend lectures. However, most of their time is spent reading and discussing traditional religious laws and their interpretations, as well as Hasidic philosophy. Younger and older students study and discuss the material together and with the teachers and rabbis who work with them. Because the different groupings of students share close quarters and their discussions tend to be animated, the yeshiva atmosphere is frequently tumultuous. Secular and religious study are combined, the mix of each varying by sect, but preparation for a religious life as a Hasidic Jew is always emphasized.

Prayers are recited three times daily—four times on Sabbath and festivals. During prayers, students concentrate and pray with reverence for themselves, their families, and the entire nation. Books in hands, they repeatedly bend over, then straighten, their heads and bodies bobbing and swaying. These ritual movements have recently been associated with the extremely high incidence of myopia among advanced yeshiva students. The continual change of focus as their eyes move closer and farther from the books they hold while they bend and straighten during prayers is the apparent reason that many of them end up wearing glasses.[18]

Learning is highly revered among the Hasidim. A boy's quality as a student is an important factor in determining his status in the community. If he is an accomplished student, that highly desirable quality will be emphasized, for example, by the matchmaker who seeks his future bride. In fact, many newly married Hasidic women who work outside the home do so primarily to permit their husbands to devote themselves full-time to continuing their (nonvocational) religious training.

A boy's education is almost always carried out within the yeshiva of his family's rebbe's court. This helps to maintain the closed boundaries of the community and facilitates the boy's transition from school to community. Occasionally, however, an especially inspiring rabbi or rebbe may attract students from a different court. The problems created by such "conversions" are profound. Within what community will a marriage be arranged? And symbolically, sons are dramatically separated from their parents if they do not follow the traditional allegiances of the family. To change yeshivas can even be viewed as failing to honor one's father and mother, thereby violating a commandment, and some parents respond by holding funeral rites for their apostate sons, permanently ending all contact with them.[19]

The Mikvah

A mikvah is a ritual bath that resembles a very small indoor pool. It is usually located in a nondescript building that contains dressing rooms and the bath itself. Immersion in the lukewarm water is considered generally beneficial, uplifting one's spirits, relieving muscular pains, sometimes even enabling cripples to walk again. An immersion is highly recommended for men prior to certain holidays and is one of a handful of rituals that is absolutely prescribed for women every month in conjunction with their menstrual cycles.

A woman is considered unclean for the length of her menstrual period and at least seven days thereafter. She remains in this state until she immerses herself in the mikvah. Every month, for this twelve-day (or longer) interval, any type of sexual relations between husband and wife are strictly prohibited. The ban even extends to actions that could arouse sexual desire; for example, sleeping in the same bed. (Sexual relations between unmarried persons are never permitted. An unrelated man and woman are not even allowed to be alone together in the same room.)[20]

After her period is over, a typical Hasidic woman walks to the mikvah and enters an outer room, in which she waits with other women. When it is her turn, she is taken by an attendant to a private room, where she very carefully and thoroughly bathes her entire body, even using cotton swabs for difficult-to-reach places. When she has finished, she puts on a white robe and presses a buzzer. An attendant comes to escort her to the bath. There she removes the robe and descends into the water. With feet apart and eyes open she slowly crouches until her body is completely immersed. Then, standing, she covers her head with a small white towel, recites a prayer in Hebrew, and immerses herself twice more. The attendant then helps her out of the bath, and she returns to her dressing room.

Observing the extended menstrual ban and the ritual cleansing is viewed by the Hasidim as enabling a married couple to strengthen the nonsexual bonds that should tie them to each other along with sexual bonds. A balance between the two types of attachment is valued by the Hasidim, who believe that if the balance is upset, unborn children can be adversely affected. For example, one Hasidic woman mentioned the retarded child of a local couple and noted that his birth had "raised suspicions" about the parents in the community.[21]

Although immersion is not rigidly prescribed for Hasidic men, many believe it fosters unity among them and elevates a participant's level of spirituality during prayer. The Hasidic movement's founding rebbe said that regular immersion may be even better for spirituality than a day of fasting—and fasting is highly valued. And one of his disciples said that a person who immerses himself in the morning will be seen by God as equivalent to a person who has fasted for the day.[22]

Outreach Programs

In most sects, the rebbe's courts are insular, almost exclusively oriented toward serving their own members. The Lubavitch, however, through the Chabad movement, have actively tried to promote religious orthodoxy among nonobservant Jews and sometimes have also tried to entice them (and non-Jews) to join Lubavitch communities. In the more than forty years he served as rebbe, Schneerson instructed his followers that they were charged with loving their fellow Jews, even the rebellious ones. Helping these nonreligious Jews adopt an observant lifestyle, he said, was their mission, and their success would hasten the coming of the Messiah. Groups of bearded young Lubavitch men, often wearing conventional business suits, spread out across New York from the Crown Heights headquarters. Many were college students at the Lubavitch yeshiva, and Rebbe Schneerson viewed them also as soldiers in a military-type campaign. For example, they were driven to neighborhoods with large Jewish populations in order to proselytize in vans called "mitzvah tanks against assimilation."[23]

One Russian-Jewish immigrant, who had not practiced Judaism in Russia, returned to his New York home one evening and announced with a grin that he had a bar mitzvah that day. "Right on Fifth Avenue. Seriously! Really! Right in the middle of Manhattan on its most famous street!"[24] He had simply been walking down the street when he passed by a group of

Lubavitchers standing in front of their van. "Excuse me, are you Jewish?" they asked. When he said yes, they asked him if he would like to do a good deed. When he said yes again, they began his bar mitzvah service. "Who ever heard of such a thing?" he asked.

In recent years the Lubavitch outreach programs have moved west across the country to places such as Salt Lake City, Utah, and Anchorage, Alaska. Many of the emissaries are idealistic young married couples, and they may spend anywhere from a few years to the rest of their lives proselytizing. In Los Angeles they have held star-studded Chabad telethons, recruiting celebrities such as the pop star Madonna. One reporter who has extensively studied the Lubavitch Chabad movement noted the irony in the use of a telethon by an antiassimilation sect, many of whose members do not even own a television set. Using technology to further their outreach, she concluded, illustrates their simultaneous engagement with and avoidance of the society that surrounds them.[25]

The Lubavitch outreach programs are run out of the sect's Crown Heights headquarters, a converted 1930s mansion. It and the adjacent building contain—in addition to the rebbe's offices, the yeshiva, and the synagogue—an educational center, a print shop, video equipment, and editorial and translation centers for disseminating the rebbe's messages around the world. Its budget in 2002 was nearly $1 billion, and the movement continues to open schools, synagogues, and outreach centers throughout the world. Prospective new members are brought for visits to the headquarters and surrounding community. Around the time of major holidays, when sect members may come from anywhere in the world, the streets around the headquarters become so crowded that police are sent to direct traffic.

Lubavitch Conflicts

Within their Brooklyn neighborhoods, the similarities in appearance and way of life of the various Hasidim stand out, especially in contrast to their African-American, West Indian, and Puerto Rican neighbors. Members of different sects have usually been willing to shop at each other's stores, exchange neighborly favors, and let their children play with each other. These informal contacts have promoted cohesion among persons from different sects living in the same neighborhoods. Members of all sects in every neighborhood have also been bound together by umbrella organizations established to promote their common interests in Brooklyn and New York City politics. Cohesion among the Hasidic sects has also been promoted by periodic conflicts between the individual sects, especially the Lubavitch, and their non-Hasidic neighbors.

Conflicts with Other Sects

There have been periodic conflicts between sects, and the outreach programs of the Lubavitchers have frequently been the cause. The most serious long-term tensions have been between the Lubavitch and the Satmar sect in Williamsburg. During the Passover holiday, for example, the Lubavitchers used to visit other sects' synagogues to present their distinctive philosophy. To Satmar Hasidim, these visits were both unnecessary and provocative. During one Passover, hundreds of Lubavitch marched the three miles from Crown Heights to Williamsburg. When they arrived, Satmar members responded by shouting, spitting, and throwing garbage cans at the marchers. Fistfights broke out between the groups, which eventually had to be separated by the police. The Lubavitch then ended their Passover marches and even rerouted their mitzvah tanks around Williamsburg.

Smaller confrontations with the Satmar have nevertheless continued, with Lubavitch outreach activities usually providing the initial spark. For example, members of the Satmar sect claimed that the Lubavitchers were intentionally using charismatic teachers to convert young Satmar males to Lubavitch views. When one such Lubavitch teacher was meeting with a Satmar teenager in the back of the youth's father's store, five Satmar men were accused of running into the room as the lesson began, throwing the teacher (a rabbi) down on the floor, holding him there, and cutting off his beard. It was not only a physical assault but a spiritual blow, because of the Hasidic prohibition on shaving. In response, the Lubavitch banned consumption of all Satmar products, claiming they were no longer kosher.[26]

The Lubavitch's conflicts with other sects have not been confined to Satmar. In 2002, a group of Lubavitchers went to Borough Park in order to convince members of a Bobover synagogue to accept the deceased Rebbe Schneerson as their Messiah. The Bobovers firmly rejected their argument, but the Lubavitch persisted, refusing to leave the synagogue until the police were finally called to confront them.[27]

Perhaps the strongest solidarity among the Hasidic sects has occurred in response to conflicts between the Lubavitch and their black neighbors. Even Satmar and Lubavitch leaders have sat side by side in City Hall when it appeared that Hasidim were the victims of attack solely because of their religion.

Conflicts with the Black Community

Relations between the Lubavitch and their non-Hasidic neighbors have usually been distant and sometimes hostile. Like other sects, the Lubavitch typically avoid contact with outsiders and even consider observant but non-Hasidic Jews to be outsiders. Their black Crown Heights neighbors, African American and West Indian, have sometimes felt that these "distant" Lubavitchers received preferential treatment in the community; for example, when major streets were closed off and police were assigned to traffic control around their Crown Heights headquarters during major holidays.

Resentment over local issues combined with growing black anti-Semitism to produce a violent riot following a tragic automobile accident on August 19, 1991. That evening, Rebbe Schneerson was returning home with a number of other Lubavitchers in a three-car procession with a police escort. One of the cars in the motorcade struck another car, then swerved onto the sidewalk, striking two black Guyanese children. One, a seven-year-old boy, died at the scene. As a crowd gathered, the driver of the errant car and his passengers, none of whom were seriously injured, were removed from the area by a private ambulance.

During that evening, hostile suppositions spread through the West Indian and African-American communities, which were unified by the racial polarization that resulted after the accident. It was rumored, for example, that the Guyanese youngster was callously left by the Hasidic ambulance to die. And because a police car had been leading the rebbe's motorcade, providing further evidence of the Hasidim's preferential treatment by the city, many black residents of Crown Heights doubted that those responsible for the boy's death would be punished. Over the next four days, there were confrontations between blacks and Jews in Crown Heights, and groups of angry young black men marched down Crown Heights streets chanting, "Kill the Jews!" One young Hasidic man was stabbed to death on the first evening, and other beatings of Jews by blacks occurred on the following days. Groups of blacks also burned or looted a number of Hasidic-owned businesses.[28]

The adequacy of the police response to the Crown Heights disturbances was a matter of some contention. Eventually, over one thousand police patrolled the streets, and hundreds of arrests were reported. However, the Hasidim and many other (especially white) New York residents were very critical of the police response, claiming it was too little, too late. Mayor David Dinkins, the city's first elected African-American mayor was at the beginning of a reelection campaign and was accused variously of favoritism, timidity, or being out of touch with what was happening. Criticism grew even stronger when the police investigation of the fatal stabbing was later shown to be sloppy, and the young African-American man, Lemrick Nelson, Jr., arrested for the murder was acquitted.

After the rioting, a precinct council, a conflict resolution task force, and various other associations were proposed to bring the African-American, West Indian, and Hasidic groups together. However, none of the umbrella associations had more than very limited and short-term success, and the different groups continued to be periodically driven apart by everyday conflicts. For example, in 1994, Labor Day fell on the eve of the Jewish New Year, Rosh Hashanah, when thousands of Hasidim travel to Lubavitch headquarters on Eastern Parkway. However, for over twenty-five years Labor Day was the scheduled date for a Caribbean parade down Eastern Parkway; a parade that attracted over one million people. The Hasidim thought the Caribbean organizers should change the date of their event, and when those planning the parade refused, the Hasidim thought they were unreasonable. When Lubavitch representatives tried to get the police to change the date of the parade permit, the Caribbean organizers in Brooklyn were enraged.[29]

Meanwhile, attempts to indict Lemrick Nelson also continued to be a source of interracial animosity. All the major Hasidic sects in New York lobbied elected representatives, urging that the U.S. attorney general reopen the case. City officials, congressional representatives from Brooklyn, and New York State's two senators were all supportive. Eventually, the U.S. Senate passed a resolution urging further inquiry, and nearly three years later the man who had been acquitted on state murder charges was rearrested on the federal charge of violating the victim's civil rights. The trial dragged on for years until in 1997 Nelson was found guilty and in 1998 was sentenced to nearly twenty years in prison. Prior to sentencing, the prosecutor described Nelson as unrepentant; considering himself to be a victim. "Damn right," Nelson muttered[30]—and he was apparently expressing the views of many in the black community. There were subsequent appeals, and Nelson was not imprisoned until 2003.

Notes

1. Daniel J. Wakin, "Rabbis' Rules and Indian Wigs Stir Crisis in Orthodox Brooklyn," *New York Times,* May 14, 2004, p. A1.
2. For a detailed description of the Hasidic way of life in the United States, see Janet S. Belcove-Shalin, *New World Hasidim,* Albany, NY: SUNY Press, 1995.
3. Jerome R. Mintz, *Hasidic People,* Cambridge, MA: Harvard University Press, 1992, p. 111.

4. David Landau, *Piety and Power,* New York: Hill & Wang, 1993.
5. *New York Times,* June 29, 1993, p. A10.
6. Philip Baldinger, "Equality Does Not Mean Sameness," in Philip L. Kilbride, et al. (Eds.), *Encounters with American Ethnic Cultures,* Tuscaloosa: University of Alabama Press, 1990.
7. Reported by Neturei Karta (Jews United against Zionism), 2003; see http://www.nkusa.org.
8. Mintz, op. cit.
9. Mordechai Rotenberg, *Dialogue with Deviance,* Lanham, MD: University Press of America, 1993, p. 165.
10. Mintz, op. cit.
11. Landau, op. cit.
12. *New York Times,* June 14, 1994, p. B1.
13. Jonathan Mahler, "Waiting for the Messiah of Eastern Parkway," *New York Times Magazine,* September 21, 2003.
14. For a review of theories and studies, see Robert P. Althauser, "The Paradox in Popular Religion," *Social Forces* 69, 1990.
15. Mahler, op. cit.
16. Quoted in *New York Times,* March 11, 1995, p. 26. At the tenth anniversary of Schneerson's death, there were still over ten thousand mourners who filed past his grave. Corey Kilgannon, "Lubavitchers Mark 10 Years Since Death of Revered Rabbi," *New York Times,* June 20, 2004, p. 32.
17. Firsthand accounts of the difficulties experienced by contemporary Hasidic women are provided in Riuka Zakutinsky and Yaffa L. Gottlieb, *Around Sarah's Table,* New York: Free Press, 2001.
18. Landau, op. cit.
19. See Mintz, op. cit.
20. To avoid close contact with women during rush hours on New York subways when Hasidic men work in concentrated numbers in areas such as the New York diamond exchange, they use the sect's school buses. Some of the bus interiors are even designed for morning and afternoon prayer services. See Robert M. Kamen, *Growing Up Hasidic,* New York: AMS Press, 1985.
21. Baldinger, op. cit., p. 168.
22. Aaron Werthheim, *Law and Custom in Hasidim,* Hoboken, NJ: Ktav Publishing House, 1992.
23. Mintz, op. cit., p. 45.
24. Fran Markowitz, *A Community in Spite of Itself,* Washington, DC: Smithsonian Institution Press, 1993, p. 163.
25. Sue Fishkoff, *The Rebbe's Army,* New York: Schocken Books, 2003.
26. Muntz, op. cit.

27. Mahler, op. cit.
28. For a chronology of the events leading to the Crown Heights rioting, see the preface to Anna D. Smith, *Fires in the Mirror*, New York: Anchor Books, 1993; and William M. Kephart and William W. Zellner, *Extraordinary Groups*, New York: St. Martin's, 1994.
29. *New York Times*, January 27, 1994, p. B8.
30. CNN, "Man Gets $19^1/_2$ Years in Crown Heights Slaying," *U.S. News Story Page*. See "Archive" for 1998 at www.CNN.com.

Some Concluding Thoughts

In this conclusion we shall examine some changes in the nature of enclaves that transcend any of the specific enclaves discussed in the preceding chapters. This will entail an analysis of the way the organization of enclaves and their residential composition have generally changed with respect to transnationalism, inclusiveness, socioeconomic status, and assimilation.

Transnationalism

The more recently an enclave has formed, the more likely are its residents to have recurrent transnational contacts, especially with people in their country of origin. The two Chinese communities in California discussed in Chapter Six vividly illustrate this age-related difference. People in San Francisco's Chinatown, the older enclave, have historically had very few contacts outside the United States beyond occasional visits home or periodically remitting money to kin. By contrast, people in the more recently formed Little Taipei outside Los Angeles have from its inception engaged in extensive international dealings, particularly with Taiwan.

The tendency for some residents of recently formed enclaves to maintain cross-national social and economic networks was noted in Chapter Seven's discussion of Little Havana. It has also been described in other cities by a number of case studies, including Salvadoran immigrants in Washington, D.C.; Asian Indian concentrations in London; people from the Dominican Republic in Boston, and so on.[1] In each of these places, an immigrant group contained entrepreneurs whose businesses required routine travel to their countries of origin and/or regular contact with business associates in those countries. A small number of persons in most enclaves fit this description of transnational entrepreneurs, but their businesses are important in creating related jobs for other residents of the enclave and for maintaining bridges between current and former countries of residence.

When immigrants establish strong ties to their countries of origin, these ties are likely to expand their notion of "home," according to Waldinger and Fitzgerald, to encompass both *here* (current place) and *there* (former place). The transmigrants' bilocal conception of home may lead to their estrangement, though. Other people in their current place of residence (i.e., *here*) may find the immigrants' foreign attachment disconcerting, particularly when the relationship between the two nations involved is strained by international events. At the same time, the immigrants' movement sets them apart from their former cohorts who remained *there.* Having left a nation almost necessarily makes them different in some respects from the people they left behind.[2] The bilocal residents of modern enclaves may therefore suffer a kind of marginality in which they do not fit anywhere, except with each other. This may, of course, increase their attachment to the enclave and make it more enduring.

Tourism can also expose a place and its residents to influences emanating from *here* and *there.* It is has often been assumed that tourist places simply cater to tourists' imaginations and, like Disneyland, present simulated versions of reality. However, Meethan argues persuasively that there are usually meaningful interactions between locals and tourists in restaurants, hotels, public transportation, shops, and street corners. Each affects the other, and they mutually shape the future directions of a place.[3] Thus residents of enclaves that are tourist attractions should on those grounds be regarded as also likely to be hybrids, molded by bidirectional cultural flows.

Enclaves based primarily upon race or ethnicity have been examined in relation to the influences of *here* and *there,* but such influences should not be thought of as necessarily confined to racial-ethnic concentrations. Recently formed enclaves based largely upon lifestyles—such as the gay community in the Castro district or the Hasidic community in Crown Heights—show similar proclivities toward high degrees of transnationalism. For example, both of these enclaves are major tourist destinations for thousand of visitors from around the world who share the residents' religious or sexual lifestyles. Tourism of this type derives from the tendency of some like-minded people to regard the enclave as being like a "Mecca" for their kind of person; hence they feel compelled to visit it, and the trip is somewhat like a "pilgrimage."[4] In addition, the Lubavitch of Crown Heights have established technologically sophisticated proselytizing centers in numerous parts of the world, such as Russia and Israel, with personnel moving to the foreign centers and back to Crown Heights.

Inclusiveness

Another notable difference between many current and historical enclaves concerns the degree to which kindred racial, ethnic, and lifestyle groups are merged. Many of today's enclaves are possible only because more encompassing, panethnic social categories, such as Asian or Latino, have evolved. Because some groups of immigrants or migrants are too small to support separate self-contained communities, enclaves could form only when there was a sufficient sense of sameness among kindred groups. As an illustration, consider the differences between the Back of the Yards in Chicago circa 1910 and Port Chester, New York, circa 1995.

In contemporary Port Chester, Latino immigrants pursuing newly created factory jobs in this suburb of New York City formed a working-class community that resembled Back of the Yards, but with one important difference. The Yards community of nearly one hundred years ago contained highly concentrated numbers of Germans, Poles, Lithuanians, and others. Despite overlap and the interpenetration of their communities, each ethnic group remained separate and distinct, shopping only at their own grocery stores, for example, and even attempted to avoid prolonged interaction with people from other ethnic groups. No shared conception of themselves as "European Americans" tied them together. In Port Chester, by contrast, countries of origin are varied, including El Salvador, Cuba, Puerto Rico, and Colombia, but the people share an overarching multicultural conception of themselves as Hispanics. Their restaurants and groceries, *botánicas* selling herbs, and *discotecas* (music stores) all stock items that cater to multiple groups. Members of each nationality group have stretched their cultural preferences to support the others rather than emphasize the historical differences that have separated their nations of origin from each other. The similarities in their language, food preferences, and so on are more likely to be emphasized in a contemporary society that places more value upon inclusiveness or multiculturalism.

One of the driving forces behind many types of inclusiveness is a shared opposition to heterosexual males of white European descent. They have typically been positioned as the center, with everyone else on the periphery. People who are "other"—because they are not heterosexual or not white European or not male—have in recent years emphasized the authenticity of their own worldviews and heritages and have frequently tried to form inclusive intergroup coalitions in order to support each other (or because they feel they were forced to by the actions of heterosexual males of white European background). A poignant example of the reach of this "other" category was provided in a Spike Lee film, *Do the Right Thing*. It examined relations among various ethnic and racial groups in a crowded inner-city neighborhood. In a confrontation with a crowd of angry African Americans, a frustrated Korean-American shopkeeper, who wanted them to appreciate his and their commonality as others, shouted, "Please . . . I black . . . like you."[5]

It is important to recognize that inclusiveness, like transnationalism, is a characteristic that need not be confined to racial-ethnic groups. It can pertain to lifestyle groups as well. For example, when gay migration to the Castro district was turning it into a distinctive enclave in the 1970s, there were marked social as well as geographical separations between the gay men and those who were openly following other alternative sexual lifestyles. As described in Chapter Nine, however, lesbians, gays, bisexual, and transgendered people have recently become parts of a more inclusive alliance that, at least for many purposes, stresses their similarities (as other than heterosexual) rather than their differences.

The Hasidic enclaves of Brooklyn provide a conspicuous exception to the recent tendency toward inclusiveness. Although they do live close to each other in some parts of Brooklyn and they do sometimes band together when one faces an outside attack, the enclaves usually remain apart socially. Further, they are often in conflict over what would appear to outsiders to be trivial differences. Perhaps their continuing separateness is due to the uncommonly high degree to which each sect is formally organized.

Food As Metaphor

The lifestyles and values of many distinctive groups are represented by their customary foods: what they choose, how it is prepared and eaten, and what foods they abstain from eating. That is why in past chapters a good deal of attention has often been paid to what people ate and drank and where they consumed it. Through their cuisine people maintain traditions and group attachments. For example, many Southeast Asians working in American hotels will forgo a free meal at work and wait until they get home, to the company of others like themselves, to eat their own food purchased in Asian grocery stores. Sharing familiar food is the most frequently relied-upon way for the Southeast Asians (and other groups) to "enjoy a sense of oneness."[6]

The epithets with which people have traditionally slurred members of various ethnic groups have also been drawn heavily from the foods and drinks associated with each. Thus, in examining the nicknames assigned to different immigrant groups, sociologist Irving L. Allen found many that were food-related: "Potato heads" (Irish), "Spags" (Italians, from spaghetti), "Hop heads" (Germans), "Rice bellies" (Chinese), and so on.[7] Pejorative terms have also been based upon foods and drinks associated with lifestyle groups based upon religious or sexual preferences.

Focusing on food provides a convenient way to summarize the preceding discussion of inclusiveness and its effects on enclaves. Let us begin by noting that in the past, the food preferences of various groups were both less likely to persist unchanged over time (because of pressures on group members to assimilate) and less likely to diffuse to members of other groups (because of weak ties among them). In Italian enclaves in Philadelphia, for example, traditional observance of Christmas Eve involved serving baccala (salted cod), calamari, fried smelts, and broccoli.[8] From generation to generation, more traditionally American seafood and vegetables came to substitute for the traditional items. A declining proportion of Italians continued the holiday food tradition (with either the original or the modified menus), and relatively few non-Italians adopted the Italians' food ritual.

To illustrate the changes in inclusiveness, consider Jack Agueros, a Puerto Rican who grew up in Spanish Harlem in New York City. He writes about types of breads as metaphors for ethnic cultures. When he says that he wishes he could obtain the flaky, soft-crusted bread baked in Puerto Rico, I believe he means that he wants both the bread and an opportunity to immerse himself in Puerto Rican life. However, both the bread and Puerto Rico are three and a half hours away by jet, so he settles for going to a nearby neighborhood where Puerto Ricans, Cubans, and Dominicans all make a very similar bread. Agueros writes that he hopes to retain his preference for authentic Puerto Rican bread and not the Americanized version of it that is more readily available. His underlying fear is that he will move to a cultural and psychological middle ground in which his identity will be diluted and lost: "not quite all Puerto Rican, not quite all American."[9]

Agueros describes how, while growing up in New York, he also acquired a taste for many other types of ethnic breads, especially crusty Italian bread baked in the Italian section of East Harlem. It, too, can be difficult to obtain, though. The bread he now sees labeled as "Italian bread" in the mass chain supermarkets seems to him to be fit only to feed pigeons! Combining Italian bread with packaged American white bread, he says, has produced a watered-down product that is neither Italian nor American. He feels sorry for the people who are so assimilated that they like this bread. He is also sorry for those people whose one ethnic tie is so strong and pure that they can appreciate only one kind of bread.

Socioeconomic Status

Another distinguishing characteristic of recently formed enclaves is the relative wealth, education, and social capital of their residents compared to people in older enclaves. Observers of immigration trends have noted these dissimilarities and have expressed them in a number of different but not incompatible perspectives. Variations in how the underlying difference is described are mostly matters of emphasis.

Some writers have tried to capture the difference, as noted in Chapter Seven, by differentiating between *immigrants* and *exiles*. The lack of economic resources and the prominence of seeking low-wage jobs are, according to this view, most typical of immigrants. Exiles, by contrast, tend to have higher socioeconomic status, and obtaining political or religious freedoms are a more important reason for their geographical movement.[10] People who have formed enclaves more recently—such as Cubans in Little Havana or gays in the Castro district—tend to have higher proportions of exiles than enclaves that formed earlier—for example, the original German settlements in southern Brazil or the Back of the Yards complex in Chicago.

A second way of dealing with socioeconomic differences between enclaves puts more emphasis upon how they are formed. More recent settlements, referred to as *ethnic communities,* are more deliberately created than earlier ones, and the term *ethnic enclave* is reserved for the latter. Enclaves, according to this view, formed primarily as a result of unintended ecological and economic constraints. By contrast, more recent ethnic communities have involved more planning and attached more weight to matters of "taste and preference."[11] We can connect this formulation with the first by noting that for a community to be deliberately planned according to people's subjective preferences, it is probably necessary for the group to contain a substantial number of high-status exiles. The earlier enclaves, on the other hand, whose shape was driven by ecological and economic considerations, would have been comprised almost entirely of immigrants.

The distinctions between immigrants and exiles and between enclaves and communities have been applied solely to ethnic-racial concentrations. However, as we have repeatedly noted, there is no reason the same kinds of distinctions should not apply when it is lifestyle rather than ethnicity that is stressed in people's ties to a place. An emphasis upon taste and preference, for example, is highly compatible with the way recent lifestyle enclaves have often been formed, and further, they have frequently been relatively planned. Thus to confine these distinctions to ethnic-racial concentrations seems unjustifiably limiting.

Finally, some observers have stressed differences in the location of enclaves. The earlier ones were almost inevitably located in central cities either because they formed prior to the large-scale development of suburbs or because most of the residents could not afford to live in a suburb. More recent enclaves are often located in suburban areas, as illustrated by Little Taipei, though they also continue to form in central cities, for example, the Hasidic enclaves in Brooklyn. In other words, it is only the more recent enclaves that are found in suburbs, but not all recent enclaves are suburban. Those that are found in suburbs are not only newer but physically more attractive and contain residents whose socioeconomic status is higher than in central-city enclaves.[12]

In sum, the above perspectives can be combined as follows: historical enclaves tended to be unplanned, comprised primarily of low-socioeconomic-status immigrants, and almost invariably located in central cities. By contrast, the more recently formed enclaves, sometimes referred to as communities rather than enclaves, are more likely to be planned, located in suburban areas, and contain a higher ratio of exiles.

Assimilation

One of the best-known ways to study assimilation of immigrants or migrants focuses upon their changing locations within a metropolitan area. When they first arrive, newcomers tend to congregate in undesirable, inner-city neighborhoods; it is all they can afford. As they become more language-proficient and acquire business skills and formal education, according to assimilation theory, they leave the inner-city enclave and move to more desirable suburban or suburban-type neighborhoods. So people move up socially by moving outward geographically; and the typical history of a group can be described as "spatial assimilation."[13]

The new communities to which people move, further from the center of the city, are typically more heterogeneous than the enclaves they left. Assimilation is then expected to occur as people are absorbed by the dominant culture and slowly lose the traditions, values, and language that formerly set them apart. The white, European heterosexual is the exemplar to be emulated, and economic rewards are expected for those who drop their unique traditions and assimilate, or at least appear not to deviate from the ideal. As a result, parents often refuse to speak to children in their native language in order to encourage the children to learn English. Similarly, gay, lesbian, and other nonheterosexual people almost always went to great lengths to hide their sexual orientations so they could pass as conventional heterosexuals.

The spatial assimilation model, the now-antiquated "melting pot" theory, and almost all of the early assimilation formulations failed to appreciate the degree to which the music, food, clothing, and other factors that were once uniquely associated with any specific group were often not lost but became incorporated into the overriding cultural pastiche.[14] In addition, these theories failed to recognize that people in distinctive groups might adopt features of the larger society and simultaneously retain unique traditions as well: become bilingual, learn to celebrate two sets of holidays, and so on; or they might confine expressions of their distinctiveness to their home or neighborhood rather than more diverse public spheres.[15] Finally, the spatial assimilation pattern described the experience of white Europeans much better than it fitted people of color.[16] Despite all of the shortcomings noted above, spatial and cultural assimilation nevertheless posited a widely shared ideal of what was supposed to occur.

In a number of ways many contemporary enclaves are organized in a manner that runs counter even to the ideal of spatial or cultural assimilation. To begin, those that are located from their inception in suburban areas make the idea of moving outward moot. And as we have seen, the newer suburban enclaves are likely to have the amenities that people historically had to move to obtain. Further, in these communities there may be economic incentives against assimilation. When exiles try to establish businesses in their homelands, attract investment capital from their homelands, or link *here* and *there* via import-export businesses or travel agencies, they maintain an advantage over "outsiders" because they share a culture and language with their counterparts in their native country. They may be able to use their common culture to build trust, a critical ingredient when business relationships are first established. To illustrate, during the 1970s, many Vietnamese government officials and professionals fled the communists and settled south of Los Angeles in a suburban enclave that came to be known as Little Saigon. The enclave established a Vietnamese Chamber of Commerce and a number of small business development centers to encourage entrepreneurship, especially directed toward dealing with Vietnam.[17] Today, the children and grandchildren of the exiles have used their "cultural capital" to advantage, opening car rental agencies, hotels, and fast-food restaurants in Ho Chi Minh City (formerly Saigon). In their visits to their ancestral homeland, they refurbish their ability to speak Vietnamese and their knowledge of Vietnamese food and cultural observances. These experiences, combined with clear economic disincentives, push them away from assimilation.

Reflecting these recent changes in the nature of enclaves and in the society's emphasis upon multiculturalism, a number of studies have indicated a tendency for current ethnic identities to be highly persistent, even under conditions that might be expected to promote acculturation. For example, a group of researchers examined all of the Asian (Chinese, Indian, etc.) and Latino (Mexican, Guatemalan, etc.) students who entered UCLA as freshmen in 1996. Three times between 1996 and 2000 the students filled out questionnaires covering many topics, including the degree to which they thought of themselves as members of an ethnic group and whether their closest relationships were with other members of that ethnic group.[18]

As entering freshmen, their ethnic identities were strongest if they came from traditional homes that did not speak English and if their high school friends were primarily of the same ethnicity. No data were provided on students' neighborhoods, though having parents who spoke in native languages and having high school friends mostly of the same ethnicity would be consistent with living in an enclave. Further, over 90 percent of the students in the sample were from California, where a large percentage of Asian and Latino immigrants do live in enclaves. In any case, over the next four years the students were in a variety of situations which could be expected to raise the salience of other identities, such as those associated with the specific fields in which they were majoring, the fraternity or sorority in which they lived, and so on. Would these others be generated at the expense of ethnic identity? Apparently not, because among both Asian and Latino students, ethnic identities remained relatively unchanged across their four years of college. Becoming a college student is one of the statuses that might be expected to increase assimilation, but it seemingly does not.

Variations in socioeconomic status have also been reported as not correlating with assimilation in the way that might be historically expected. Specifically, if moving upward socially were associated with moving outward geographically and with cultural absorption, then the second-generation offspring in middle-class ethnic families should have weaker ethnic identities than their counterparts in lower-class families. In fact, however, the actual relationship has been just the opposite. Among Haitian high school and college students in Brooklyn, for example, those who were from lower-income families were found to have a less strong sense of membership in a separate ethnic group than those in middle-income families.[19] Thus assimilation does not seem to be occurring where it would historically have

been most expected, and changes in enclaves are one of the important reasons for the apparent change. This also suggests that contemporary enclaves may be more enduring than their historical counterparts.

Notes

1. For a discussion of these studies, see Peggy Levitt, "Transnational Migration," *Global Networks* 1, 2001; and Alejandro Portes, William J. Haller, and Luis E. Guarnizo, "Transnational Entrepreneurs," *American Sociological Review* 67, 2002.
2. Roger Waldinger and David Fitzgerald, "Transnationalism in Question," *American Journal of Sociology* 109, 2004.
3. Kevin Meethan, *Tourism in Global Society,* New York: Palgrave, 2001.
4. See the similar description of tourism to malls and other large shopping venues in George Ritzer, *Enchanting a Disenchanted World,* Thousand Oaks, CA: Pine Forge Press, 1999.
5. Quoted and discussed in Robert D. Manning, "Cultural Diversity of Diverse Cultures," *Proteus* 10, 1993.
6. Trans Minh Tung, "Southeast Asian Expatriates," in Ernest R. Myers (Ed.), *Challenges of a Changing America,* San Francisco: Austin & Winfield, 1994.
7. Irving L. Allen, *The Language of Ethnic Conflict,* New York: Columbia University Press, 1983.
8. See Judith G. Goode, "Meal Formats, Meal Cycles and Menu Negotiation in the Maintenance of an Italian-American Community," in Mary Douglas (Ed.), *Food in the Social Order,* New York: Russell Sage Foundation, 1984.
9. Jack Agueros, "Beyond the Crust," in Kathleen Aguero (Ed.), *Daily Fare,* Athens: University of Georgia Press, 1993, p. 220.
10. Georges Sabagh and Mehdi Bozorgmehr, "Are the Characteristics of Exiles Different from Immigrants?" *Sociology and Social Research* 71, 1987.
11. John R. Logan, Richard D. Alba, and Wenquan Zhang, "Immigrant Enclaves and Ethnic Communities in New York and Los Angeles," *American Sociological Review* 67, 2002, p. 300.
12. Richard D. Alba, John R. Logan, Brian Stults, Gilbert Marzan, and Wenquan Zheng, "Immigrant Groups in the Suburbs," *American Sociological Review* 64, 1999.

13. For a summary, see Douglas S. Massey, "Ethnic Residential Segregation," *Sociology and Social Research* 69, 1985.

14. The change from "melting pot" to multiculturalism is discussed in Nathan Glazer, *We Are All Multiculturalists Now*, Cambridge: Harvard University Press, 1993.

15. For a qualified view of cultural absorption, see Peter Salins, *Assimilation American Style*, New York: Basic Books, 1997. For a critique of that conception, see Richard Alba "Immigration and the American Realities of Assimilation and Multiculturalism," *Sociological Forum* 14, 1999.

16. The model's poor fit with the experiences of blacks is discussed in Douglas S. Massey and Nancy Denton, *American Apartheid*, Cambridge: Harvard University Press, 1993.

17. For further information, see www:info@littlesaigon.com.

18. David O. Sears, Mingying Fu, P. J. Henry, and Kerra Bui, "The Origins and Persistence of Ethnic Identity among the 'New Immigrant' Groups," *Social Psychology Quarterly* 66, 2003.

19. Flore Zephir, *Trends in Ethnic Identification among Second-Generation Haitian Immigrants in New York City*, Westport, CT: Bergin & Garvey, 2001.

INDEX